International Re
and Jeremy Bentham

Jeremy Bentham (1748–1832) is best known amongst political theory scholars as the vast proportion of his work addressed legal theory, reform, and the ideal relationship between the governors and the governed.

This book offers the first comprehensive presentation and discussion of Jeremy Bentham's contributions to international relations theory. It rectifies many of the erroneous assumptions made about Bentham's contributions to the field, and critically examines his place within the confines of the liberal theoretical tradition, arguing that Bentham's preoccupation with security resulted in often conflicting and inconsistent ideas about the conduct of nations in the international realm. International relations scholars have long needed clarification and an accurate presentation of Bentham's work, but additionally, his constant struggle to ensure security of expectation resulted in a striking ambivalence about world politics and how states ought to engage them. Bentham's work was pivotal to the development of the international climate we now face – he coined the word 'international' – and was one of the first thinkers to consider the globalized community that we see before us. He also struggled, sometimes in vain, to reconcile such a globalized community with the need to ensure security. His struggle was essentially no different than that facing international relations scholars today.

Within the context of Bentham's work, this book also addresses the broader context of international relations theory itself, and demonstrates the strengths and weaknesses of the international relations theory traditions, in particular, liberalism and realism. This book will be of strong interest to students and scholars of international relations and political theory.

Gunhild Hoogensen is Associate Professor and a Senior Researcher in the Department of Political Science, University of Tromsø. Her research interests include international relations and security theory.

Routledge Advances in International Relations and Global Politics

International Relations, Security and Jeremy Bentham

Gunhild Hoogensen

Routledge
Taylor & Francis Group

LONDON AND NEW YORK

First published 2005
by Routledge
2 Park Square, Milton Park, Abingdon, Oxfordshire OX14 4RN

Simultaneously published in the USA and Canada
by Routledge
711 Third Avenue, New York, NY 10017

First issued in paperback 2014
*Routledge is an imprint of the Taylor and Francis Group,
an informa company*

© 2005 Gunhild Hoogensen

Typeset in Times by
Florence Production Ltd, Stoodleigh, Devon

British Library Cataloguing in Publication Data
A catalogue record for this book is available form the British Library

Library of Congress Cataloging in Publication Data
Antony Rowe Ltd, Chippenham, Wiltshire

ISBN 978-0-415-36578-9 (hpk)
ISBN 978-0-415-75913-7 (pbk)

Contents

Acknowledgements

To successfully complete this book I received wonderful support, and thus incurred a number of debts. I do not have the space to acknowledge each and every one, but a few deserve special mention. First and foremost I owe considerable debt and thanks to my very supportive husband Duane Campbell, and our three patient children, Arne, Brontë and Liesbeth, who spent their infancies on their mother's lap in front of the computer. My father-in-law, Graham Campbell, has kept our family smiling, and my parents, Marga and Chris Hoogensen, have provided me with infinite understanding and support over the years, without which I probably would never try to do the many things that I do.

My debts extend to the academic realm as well. As is often said 'all the errors in this book are mine', but I want to thank very much those who have helped me think through these ideas, good and bad, along the way. Many thanks to Philip Schofield, Fred Rosen, Tom Keating, Kim Richard Nossal, Tom Pocklington, with extra special thanks to Larry Pratt. Last, but not least, many thanks to my dear friend Allison Dube, who got me 'hooked' on Bentham in the first place.

1   Introduction

> In the second place, with regard to the *political quality* of the persons whose conduct is the object of the law. These may, on any given occasion, be considered either as members of the same state, or as members of different states: in the first case, the law may be referred to the head of *internal*, in the second case, to that of *international** jurisprudence.
>
> (*The word *international*, it must be acknowledged, is a new one; though, it is hoped, sufficiently analogous and intelligible. It is calculated to express, in a more significant way, the branch of law which goes commonly under the name of *law of nations*: an appellation so uncharacteristic, that, were it not for the force of custom, it would seem rather to refer to internal jurisprudence.)[1]

Jeremy Bentham (1748–1832) is best known among political theory scholars, since the vast proportion of his work addressed legal theory, reform, and the ideal relationship between the governors and the governed. His work has had an acknowledged impact on international relations theory, but generally speaking, the man and his contribution to international relations thinking have to date remained unexamined and unknown. Bentham's work, however, has a great deal to offer to international relations scholarship. Bentham lived during, and responded to, a number of critical events that took place in the late 1700s and early 1800s, including the American and French revolutions and the Napoleonic wars. These events, as well as the circumstances of his life, had an impact on his writing in international affairs, providing us with many worthwhile insights into his work in particular, and international relations theory in general.

In this book I offer the first comprehensive presentation and discussion of Jeremy Bentham's contributions to international relations theory. The breadth of Bentham's contribution is revealed, and a novel analysis is introduced, using Bentham's own 'disappointment-prevention principle' and his preoccupation with security as the point of departure. Within the context of Bentham's work, this book also addresses the broader context of international relations theory itself, and demonstrates the strengths and weaknesses of the international relations theory traditions, in particular liberalism and realism. Bentham tried, sometimes in vain, to reconcile present and future security needs (often associated with realist preoccupations) with such liberal notions as equality, freedom and commerce. Bentham's work illustrates the profound difficulties in achieving such a reconciliation, and speaks to those continuing to seek the ways in which security can be reconciled with the powerful forces of globalization to which liberal ideas have strongly contributed including Bentham's own.

Bentham's connections with the international realm

A central problem in assessing Bentham's work is his reputation among scholars. Especially in his later years, Bentham's eccentric lifestyle made him prone to ridicule and caricature, with John Stuart Mill providing one of the more influential critiques of Bentham's life, often discrediting his years of work:

> In one of two extremely interesting essays which [Mill] wrote about Bentham after his death, Mill applauded many of his ideas and achievements, but portrayed him as childlike, cloistered, equable, and emotionally shallow – as someone who had never known adversity or dejection, and whose knowledge of human affairs and human nature was very confined.[2]

Mill's characterization was not entirely accurate, as Bentham was familiar with dejection, and he often addressed many prominent leaders of his day, Catherine the Great and William Pitt the Younger among them, in response to various political events. Nevertheless, even though '[N]ot many philosophers – though Mill himself was one of the exceptions – have had as much contact with the world of affairs as Bentham did',[3] his contact was often awkward and diffident.

Although Bentham was continually interested in the political events unfolding around him, he was not predisposed to an actively public life. Born in February 1748, Bentham experienced childhood within a prosperous middle-class London family. His father was a successful lawyer and played a dominant, if not domineering, role in Bentham's life, even more so when his mother died when he was 10 years old. His intelligence was recognized early and encouraged by a proud and determined father; the small Bentham began Latin studies at the age of three, entered Westminster at the age of seven, and moved quickly on to Queen's College, Oxford at the age of 12. More than able to meet the intellectual challenges of school, Bentham was otherwise unhappy. He was smaller than his schoolmates, and much younger than his colleagues at Oxford: 'kept very short of money by his father, he lived an isolated and restricted life, and meanwhile gained little satisfaction from the desultory and pedestrian teaching offered by his tutors'.[4] Trained as a lawyer, Bentham did little to pursue an active law career, never tried a case, and gave up any notion of practising shortly thereafter. He was aghast at the disorder disguised as the English legal system. He turned to addressing that disorder, and spent the rest of his life writing about the legal system and how it could be improved.

His life as a writer and philosopher did not differ a great deal from his school years. Describing himself as 'working hard, though in a manner underground, and without producing any apparent fruits',[5] Bentham spent his life in relative detachment from the rest of the world. He was not completely isolated, however, as he did entertain the notion of marriage in the mid-1770s, a notion quickly dispelled by his father. For the most part, however, Bentham's attention was focused on his writing, producing at this time *An Introduction to the Principles of Morals and Legislation*, *Fragment on Government*, and *Of Laws in General*, to name a few. Of these, *Fragment on Government* was the only one published immediately but anonymously, and receiving high acclaim until its true authorship was discovered: 'Acutely aware that he was a nobody, he had wishfully taken refuge in drafting letters to great figures of the Continental Enlightenment such as Voltaire, d'Alembert, and Catherine the Great, in which he described the nature of his work and sought their interest and approval.'[6] Bentham had hoped to present Catherine the Great with an immense code of law, and went to Russia in 1785, in part with this endeavour in mind. 'But Catherine never saw either the Code or its author. Bentham remained secluded in western Russia, translating his work into French; and when the empress visited the district he stayed – stubbornly diffident – in his cottage. So it had been time and time again with Bentham.'[7] He had many grand schemes, and plainly wished them to be adopted, but he failed miserably in promoting his own work.

This was also the period during which the Americans fought for independence, and the French for 'liberté, égalité, et fraternité,' and the isolated Bentham nevertheless sought to make his views plain to the Americans and the French by writing vociferously to the policymakers and citizens of each state. Bentham supported the British policy on America in 1775 and 1776, and made anonymous contributions to John Lind's *Remarks on the Principal Acts of the Thirteenth Parliament of Great Britain*, which:

> was designed to show, by an exhaustive review both of the charters granted to the colonies and the history of British legislation as well as by examination of constitutional principles, that Parliament had had full power to enact the so-called 'Intolerable Acts' of 1774 – including the act shutting the port of Boston – which had aroused such great indignation in America.[8]

Bentham's greatest preoccupation with the American strategy was with its declaration of rights, a notion he found baseless and weak. As such, any justification for rebellion and self-determination on the grounds of natural right was untenable. Bentham took issue with the work of Richard Price, a prominent advocate of the American cause, who wrote *Observations on the Nature of Civil Liberty, The Principles of Government, and Justice and Policy of the War with America*:

> This was an attempt to demonstrate, on the basis of a theory of a natural right to liberty, that democracy, direct or indirect, was the only legitimate form of government. Price defined liberty as "self-government" and for him laws made without the participation of those governed reduced subjects to the condition of slavery. So the maxim by which sound political thought should be guided was "every man his own legislator." On Bentham, Price had a profoundly irritating effect. Price's slogan "every man his own legislator" seemed to him the height of absurdity and years later, in explaining why he had taken the government's side against the Americans who had so reasonable a cause, Bentham said, "Dr. Price with his self-government made me an anti-American."[9]

Bentham's reaction to American independence was typical of his person and work throughout his life; his many commentaries and diatribes were often made anonymously or were never published until after his death, and his views often altered, not so much with time but with circumstance.

Bentham later became an advocate of the democracy he witnessed developing in the United States, but for some time he was in favour of the British constitution and those in power: 'I was a determined aristocrat [in 1776] – a prodigious admirer of Lord Mansfield and the King. I was, however, a great reformist; but never suspected that the people in power were against reform. I supposed they only wanted to know what was good in order to embrace it.'[10] For some years after the American Revolution, Bentham considered the British constitution to be 'the best beyond comparison that has hitherto made its appearance in the world; resting at no very great distance, perhaps, from the summit of perfection'.[11] By 1789 his views had altered somewhat as Bentham was praising America as the most enlightened state on the globe,[12] but by that time he had already turned his attention to the continent.

Bentham was attracted not only to the events taking place in France, but to British foreign policy regarding Russia. Although '[I]n 1783 Britain was widely regarded as having been reduced to the status of a second-rank power',[13] Bentham did not agree. Much of his writing at this time emphasized the significance of the great power that Britain wielded, and its capacity to dictate the norms of international behaviour. British foreign policy did not reflect Bentham's confidence, and instead 'Pitt the Younger and his first foreign secretary, the marquess of Carmarthen, sought a European alliance to end their country's isolation and vulnerability'.[14] In

1787 and 1788 the British forged an alliance with the Dutch and the Prussians, the 'Triple Alliance', enabling Britain to exert greater pressure on the international community than ever before. The British were instrumental in forcing Denmark to withdraw support from Russia when Sweden declared war against it. 'Only when the government backed down during the dispute with Russia over possession of the Turkish fortress of Ochakov on the Black Sea coast, were the limits of British power fully exposed.'[15]

It was Britain's actions against Russia that enraged Bentham. Britain had no business interfering with the affairs of Russia, as he argued in four letters published in the *Public Advertiser* between 15–16 June and 23 July 1789, signing them 'Anti-Machiavel.'[16] Bentham's brief tenure as 'Anti-Machiavel' was initially a response to a letter signed 'Partizan' in the *Public Advertiser*; 'Partizan' applauded British foreign policy initiatives, claiming that any commercial treaty with Russia was not necessary (goods could otherwise be obtained from the Baltic countries, or from the colonies), and that British support of Sweden and Turkey (both at war with Russia) would eliminate any advantage the French had in those countries. Bentham attacked Britain's policy of forcing Denmark to betray its defensive alliance with Russia, and took issue with the claim that Britain should continue to plunder the colonies for trade. He argued 'that the government's actions were likely to plunge Britain, and indeed much of Europe, into hostilities'.[17] Bentham wrote to Pitt personally, to dissuade him from pursuing the anti-Russia policy. He intended to write a pamphlet addressing this error in British foreign policy, expanding on the comments and ideas expounded in his 'Anti-Machiavel' letters, but, like many of his potential projects, this pamphlet never came to fruition. Perhaps this inaction was understandable, as there were other important matters afoot, namely the French Revolution.

When revolution dawned in France, Bentham saw opportunity: 'He came to see that a new order across the Channel might afford him the chance he had so far failed to find'; namely the chance to be hired as a codifier for a new constitution.[18] He continued his crusade against natural rights using the French 'Declaration of the Rights of Man and the Citizen' as his target, but opted for a less vehement stance against this notion than during the American Revolution.[19] Bentham concentrated on the French situation, writing *Essay on Political Tactics* on parliamentary procedure, and *Draught of a New Plan for the Organization of the Judicial Establishment in France*, sent to the French Parliament with the aim of having his ideas adopted. Although Bentham received substantial encouragement from some of his contacts in the National Assembly, it all came to nothing:

> The latter part of 1790 was indeed a time of disappointment for Bentham. On top of the indifferent success of his plans for the French judiciary came the failure of his hopes of a seat in parliament through

Landowne's patronage. On the French side, only the belated appearance of a translation of the *Defence of Usury* could be set against the record of failure.[20]

At this time Bentham began his Panopticon plan, resulting in a ten-year preoccupation with prison reform. He sent a copy of his Panopticon scheme to the French National Assembly along with his offer to come to France personally and establish a model prison, both of which were 'received with applause by the Legislative Assembly on 13 December [1791]'.[21] Like his other initiatives, however, the Panopticon proposal never came to fruition. France was on the brink of revolutionary war, and had no time for prison schemes.

While order broke down again in France and Bentham harboured refugees fleeing the unstable country, the status of honorary citizen was conferred upon him by the French National Assembly.[22] But Bentham's previous infatuation with the political change in France now turned to horror: 'After 1792, however, he became deeply alarmed, like many others of his class, by the course of events in France, and especially by the threats to the security of life and property that seemed to be developing there; and he reacted strongly against democracy.'[23] Not until 1809 did Bentham again consider parliamentary reform. His reaction was not anti-French, but anti-revolution. 'Peace, when peace could be securely obtained, was to Bentham by far the better alternative.'[24] Henceforth for Bentham, reform would be acceptable only if security was not compromised. This concern about security would resonate throughout his work until his death in 1832.

The years between the mid-1790s and the first decade of the nineteenth century were largely devoted to economic concerns, producing *Manual of Political Economy*, and *Institute of Political Economy* both essays including discussions on international trade, but he discontinued writing on the subject in 1804, when his interests and thoughts moved back to codification. Bentham's constitutional code became his passion, and occupied his thoughts for the rest of his life. His more active involvement in international affairs subsided after the French Revolution, and he did not pay explicit attention to international relations until 1830, when he drafted a loose proposal of international law to be promoted by his friend Jabez Henry. Bentham's focus on codification did not inhibit his attempts to contact various heads of state, however. Bentham looked to the Americas as a potential 'market' for a constitutional code, writing to President Madison of the United States in 1811 and offering his services as a codifier, and making a similar offer to Alexander I of Russia in 1814.[25] Madison wrote back five years later, only to refuse Bentham's offer, but his letter expressed enough optimism about Bentham's ideas being used in America for Bentham to misinterpret Madison's words as an invitation to approach each state of the union individually.[26] Bentham did so in 1817, and again, it came to nothing:

indeed the most concrete acknowledgements that he received were professions of admiration for his genius and fame, and the report (from Governor Plumer of New Hampshire) that the distinguished American lawyer, Mr. Edward Livingstone, had said more than once that his own project of a new penal code for the State of Louisiana had grown out of what he had learnt of Bentham's views in the French translation published by Dumont.[27]

Bentham pursued the Americans once more in 1830, two years before his death. He wrote to President Jackson to 'express his intense admiration of his inaugural address', and again offered his superior skills in codification.[28] He received no reply.

By this time Bentham had also included the Iberian Peninsula in his solicitations. It was in large part thanks to Étienne Dumont, a Swiss Calvinist ex-minister who was exiled from France at the time of the Revolution, that Bentham's work became widely known. Bentham's awkward writing style and poor editorial skills were largely smoothed over through Dumont's translation skills: 'the versions of Benthamite doctrine which, first in French, and then in translations into many languages (including English) made Bentham's ideas current in a fashion their originator could never had contrived.'[29] The Spanish and Portuguese gained access to Bentham's work 'in the wake of Napoleon's invading armies'.[30] Toribio Nunnez, a librarian at the University of Salamanca in Spain, used the Dumont translations to produce two volumes presenting Bentham's ideas.[31] After the Portuguese and Spanish revolutions of 1820 Bentham's ideas garnered a great deal of interest by those in both Cortes, including a request from the Portuguese Cortes that Bentham submit a set of codes. Once more Bentham's hopes were dashed against the counter-revolutions that took place in Spain and Portugal in 1823. Bentham took up correspondence with Greece during its war of independence against Turkey, and after that the new states of Latin America.[32] Each turn was thought to give new promise, but each was pursued in vain.

While peddling his wares to various states engaged in rebellion, Bentham also enjoyed a happy old age. In 1813 he was granted a large sum from Parliament as compensation for not pursuing his Panopticon plan. He entertained often, helped launch the *Westminster Review* in 'rivalry with the established Whig and Tory quarterlies', and enjoyed the tributes that 'arrived in profusion from overseas'.[33] Although some people found Bentham to be charming and generous, there were others who found his vanity and narrow-mindedness unbearable.

He was vain and egocentric, and surrounded himself with uncritical admirers much younger than himself . . . With friends who were closer to his own age and stature he tended to quarrel, as he did with James Mill and Dumont, and he could be ungenerous and ungrateful. When

Dumont applied to him for help in 1820–1 over a projected penal code for Geneva he was unresponsive, apparently because he regarded the Genevan republic as too small and unimportant to claim his attention when he was busy with other schemes of greater potential scope.[34]

The image of a vain old man, as opposed to enlightened and influential philosopher, is probably best illustrated in Bentham's decision to have his body mummified and displayed after his death. This gruesome oddity has undoubtedly played an unfortunate and misleading part in subsequent interpretations of the quality and seriousness of Bentham's work. Overshadowed by his complicated writing style, poor editorial support, as well as his eccentricities and post-mortem status, Bentham's reactions to the many international political events of his day, his attempts to benefit from them, and his resulting thoughts on international politics have not received adequate attention or analysis, especially given his significant contributions, known and unknown.

Bentham despaired over the results of the French Revolution, and henceforward never advocated revolutionary change, but he was willing to profit from newly formed governments, revolutionary or no, as potential consumers of his wares. Known for his peace-loving sentiments, he nevertheless found no difficulty in suggesting to his brother that they profit from the Napoleonic wars.[35] His writing, like his eye for opportunity, was often riddled with contradiction. Bentham's writings on international relations take twists and turns that are difficult to explain, important to identify, and highlight the very complexities of the international relations theory traditions themselves. It is the object of this work to present a thorough identification and evaluation of his essays and offer such an explanation.

Bentham and international relations theory

During his lengthy writing career Bentham devoted significant effort to international affairs, although, as shown above, the vast proportion of it was written before the 1790s. Bentham's essay *A Plan for an Universal and Perpetual Peace*,[36] is his best-known work on international matters, but within his many other essays and texts there lies a rich and substantial contribution to international relations thinking that is largely untapped. Consequently our understanding of Bentham's contribution in international relations is limited and deficient. Additionally, international relations scholars studying his work, rooted in the various theories of international relations, have often included Bentham within the liberal tradition.[37] Bentham's international essays cannot be so hastily assessed.

The first problem arises from Bentham's work itself; an incomplete and inaccurate published presentation of his main international essays, combined with a limited, if not non-existent, examination of the scope of Bentham's work in international relations, have resulted in a largely superficial analysis of his contribution. Second, international relations theory seeks to place theorists and their ideas in the hope of better understanding their work. Such categorization, however, can be quite limiting in that any inconsistencies in a theorist's work cannot be adequately explained and must ultimately be ignored if the categorization is to be sustained. This is precisely the difficulty found with Bentham's work. Bentham was not an idealist; nor was he a realist. Bentham's work in this area stands in a unique place in the history of international relations theory. His ideas transcend the categorization of the theoretical traditions because they reveal a distinct discomfort with the principles that the international relations theory traditions attempt to impose.

To date there has been no comprehensive compilation and examination of Bentham's works on international relations. This book is an attempt to remedy that, not only by bringing together his international relations work and making it more accessible, but also by clarifying, if not correcting, the presentation and understanding of his work, and its place in the development of international relations theory. Upon re-examining Bentham's known works in international relations, and examining other pieces hitherto not considered, particular themes come to the fore. The result is not only a broader and more comprehensive presentation of Bentham's contribution to international relations theory, but a fresh understanding of the issues important to Bentham, and how his concerns could be interpreted through, the international relations traditions. I want to emphasize that it is Bentham's work as it relates to international relations and international relations theory that has been examined, by an international relations scholar. I have included a broader range of Bentham's essays than has customarily been examined by international relations scholars to present a complex and detailed picture of Bentham's contribution to international relations thinking, but as Bentham wrote exhaustively upon numerous subjects, it is possible that even more essays could shed further light on these contributions. If nothing else, this book can serve as an introduction to Bentham's ideas on international relations.

The point that Bentham's work does not entirely fit the traditional paths assigned to his predecessors and contemporaries such as Kant, Rousseau and the Abbé St. Pierre is not new. F. H. Hinsley notes the very same in his seminal work *Power and the Pursuit of Peace*.[38] The distinctiveness of Bentham's position is largely bypassed as it is clear that Bentham espoused many of the tenets of idealist, or more broadly speaking liberal, thinking: he detested war, thought commerce promoted peace, and respected notions of international law. In these ways, Bentham clearly fits the mould.[39] The realist is apparent in Bentham as his ideas were couched in terms of interest, not just of individuals but often including the interest of those who were in power. The conclusion of some analyses in political philosophy is that Bentham was very much a realist because of his emphasis on self-interest (among other things), and not an idealist.[40] Especially in his earlier writings, Bentham's words were frequently directed to the powerful states of Europe, trying to convince them of the ways in which they could best profit.[41] Most importantly, however, is that Bentham's concern for security in all its manifestations often speaks to a more realist interpretation of his work. Bentham was preoccupied with ensuring security, and this has occasionally given him a reputation as an authoritarian. As a result, it is difficult to state categorically that Bentham's ideas should be associated more with one than with another tradition.

It should be noted that the purpose here is not to identify Bentham as particularly realist or liberal, but to understand his work within and beyond these frameworks. I am examining Bentham's work in relation to the realist and liberal traditions only, thus do not include the contributions and insights of the critical theory or constructavist traditions. Part of the problem lies in how the traditions are identified, especially those that are not realist.[42] 'Non-realists' are labelled, among other things, as idealists, rationalists or revolutionists, or are encapsulated within the catch-all label of 'liberal'. But what is 'liberalism' within the context of the international relations theory traditions? If being a liberal means that one can assume all the trappings of realism but accept the possibility of progress, or on the other side of the spectrum, advocate the union of all states under a world or cosmopolitan government, then the efficacy of understanding various ideas through the liberal lens becomes seriously diluted.

Although it is fair to say that interpretations of Bentham's writings were influential for subsequent liberal thinkers, this does not mean that, conversely, the liberal tradition defines his work. It is also not a matter of contrasting ideas from his youth with his later writings since, as will be seen, his views fluctuate. To say that his fluctuating opinions reflected particular philosophical transitions (from Toryism to radicalism, for example) also denies the fact that in each instance there still remains an inconsistency of ideas. To say Bentham was ambivalent merely states the obvious and does not explain why. To say that his definitive guiding principle, the principle of utility, was the source of his various, often contradictory, directives[43] is to suggest that the principle is highly subjective and more arbitrary than a guiding principle should be.

The difficulties in defining Bentham's position has not been properly evaluated in his international relations work, but the problems have been obvious with his writing in general: 'Was the radical individualist really a precursor of what is sometimes called "totalitarian democracy"?'[44] The 'liberal' Bentham is questioned when it becomes apparent that for Bentham's ideas to be carried through, the government must compel its citizens to understand that their interests coincide with the overall public interest. Bentham's government must likewise compel the people to behave in a particular manner that is consistent with the objective of security.[45] The state becomes the paramount factor, and the security of the individual is integrally linked to the security of the state. Fred Rosen, a Bentham scholar, states that Bentham would not have agreed that 'totalitarian democracy' was the result of his work, and that Bentham 'believes that the people themselves will largely seek security and subsistence as ends so long as they are not misled by corrupt government and sinister interests'.[46] Others have interpreted Bentham's thought in a different light, taking the view that he advocated close government control. Both of these interpretations are illustrative of the battle that ensued within Bentham's thoughts and work.

The disappointment-prevention principle

Bentham often provided an exit, in his later writings articulated as the disappointment-prevention principle, from any liberal constraints that might affect the security of common practice and expectations, in particular with regard to property. The disappointment-prevention principle seeks to secure expectation – it is rooted, for the most part, in maintaining the status quo, or in gradually altering expectations so that no insecurity results from reforms. The principle was developed late in Bentham's career,[47] and for that reason alone one might argue that any suggestion that it was integral to any of Bentham's earlier writings is misguided and inaccurate. However, it is apparent that this principle is a fundamental underlying concern throughout Bentham's work.[48]

The principle is a reflection of his concern over the place of security in legislation. The disappointment-prevention principle 'might be said to form, for Bentham, under the overall authority of the greatest happiness principle, a principle of justice'.[49] Security and justice become intertwined. 'If, for Bentham, happiness in its basic sense means the establishment of security (as opposed to the simple satisfaction of wants), the disappointment-prevention principle, in providing security of property, would seem to operate as a necessary condition for happiness.'[50] The state, through proper legislation, offers such security.

When Bentham closely re-evaluated the principle of utility, or the greatest happiness principle in order to address any deficiencies,[51] it is arguable that his evaluation was, in part, prompted by the struggle evident throughout his work. Bentham's writing, at least with regard to international relations issues, is riddled throughout with a tension over the issue of security. How much security is necessary to produce the greatest happiness for the greatest number? That he later associated the importance of security to establishing the greatest happiness through a 'new and improved' principle illustrates its importance. The disappointment-prevention principle, rooted in the security of property, is directly linked to Bentham's concerns in international affairs, his concerns with property extending to those of state territory, sovereignty, international relations and law.

Security: the key to understanding Bentham

It can be argued that Bentham's definition of security significantly differs from that of any realist predecessors, and that his concerns still reflect strictly liberal, or idealist, notions. Bentham places security as one of the four subordinate ends of the greatest happiness principle, and ultimately the most important end:

> Security admits as many distinctions as there are kinds of actions which may be hostile to it. It relates to the person, the honour, to property, to condition. Acts injurious to security, branded by prohibition of law, receive the quality of offences.
> Of these objects of the law, security is the only one which necessarily embraces the future. Subsistence, abundance, equality, [the other subordinate ends] may be considered in relation to a single moment of present time; but security implied a given extension of future time in respect to all that good which it embraces. Security then, is the pre-eminent object.[52]

Of course, anyone would desire a sense of security, liberal or realist. So perhaps this distinction is really not so significant. But then what is the difference – the method by which this security is achieved? Bentham sees the 'principal object of law' as the 'care of security':

> That inestimable good, the distinctive index of civilization, is entirely the work of law. Without law there is no security; and, consequently, no abundance, and not even a certainty of subsistence; and the only equality which can exist in such a state of things is an equality of misery.[53]

Law has the greatest power to provide security:

> Law alone has done that which all the natural sentiments united have not the power to do. Law alone is able to create a fixed and durable possession which merits the name of property. Law alone can accustom men to bow their heads under the yoke of foresight, hard at first to bear, but afterwards light and agreeable . . . security is assailed on every side – ever threatened, never tranquil, it exists in the midst of alarms. The legislator needs a vigilance always sustained, a power always in action, to defend it against this crowd of indefatigable enemies.[54]

And as such, law is all-important, as it ensures the security that is the pre-eminent concern of all humanity:

> To form a precise idea of the extent which ought to be given to the principle of security, we must consider that man is not like the animals, limited to the present, whether as respects suffering or enjoyment; but that he is susceptible of pains and pleasures by anticipation; and that it is not enough to secure him from actual loss, but it is necessary also

to guarantee him, as far as possible, against future loss. It is necessary to prolong the idea of his security through all the perspective which his imagination is capable of measuring.[55]

Bentham wishes to secure expectations: not just present conditions, but also future ones. When and if security is threatened, and security includes but is not limited to self-preservation, then the law must intervene decisively to ensure that self-preservation, and hence security, is maintained.

Security, especially as understood by Bentham, can be examined through the notion of liberty. At first glance, one could claim that the fact that security has been in any way, linked to liberty is a liberal notion, and the argument about inconsistency or confusion can be closed. However, since 'Bentham dwells throughout his life on the importance of security as the primary end of government',[56] and he frequently links his view of security with that of liberty, this connection has not prevented some from claiming Bentham's 'emphasis on security as revealing his real interest in order and social control rather than liberty'.[57]

Liberty can be evaluated from two different perspectives as far as it relates to law, according to Bentham. The first, and consistent with the liberal approach, is the perspective of negative liberty, whereby there is limited intervention by the law to ensure maximum liberty of individuals to pursue their interests. In this sense law is that which limits liberty. Law protects individuals and property through a sacrifice of liberty.[58] At the same time, however, law can also ensure that other liberties can be obtained; these liberties are often known as civil or social liberties.[59] As Fred Rosen states, 'Bentham recognizes that liberty has this second sense, but he distrusts the way that other writers and supporters of liberty fail to see that the creation of civil liberty requires the sacrifice of "natural" liberty.'[60] Bentham therefore replaces this second notion of liberty with his idea of 'security':

> As to the word *liberty*, it is a word, the import of which is of so loose a texture, that, in studied discourses on political subjects, I am not (I must confess) very fond of employing it, or of seeing it employed: *security* is a word, in which, in most cases, I find an advantageous substitute for it: *security* against misdeeds by individuals at large: *security* against misdeeds by public functionaries: *security* against misdeeds by foreign adversaries – as the case may be.[61]

Bentham's concern was with legislation, and therefore with that which would restrict liberty in the first sense described ('natural' liberty). However, 'natural' liberty as understood by Bentham was consistent with that understood by Hobbes, and is that which required legislation to ensure that individuals did *not* suffer a life that was 'solitary, poor, nasty, brutish, and short'.[62] This perception of security the dynamics between security and liberty, and the way in which many have subsequently chosen to interpret it is at the root of the difficulty in understanding Bentham's work.

Fred Rosen notes this problem in his analysis of Bentham's work on the *Constitutional Code*. One can argue that Bentham's preoccupation with security is merely his way of ensuring that particular liberties are available that otherwise would not be if the legislation did not exist. Liberty becomes central to Bentham's whole system. However, as argued by others, 'Material security, like health and knowledge, may be a condition for liberty, suggests Berlin, but to provide for increasing security is not the same thing as expanding liberty'.[63] The liberty, and therefore security, that Bentham sought through adequate legislation requires obligation, not freedom, to obtain it. The question is, how extensive do these obligations need to be to provide the security Bentham expects, such as security against invasion or hunger or crimes against one's property? Even Bentham scholars find this question difficult to answer:

> If a government sets out methodically to prevent crime without any limits on its measures to maximize security, the constant surveillance necessary to achieve this end might create conditions which would make life secure though rigidly organized. Even though the measures are rational and justifiable (and thus do not represent an abuse of government power), they may still seem destructive of dignity. In depicting the paupers of Bentham's Panopticon for the poor, Bahmueller argues that they 'were to be divested of personality and formed into a common mould, much like soldiers upon joining an army.'[64]

Fred Rosen, concedes that Bentham's emphasis on security could open a Pandora's Box of coercive initiatives on behalf of the government.

> Bentham might admit that to maximize security (and liberty) government activity must be considerable, but he would argue that it need not be arbitrary and tyrannical. A well-ordered society, based on rational principles of security, need not be a totalitarian one.[65]

Rosen states that Bentham's society would never take the need for security too far. Using the disappointment-prevention principle as the tool, it is possible to explore how Bentham's ideas in international relations contribute to this debate.

One cannot ensure security of expectations if one's immediate security is still threatened. However, the *security of expectation* ensures that immediate security will never need to worry about any threats because it expands beyond immediate threats (physical and material) and tries to anticipate future needs. Thus security is an integral part, if not the paramount concern, of the legislator because this broadened approach reflects the way people in fact think about their security. Bentham claimed that

that the 'presentiment, which has so marked an influence upon the fate of man, is called *expectation*'.[66]

> It is hence that we have the power of forming a general plan of conduct; it is hence that the successive instants which compose the duration of life are not like isolated and independent points, but become continuous parts of a whole. *Expectation* is a chain which unites our present existence to our future existence, and which passes beyond us to the generation which is to follow. The sensibility of man extends through all the links of this chain.
>
> The principle of security extends to the maintenance of all these expectations; it requires that events, so far as they depend upon laws, should conform to the expectations which law itself has created.
>
> Every attack upon this sentiment produces a distinct and special evil, which may be called a *pain of disappointment*.[67]

What is interesting is that Bentham's own ideas of what today we call "development" are integrally linked to this disappointment prevention principle. Our expectations develop with our apparent propensity to acquire, in which our security is rooted:

> [The right of property] has vanquished the natural aversion to labour; which has given to man the empire of the earth; which has brought to an end the migratory life of nations; which has produced the love of country and a regard for posterity. Men universally desire to enjoy speedily – to enjoy without labour. It is that desire which is terrible; since it arms all who have not against all who have. The law which restrains that desire is the noblest triumph of humanity over itself.[68]

Law is the tool by which the legislator should maintain the security of expectations, even when such maintenance would require security to prevail over equality for the 'subject many', keeping in mind that '[T]he goodness of the laws depends upon their conformity to general *expectation*'.[69]

It is my contention that the disappointment-prevention principle articulates the concern for security that is so prevalent in Bentham's writing. Because this is such an important feature in his work, it cannot be ignored by international relations theorists. The principle is, in my view, also the source of ambivalence and inconsistency that is apparent to the many scholars who have examined Bentham's work more closely. It is for this reason that the disappointment-prevention principle plays a central role as the analytical tool in this book. In identifying this principle for international relations scholars, a greater understanding and a more accurate representation of Bentham's work is the result. In addition, it is hoped that illuminating this important feature of Bentham's attempt to wrestle with the 'is' and the 'ought' of international relations, through the measure of security, will provide insight into international relations theory as it has developed over the ages.

The following chapters address, in different contexts, this need for security and its articulation through the disappointment-prevention principle. Chapter 2 reviews Bentham's notions of 'human nature' in relation to conduct in the arena of international relations in order to set the terms of analysis which follow. Chapter 3 addresses the origins of confusion surrounding Bentham's writing. An examination of Bentham's original manuscripts against the well-known published essay *A Plan for an Universal and Perpetual Peace* reveals the origins of the essay and the subsequent problems that arise, including subsequent interpretation of Bentham's work in international relations theory. Chapter 4 presents an overview of the theoretical traditions in international relations as they relate to Bentham's work. The ideas of Machiavelli, Grotius and Kant, as influential predecessors or contemporaries, set the stage for the subsequent evaluation of Bentham's contribution to the international relations discipline. In Chapter 5, Bentham's ideas on sovereignty are presented. Sovereignty is fundamental to Bentham's rationale in his international writing; it is integrally linked to security issues, and by understanding the nature of sovereignty, features of Bentham's international writings gain clarity. As such the stage is set for Chapter 6, examining the works most familiar to international relations scholars, the essays and fragments composing *A Plan for an Universal and Perpetual Peace*. The strength of Bentham's liberal thinking is obvious in many of the pieces evaluated, as his reputation in international relations theory emanates almost solely from portions of *Plan*. The authority of the liberal interpretation comes into question in Chapter 7, however, when investigating Bentham's position on war. Security concerns override many of his idealist exhortations found in *Plan*, and a less than liberal character emerges. Chapter 8 delves into the question of colonies, again an area in which many have felt confident about Bentham's position but, which rather, illustrates the depth of Bentham's problems. Finding an appropriate balance between ideas of emancipation, and those echoing the economic and population concerns of his time, becomes a difficulty that Bentham fails to address adequately. Chapter 9 continues on the economic theme, focusing on Bentham's other international political economy writings, including the financing of war, supporting the thesis that security, and security of expectations, play a paramount role in his thinking. Chapter 10 takes some of Bentham's ideas about international relations and compares them with current liberal thinking in the context of 'human security'. Can Bentham's work contribute to current debates in international relations? An examination of current debates which reflect the older, liberal ideas of Bentham and other theorists illustrates the extent to which we can and should turn to the works that preceded us. Chapter 11 concludes the work, highlighting recurring ideas throughout the book and how they are connected through the security of expectation, or disappointment-prevention principle.

It has been said that in international relations theory, Bentham is a liberal, keeping company with Immanuel Kant, Thomas Paine and other kindred spirits. On the other hand, scholars such as Meineke considered utilitarianism to be linked to such notions as raison d'état, a concept linked to the realist tradition.[70] Through a cursory reading of Bentham's works, it becomes clear that too many difficulties arise if one expects to keep Bentham locked in the liberal tradition. To complicate things further, the difficulties of locating Bentham in the liberal tradition do not imply that his is, therefore, a realist approach. Apart from the fact that Bentham's place in the liberal tradition is based on the evidence offered in *A Plan for an Universal and Perpetual Peace*, there is ample evidence, especially as seen from the perspective of the disappointment-prevention principle, that Bentham cannot and will not be placed within one of the theoretical traditions at all.

Bentham does not appear to have arrived at any definitive conclusions on the many issues he raised in his international writings. His aspirations are idealist, his senses are realist, and so the battle ensues. There is no doubt that Bentham is a *contributor* to the liberal tradition that was evolving during his time. However, his theoretical conundrums not only allow us to understand part of the development of international relations thought, but also give us cause to consider the efficacy of these theoretical traditions altogether. There is merit in all of these positions, and attempting to reify one or the other as the correct perspective or even 'truth', can be both fruitless and deceiving.

Notes

1 The first use of the word 'international', coined by Jeremy Bentham and used in *An Introduction to the Principles of Morals and Legislation* (New York: Hafner Publishing, 1965), p. 326. Bentham was dissatisfied with the term 'law of nations' and sought an alternative that he hoped would more clearly articulate the concept intended. Bentham had this work printed by 1780, but it was not published until 1789.

2 John Dinwiddy, *Bentham* (Oxford: Oxford University Press, 1989), p. 19.

3 Ibid.

4 Ibid., p. 1.

5 Ibid., p. 4.

6 Ibid., p. 5.

7 J. H. Burns, 'Bentham and the French Revolution', *Transactions of the Royal Historical Society*, 5th series, xvi (1966), p. 95.

8 H. L. A. Hart, 'Bentham and the United States of America', *Journal of Law and Economics*, Vol. xxi (1967), p. 549. John Lind was an ex-clergyman and active lawyer, 11 years older than Bentham, and a very close friend. Lind was the one to suggest a critical commentary against Blackstone's famous commentaries, part of which became Bentham's *Fragment on Government*.

9 Ibid., p. 553.
10 John Bowring, 'Memoirs of Bentham', *Bentham's Works*, Vol. I, p. 66. Found in Hart, p. 557.
11 Ibid., p. 558.
12 Ibid., p. 557.
13 Stephen Conway, 'Bentham versus Pitt: Jeremy Bentham and British Foreign Policy 1789', *Historical Journal*, Vol. 30, No.4 (1987), p. 791.
14 Ibid.
15 Ibid.
16 Ibid., p. 792.
17 Stephen Conway, 'Bentham on Peace and War', *Utilitas*, Vol. 1, No. 1, (1989), p. 85.
18 Burns, p. 96.
19 Ibid., p. 112.
20 Ibid., p. 106.
21 Ibid., p. 107.
22 Ibid., p. 109.
23 Dinwiddy, p. 12.
24 Burns, p. 112.
25 Dinwiddy, p. 14.
26 Ibid., and Hart, pp. 565–6.
27 Hart, p. 566.
28 Ibid.
29 Burns, p. 114.
30 Ibid. In his capacity as honorary citizen of France, Bentham voted in favour of 'the consulship for life' for Napoleon in 1802. (ibid.).
31 Dinwiddy, p. 15.
32 Ibid.
33 Ibid., p. 17.
34 Ibid., p. 18.
35 For more on Bentham's history with the peace movement see Steven Conway, 'Bentham, the Bethamites and the Nineteenth-Century British Peace Movement,' *Utilitas*, Vol. 2, No. 2, (1990), pp. 221–43. Bentham's penchant for opportunism led him to write to his brother on 24 April 1811, asking him to 'assist in a project to fit out a privateer'. This was to be no ordinary privateer, but a primitive submarine piloted by the notorious smuggler 'Captain' Johnson. Bentham explained: 'If this man fails and perishes, he can be better spared than a better and less mischievous man.' Bentham's primary motive seems to have been financial: it was the 'probable prospect of pecuniary advantage' that attracted him.* (* Even on this score Bentham's proposal was curious. In 1789 he had written that 'the profit of privateering had been thought to be not greater upon the whole than that of other businesses, but rather less'. UC XXV.130. Moreover, at about the same time he had recommended the abolition of privateering. See ibid., p. 120.)' Conway, 'Bentham on Peace and War', p. 84.
36 Hereafter referred to as *Plan*.
37 For a more thorough elucidation of the realist and idealist, or liberal, theoretical traditions in international relations see Chapter 3.
38 F. H. Hinsley, *Power and the Pursuit of Peace* (Cambridge: Cambridge University Press), 1963.
39 Bentham as the idealist is noted in the writings of Hans Morgenthau, E. H. Carr, Kenneth Waltz, F. H. Hinsley, Arnold Wolfers and J. W. Burton, to name a few. Those who read his work as that of a rationalist, also part of the liberal tradition, are Martin Wight, K. J. Holsti, Michael Donelan, Brian Porter and Stanley

Hoffmann. Generally speaking, then, there appears to be agreement among many international relations scholars as to Bentham's solid roots in the liberal tradition.

40 For example, see Norman E. Bowie and Robert L. Simon, *The Individual and the Political Order: An Introduction to Social and Political Philosophy* (New Jersey: Prentice Hall, 1977), pp. 32–33.

41 In later writings, Bentham often addressed his words to the people of the state in question and not just the legislator. See *Rid Yourselves of Ultramaria* for an example. One of his earliest pieces, *Emancipate Your Colonies!*, was also directed toward the citizens (of France in this case); however, *Colonies and Navy*, written at roughly the same time, spoke to the states of France and Britain themselves.

42 The 'ambivalence' argument is used by Donald Winch. See Chapter 3.

43 This argument, that Bentham cannot be regarded as inconsistent because his various and often conflicting conclusions are based on the greatest happiness principle, is used by Lea Campos Boralevi. See Chapter 6.

44 J. A. W. Gunn, 'Jeremy Bentham and the Public Interest', *Canadian Journal of Political Science*, I (1968), p. 408. Provided by F. Rosen, *Jeremy Bentham and Representative Democracy: A Study of the Constitutional Code* (Oxford: Clarendon Press, 1983), p. 31.

45 Ibid., p. 31

46 Ibid.

47 Ibid., p. 104. Rosen states that the principle itself appears in the first volume of the *Constitutional Code*, but only in material added in 1830. The earliest appearance of the principle is in 1826 in *A Commentary on Mr. Humphreys' Real Property Code* (Rosen, p. 104).

48 Rosen discredits this point by stating that instead of reflecting an 'older conception of security, and especially security of expectations' as argued by Doug Long, the disappointment-prevention principle 'receives a new emphasis and application in Bentham's later writings.' (Rosen, p. 104n). As a coherent and fully articulate 'principle', Rosen may be correct. Nevertheless, it is quite clear that this very principle emanates from Bentham's consistent and overall concern with security.

49 Ibid.

50 Ibid., p. 105.

51 Ibid., p. 104.

52 J. Bentham, *The Theory of Legislation*, pp. 96–97.

53 Ibid., pp. 109–10.

54 Ibid.

55 Ibid.

56 Rosen, p. 68.

57 Ibid. Rosen cites Bahmueller, *The National Charity Company*, (Berkeley, CA: University of California Press 1981), pp. 154–6; and D. Long, *Bentham on Liberty* (Toronto: University of Toronto Press 1977), pp. 215 ff., as examples of this type of charge.

58 Ibid., p. 69.

59 Ibid.

60 Ibid.

61 Ibid. From Bentham's *Letters to Count Toreno on the Proposed Penal Code* in Bowring, Vol. VIII, pp. 509–10.

62 Thomas Hobbes, *Leviathan: Or, the Matter, Forme & Power of a Common wealth, Ecclesiastical and Civill* (Cambridge: Cambridge University Press, 1904) p. 84.

63. Ibid., p. 71.

64. Ibid., p. 72.

65. Ibid.

66. Ibid. J. Bentham, *Theory of Legislation*, p. 111.

67. Ibid.
68. Ibid., p. 114
69. Ibid., pp. 120, 148. Equality is still a desired end as long as security remains the supreme principle; security is even able to lead indirectly to equality. Equality, however, is a result that, though desired, is a final priority where the subordinate ends of utility are concerned.
70. F. Meinecke, *Machiavellism: The Doctrine of Raison d'État and its Place in Modern History* (New Haven, CT: Yale University Press, 1957), p. 3.

2 Who We Are versus Who We Want to be: Bentham and Nationalism

All political theory presupposes some kind of theory about human nature, some basic, anthropological theory.[1]

In peace and prosperity states and individuals have better sentiments, because they do not find themselves suddenly confronted with imperious necessities; but war takes away the easy supply of daily wants, and so proves a rough master that brings most men's characters to a level with their fortunes.[2]

Idealists railed against realism during the first debate and sought to mold international relations to reflect the supposedly cooperative standards of domestic politics in liberal states. In emphasizing peace and altruism, the idealists appropriated for international relations certain traits commonly assigned to the nonpolitical western 'women,' and they did so without offering gender attributions for their ideas.[3]

There is a third way between Utopianism and despair. That is to take the world as it is and to improve it; to have faith without a creed, hope without illusions, love without God. The Western world is committed to the proposition that rational man will in the end prove stronger and more successful than irrational man.[4]

How does the political philosopher develop a theory of the relations between individual and state without making fundamental assumptions about troublesome human nature? The difficulty of identifying particular traits of human nature which can be taken as universal, and therefore also as universally applicable is often illustrated in international relations discourse through the positions articulated by those referred to as realists, idealists, or rationalists.[5] Although varying assumptions exist within these particular approaches, most, if not all, of them rely on reifying some characteristics emanating from the elusive concept 'human nature'.

This chapter examines the difficulty Jeremy Bentham had in reconciling the discrepancy between what he thought *ought* to be the fundamental, ruling principles of human nature, and what he observed in both himself and his fellow citizens that tended to contradict those assumptions, and that subsequently led to political solutions often contrary to others he allegedly espoused. The purpose of this exercise is not only to illustrate the dynamics behind the development of Bentham's thinking in the area of international relations, but also to set the terms for subsequent analysis. In deliberately choosing one set of assumptions over another, even while recognizing the validity of both, Bentham inevitably laid himself open to criticism. An example can be seen in a discussion of nationalism and Bentham's response to nationalist sentiments.

Human nature

What is meant by the term human nature? What have been some common assumptions about human nature and what have they meant for political thought and international relations theory in particular? Kenneth Waltz examines some of these assumptions in *Man, the State, and War*. Reviewing the works of such thinkers as Augustine, Spinoza, Niebuhr, and Morgenthau, among others, Waltz provides a simple delineation whereby he divides views of human nature into two groups – the optimists and the pessimists.[6] Both camps, in general, have no difficulty in recognizing human beings as inherently evil, but, argues Waltz, the pessimists do not envision a solution to combat this inherent trait, whereas the optimists look to reason, nature, or another external factor to impell humanity towards progress. This impulsion includes, if not centres on, the elimination of war as an objective.[7]

Before considering Bentham's own struggle with assumptions about human nature it would be useful to discuss how these perceptions have been dealt with by others. A useful point of departure for such an examination are the views of Isaiah Berlin. The position of Berlin, a present-day theorist, on the 'human nature question' is largely derived from his evaluations of Enlightenment and Counter-Enlightenment thinkers.[8] As Bentham was a philosopher of the Enlightenment era, Berlin's critique and evaluations provide useful tools for analyzing Bentham's position.

Another reason for introducing Berlin's work here is that his conclusions about human nature, to the extent that he recognizes that we have one, reveal a similar ambivalence about categorizing and reifying human behaviour, but unlike Bentham, Berlin refuses ultimately to rely on a universal-izing principle with which to assess and drive political development. It can be argued that Berlin has had the additional advantage of the insights of Counter-Enlightenment thinkers, especially those of Hamann, Herder, and Vico. Nevertheless, Berlin's assessment as a critique of Enlightenment thinking can be useful when we address the issue of how one Enlightenment philosopher sought to address the question of human nature.

Instead of desiring a universal characteristic of human nature which might inform a principle by which society would be able to shape itself towards the ideal state of the 'good', Berlin accepts the diversity and variety of actions, values, and decisions of various peoples which have been evident throughout history. Bentham had noticed similar tensions, value differences, and 'incommensurables' as Berlin terms them,[9] but as will be seen below, Bentham was apparently not as able to embrace these incommensurables as did Berlin. Berlin's value-pluralism recognizes that which Bentham could not accept; sometimes one must choose between values without being able to determine if one value is better than the other. Whereas an overriding principle would dictate the direction in which a society could progress, value-pluralism recognizes that a 'best state of affairs' is impossible to determine.[10]

John Gray points out an interesting contrast between Berlin's value-pluralism and utilitarianism: 'It is worth considering further the implications of Berlinian pluralism for ethical theory and, thereby, for political thought. Perhaps the most straightforward implication is the death blow it deals, if it is true, to utilitarianism.'[11] As Gray argues, the utilitarian approach dictates that all values must be comparable for the purpose of evaluation and subsequent rational decision making. In this instance Gray relies on John Stuart Mill's version of utilitarianism; however, much of Gray's discussion depends on a general account of utilitarianism and many of his comments have a bearing on Bentham's thinking. Gray identifies a tension which plagues the philosophy of both Mill, and Bentham: 'It was one of Mill's chief contentions that the demands of happiness or flourishing differ in individual cases, perhaps because individuals have natures, or quiddities, containing endowments and needs that are in many respects unique or particular to them. A liberal society is commended because, via 'experiments in living', it will shelter many varieties of individual flourishings.'[12] Although taken from Mill, this position is also consistent with the importance Bentham placed on negative liberty, an importance recognized by both Gray and Berlin.[13] Yet one cannot deny that, ultimately, Bentham opted to design a principle which would dictate a particular path for humanity, so much so that he developed a constitutional code that he hoped most, if not all, nations would assume.[14] Naturally, one constitutional code informing the political practices of so many nations ultimately presupposes, implicit though it may be, a homogenization of ideals, values, and peoples. Such a scenario is entirely contradictory to Berlin's value-pluralism as well as to the evidence born out by world history. It also contradicts many of Bentham's own observations as will be seen below.

The dilemma experienced by Bentham in deriving what he felt to be an accurate understanding about human nature can be illustrated by the ongoing debate regarding Bentham's place in liberalism as a whole.[15] Although a more extensive discussion of this debate will take place in a later chapter, and especially with regard to Bentham's place in the international relations theory traditions, an introduction may be provided here for the purposes of elucidating the tensions within Bentham's work.

For our purposes, this debate aptly demonstrates not only the obvious difficulty Bentham had in reconciling some of his views with his others, but also the difficulty of subsequent theorists and scholars of the history of ideas have had in isolating Bentham's position accurately. And even the attempts to categorize Bentham's thinking are telling; different essays and bodies of work are referred to depending on the case being made, and there seems to be no room to question whether Bentham is either an 'individualist', because of his liberal views, or an 'authoritarian', reflecting his more illiberal aspects.[16] The debate does not allow for a value-pluralist interpretation (assuming that one is warranted) whereby Bentham may have seen the validity of various contradictory views and have possibly accepted them as such, while in fact committed to a 'principle' which could draw on either liberal or authoritarian premises as circumstances dictated. [17] Whether this is the case or not, at this point it is important to recognize the broad scope of Bentham's thinking, often based on his varying views of human nature.

It is therefore worthwhile to present this dilemma for the purposes of coming to know and understand Bentham as a contributor to international relations thought, and to speculate how and why Bentham dealt with the issue of human nature. Crimmins states that Bentham was no different from his contemporary and later 'nineteenth century liberals [who] wrestled with the conundrum: how far could democratization go without trampling underfoot the liberty of the middle classes? The uncertainty of the response is amply illustrated in Bentham, and it should not surprise us that disciples could draw strikingly different messages from his writings'.[18] However, is this enough to explain Bentham's work in regard to his place as a theorist and his difficulty in evaluating human nature? The following pages map some of the contradictions and tensions which pervade Bentham's work, especially in international relations, and comment on the apparent decision he made to choose one view of human nature rather than another. This will illuminate the question as to where his true home resides, in liberalism or elsewhere.

A final thought on human nature, which might assist subsequent evaluation, comes from Kenneth Waltz. Waltz provides a critique of human nature based political theories by suggesting that it is ineffectual to develop ideas of good government on the basis of one 'theme' of observations. Waltz points out the obvious fact that humanity has exhibited tendencies which range from the selfishly horrific to the selflessly heroic; no matter where one looks in history one will find ample evidence to support one's theory, whether pessimist or optimist. It is on this basis that Waltz chooses to eliminate, or at least minimize the importance of theories based in human nature in favour of alternative theories, such as those which see the state, or better yet, international structures, as primary factors in deriving an effective theory and therefore explanation of world politics. However, Waltz's critique of human nature theorists is useful if for no other reason than to try to understand thinkers such as Bentham would not have been able to formulate Waltz's critique themselves.

Human beings throughout history have committed atrocities and good deeds alike: who is to say which quality predominates in us? Berlin makes the same observation, but he does not abandon the actions of the human being as a result. Focusing on the individual, Berlin adjusts his theory to enable one to acknowledge the different decisions made by people, but still respect those individuals as those who have influenced political and cultural development in general. In this way, too, Berlin does not abandon the philosophers of the Enlightenment. But given such modifications as are made by Berlin, is Waltz's critique of human nature theorists still helpful? Are the works of theorists such as Machiavelli, Kant, Bentham, Augustine, Spinoza, and Morgenthau too narrowly focused to accommodate Waltz's obvious point? Were they incapable of seeing either the good or the bad in human nature that some of their predecessors or successors observed?

It is an understatement to suggest that it is difficult to 'know' exactly why a scholar opts for particular assumptions, but these questions are worth addressing and prompt some cursory speculations, if not precise answers. Waltz's dismissal of human nature theorists is too easy, and devalues the work of these important thinkers. Using Bentham as an example, we can see that he was not oblivious to contradictory features of human behaviour and was troubled by this dilemma himself. And as will be shown below, although he readily recognized that humanity could exhibit traits both evil and good, he ultimately settled on one of those observations as the basis for his theorizing.

Bentham and human nature

Printed in 1780 and finally published in 1789, Bentham's first paragraph of *An Introduction to the Principles of Morals and Legislation* presents one of his earliest and certainly most celebrated comments on the nature of humankind:

> Nature has placed mankind under the governance of two sovereign masters, *pain* and *pleasure*. It is for them alone to point out what we ought to do, as well as to determine what we shall do. On the one hand the standard of right and wrong, on the other the chain of causes and effects, are fastened to their throne. They govern us in all we do, in all we say, in all we think: every effort we can make to throw off our subjection, will serve but to demonstrate and confirm it. In words a man may pretend to abjure their empire: but in reality he will remain subject to it all the while. The *principle of utility* recognises this subjection, and assumes it for the foundation of that system, the object of which is to rear the fabric of felicity by the hands of reason and of law. Systems which attempt to question it, deal in sounds instead of sense, in caprice instead of reason, in darkness instead of light.[19]

Self-interest is the expression of that pleasure and pain; one attempts to augment pleasure and diminish pain. However, the principle of utility extends that sense of self-interest to include as many other 'selves' as possible, thereby 'maximizing the greatest happiness for the greatest number.' It is this principle of utility that is meant to guide the legislator when determining what sort of legislation would best reflect the interest of all of the individuals composing the community. Although this principle is rooted in the notion of self-interest, a notion which is commonly recognized and utilized by international theory realists,[20] Bentham incorporated within it an element of social regard, or regard for others.[21] Therefore one central manifestation of our self-regarding actions, at least according to Bentham, are those which are also other-regarding.

Interpretations of Bentham's thinking have been plagued by subsequent ahistorical analysis such that his definition of the principle of utility has not really been explored beyond the early definition provided in *An Introduction to the Principles of Morals and Legislation*. Therefore his struggle with notions of human nature, which provide the basis for his thinking, have never really been recognized.[22] However, in reading Bentham's correspondence over the years in which he reflected often on such subjects, together with his writings on international affairs and other texts such as *Evidence* and the *Rationale*, we find evidence of a definite struggle to define adequately the greatest happiness principle.[23]

What follows is a brief discussion of this struggle and the attempts Bentham made to refine and improve his guiding principle. Examining the process of Bentham's thinking, both in general and particularly in the area of international relations, provides a more complex picture of how Bentham arrived at his conclusions and at the same helps to clarify the problem of over-simplifying certain aspects of his ideas, such an examination also helps us in better understanding some of the twists and turns Bentham made during his years of writing; his economic texts, which are central to his thinking in international relations, are an excellent example.

This chapter is a contribution towards reconciling Bentham's position on human nature and the issue of nationalism. Late in life Bentham finally concluded that individuals do not function in accord to how their actions affect others, and that 'reason' is not necessarily always at play. Nevertheless, as much as he does try to recognize this fact, and reflect it in his greatest happiness principle, he is still a product of his Enlightenment upbringing, and 'rational' action ultimately prevails.

Understanding human nature

Bentham's understanding of human nature did change over time; where he initially, and for the greater part of his life, believed that human beings were endowed with a capacity for virtue which was evidenced by social-regarding actions, he subsequently changed his mind such that the notion of virtue drops from his thinking and human beings only function with regard to self-preference and with no social-regarding element present whatsoever.[24] Even so, Bentham found a way to express this new 'self-preference' in such a way that individuals do become capable of acting with the interests of others in mind. The concupiscent appetite of each individual experiences a check from the prospect of the evil effects produced to their own detriment by the operation of irascible appetite in other individuals whose pain or loss of pleasure is a consequence of those selfish appetites. In this way injury to others finds its first restraint in the fear of the eventual retaliation and retribution – the natural consequences of resentment.

> And thus it is that out of the self-regarding affection rose by degrees the sympathetic affection; out of that, the power of the popular or moral affection – and both of them, in their main tendency, operating in conjunction to the increase of the aggregate of happiness.[25]

The 'concupiscible' and 'irascible' appetites refer to the physical and 'dissocial affections' to use Bentham's term, neither of which considers the interests of others. This evaluation of human nature fundamentally differs from Bentham's previous and long-standing assumption that virtue was an inherent element of human nature, a shift in his thinking did not begin to take place until 1809. But as much as virtue was supposed to be an inherent quality for Bentham, he still noted that 'it has seldom, as yet, been consistently pursued.'[26] Bentham's new understanding attempted to rectify this problem by completely eliminating the notion of virtue and focusing solely on the notion of self-preference. In this way the foundation of the principle of utility, or greatest happiness principle, was radically altered:

> As an 'is', a principle of human nature which involved taking the pleasures of the whole society as a concern of calculation for the individual, it was rendered illusory by the *self-preference principle* which made the calculation of pleasure for the individual the whole of the individual's concern. As an 'ought', it was no longer a solicitation of virtue guided by reason, but rather an expression of a desire for peace by self-preference cognisant of its own dependence and vulnerability – 'a declaration of peace to all mankind.' [Footnote: Bentham, *First Principles Preparatory to Constitutional Code*, (*CW*), pp. 231–2n; (*Works*), IX, pp. 4–5.][27]

Although Bentham's principle, by which he measured all action, had changed to reflect self-preference, that same principle was still supposed to lead to progressive and positive outcomes when followed. Bentham's pleas for the emancipation of colonies, for the establishment of some level of international law, and for the implementation of his constitutional code, all of which he considered well into the 1820s, were based on the greatest happiness principle even after this shift of emphasis to self-preference had occured.

The fact that the principle of utility was based on self-interest at all was still unique for a philosophy soon to be included under the banner of liberalism. Stanley Hoffmann expresses discomfort with the utilitarian approach[28] in that he considers it to be cold, calculated, and more a method of justification than a guide to moral development:

> Utilitarianism is better at giving one a good conscience than at providing a compass ... The morality of international relations will simply have to be a mix of commands and of utilitarian calculations. The commands cannot be followed at any cost; 'Thou shalt not kill' or 'Thou shalt not lie' can never be pushed so far that the cost clearly becomes a massive disutility to the national interest.[29]

Friedrich Meinecke also discusses his discomfort with utilitarianism in stating that

> [I]f he [the statesman] acts out of consideration for the well-being of the State – that is to say, from *raison d' état* – then there at once arise the very obscure question of how far he is guided in doing so by a utilitarian and how far by an idealistic point of view ... the advantage of the state is always at the same time blended too with the advantage of the rulers. So *raison d' etat* is continually in danger of becoming a merely utilitarian instrument without ethical application, in danger of sinking back again from wisdom to mere cunning, and of restraining the superficial passions merely in order to satisfy passions and egoisms which lie deeper and are more completely hidden.[30]

Bentham's utilitarian approach to world politics differs markedly from the above interpretations of utilitarianism however. Bentham had hoped to direct legislators in such a way that although the foundation of the principle of utility, self-interest, is taken into account, it generally directs policy toward cooperation, open dialogue, prosperity and peace among states.[31] But, as will be shown below, Bentham was also not unaware of the more cynical view and sinister results of self-interest.

Bentham required that judgements of others ought not rest with uneducated, irrational assumptions, but he himself had difficulties overcoming his own prejudices and negative thinking when it came to other cultures. This fact is interesting for two reasons; on the one hand in order to warrant a universal principle of action Bentham had to argue that human beings behaved in a universal fashion, but on the other hand he had occasional negative reactions to cultures which differed from his own and these reactions did not seem to reflect any similarity or potential kinship between peoples. In evaluating human nature Bentham often looked to his own sentiments and actions as illustrations of what human beings are capable of doing or feeling. Upon this and his observations of the human race, at least from his standpoint, Bentham derived assumptions and a correlative political theory which he believed would enable people to live in peace and prosperity. However, if one so learned as Bentham could generate opinions about others which were demeaning, low, and frequently based on a lack of understanding,[32] how could he possibly expect the whole human race to overcome its various prejudices, perceptions of superiority, and mistrust in favour of fair treatment, cessation of war and free trade?

As an example, one may look to Bentham's opinions about the Jews; it is quite true that from a juridical point of view, Bentham could not see the sense in legislating discriminatory codes and thus sanctioning discriminatory behaviour against Jews, as against any other individual or group.[33] Nevertheless, his more visceral sentiments about Jews are less than complimentary, and illustrate the type of characteristics, attitudes and attendant behaviours that Bentham thought could be opposed. Of course he did not discuss these attitudes within his formal writings, but they are found in his correspondence to his brother and his father while travelling to Russia in 1786. Many of his personal reflections are contained within his correspondence, not only his sentiments towards Jews but also his thoughts on relationships, and family affairs, the politics of the day and especially the doings of the Prime Minister William Pitt and King George III, and his admiration for Catherine the Great of Russia. The letters provide scholars with an excellent source of Bentham's private observations which frequently informed his more formal writings.

After years of planning, Bentham finally visited Russia, a country for which he had no lack of praise. However, his travels required him to meet and stay with people who really did not suit his tastes, to say the least:

> From Chekanofka even unto Bohopol, a space of not less than 144 miles, not an Inn have I entered that has been in any other hands than those of the race of Israel: a people by inbred filthyness the worst qualified, and by religious scruples, one should think the least disposed, to engage in such a business . . . I am now satisfied that the sufferings of the forefathers were no more than a just retribution for those which the children have inflicted on me. *Qui fit Maecenas*, that in all Poland a man can not get a rag to cover him, nor a piece of lack bread to eat, nor a beast to carry him, nor a hog-stie to lay his head in, but he must have a Jew to help him to it? – O but they *have* a head! – 'Yes' replied I, 'but it is a lousy one' –.[34]

To consider suffering a just retribution for anyone suggests that the wickedness of these particular individuals is somehow evident to Bentham and that the retribution is therefore deserved. Nor is there evidence here that these evils reflect on humanity as a whole rather than one group. This puts Bentham's principle and overall philosophy at odds with his feelings regarding a particular culture, and negative though the thoughts may be, show at least an inner recognition of differences between people. It is certainly true that Bentham was able to overcome his personal feelings about Jews and to provide them support at least in a political sense. But this altruism is also what he expects of all persons at all times, and most other people have not had the privilege of his education or his travels to broaden their opinions.[35]

Although Bentham tried to transcend his own prejudices in the above example, in his essays on international relations he also recognized that the rest of humankind had characteristics which ran counter to his rationalist thinking, and he recognized that overcoming these characteristics on such a large scale might be insurmountable. Although he wrote the bulk of the more internationally focused essays in the 1780s, long before he found himself 'forced to accept that more fundamental principle [of self-preference]',[36] his ambivalence about the nature of humanity was readily apparent.

> The moral feelings of men respecting national morality are still so far short of perfection, that in the scale of estimation justice has not yet gained the ascendant over force . . . as I have observed, men have not yet learnt to tune their feelings in unison with the source [of] morality on these points. They will feel more pride at being accounted strong, than resentment at being called unjust; or rather the imputation of injustice will appear flattering rather than otherwise, when coupled with the consideration of its cause. I feel it in my own experience. [B]ut if I, listed as I am in the professed and hitherto only advocate in my own country, in the cause of Justice, set a less value on Justice then is its due, what can I expect from the general run of men.[37]

In this small essay, *Pacification and Emancipation*,[38] Bentham has presented both himself and his readers with an immense problem. If human beings function on the basis he has observed, what is the likelihood that they will ever endeavour to do as he requests? Notions of justice will more than likely fall on deaf ears, and anything honourable manifests itself in activities which prove to be far more harmful than beneficial to humankind. Still, Bentham's answer to this problem, remote though the solution may appear, is also revealed in the above passage: a reliance upon a person's capacity to learn the proper thing to do. How influencial education could be is open to debate, but the possibility still existed according to Bentham.

In what way does Bentham plead the cause of emancipating colonies, establishing international law, and ceasing war? Although he did articulate notions of justice which ought to apply when evaluating national and international policy, he gave equal, if not more attention, to the glory and honour which would be endowed upon those who participated in his plan.

> Whatsoever nation got the start of the other in making the proposal would crown itself with everlasting immortal honour. This risk would be nothing: the gain certain. This gain would be, the giving an incontrovertible demonstration of its own disposition to peace, and of the opposite disposition on the other nation in case of its rejecting the proposal. . . .
>
> O my countrymen! [P]urge your eyes from the film of prejudice: extripate from your hearts the black specks of excessive jealousy, false ambition, selfishness and insolence. The operations may be painful: but the rewards are glorious indeed!! As the main difficulty, so will the main honour be with you.[39]

Making a case for honour and glory reveals the difficulty Bentham had in relying on other-regarding tendencies in human nature, even though the principle of utility, at this point in Bentham's writings, assumes that such tendencies exist. Instead he must show how self-regarding factors will be enhanced to bring his fellow countrymen on side.

This ambivalence being so obviously present, why did it take so long for Bentham fundamentally to adjust his thinking on the principle of utility? Don Jackson discusses this development drawing on more extensive examples from Bentham's work,[40] but it is possible to see where his thinking was taking him in the 1780s with his international writings, and perhaps understand, to some degree, what made Bentham persist with his 'other-regarding' assumptions. One example of what Bentham believed to be a superb illustration of the appropriate behaviour of statesmen was the negotiating team of De Witte and Temple:[41]

> Jealousy is the vice of narrow minds. Confidence the virtue of enlarged ones. To be satisfied that confidence between nations is not out of nature when they have worthy ministers one need but read the account of the negotiation betwixt De Wit and Temple as given by Hume. I say by Hume: for as it required negotiators like De Wit and Temple to carry on such a negotiation in such a manner, so it required a historian like Hume to do it justice ... Temple and De Wit whose confidence in each other was so exemplary and so just, Temple and De Witt were two of the wisest as well as most upright honourable of men in Europe. The age which produced such virtue was the age of the Pretended Popish (?) plot, and of a thousand other enormities which now can not be thought of without horror. Since then the world has had upwards of a century to improve itself in experience, in reflection and in virtue. In every other line at least its improvements in that line have been unquestioned and immense. It is too fond a hope to expect

that France and England might produce not a Temple and De Witt, virtue so transcendent as theirs would not be necessary, but men who in happier times might achieve a work like theirs, with less powers of virtue.[42]

Bentham did not think it impossible that states, through their government ministers, could act in an honourable and 'enlightened' fashion, and that improvements in the conduct of world affairs were feasible. And given the above example, the world did not even require people as 'virtuous' as Temple and De Witte; it can therefore be assumed that, at times, Bentham did not think that it would take much effort to produce a better breed of citizens who would be less inclined to war and more toward peaceful negotiation and mutual prosperity.

Bentham applauded the successes of DeWitte and Temple while at the same time acknowledging that these were two exceptional people on the international stage. His only hope was that people with considerably less virtue could nevertheless accomplish similar feats. This, in turn, speaks to the issue of our human nature and the extent to which this nature will embrace actions which are other-regarding rather than only self-regarding. It appears that Bentham was not about to commit himself to actions which he did not consider realistic.[43] Given the struggle Bentham has in determining human nature, how does he see the transformation to even a moderately virtuous state taking place?

> Though in the generating of this disposition [of emancipating colonies], unjust ambition has doubtless had but no great share: yet jealousy, sincere and honest jealousy must be acknowledged to have had no inconsiderable a one. Vulgar prejudice, fostered by passion, assigns the heart for the seat of all the moral diseases it complains of: but the principle and more frequent seat is really in the head: it is from ignorance and weakness that men deviate from the path of rectitude, more frequently than from selfishness and malevolence. This is happy: for the power of information and reason over error and ignorance is much greater and much surer than that or exhortation and all the modes of preaching, over selfishness and malevolence.[44]

Education is the weapon we can use against the more visceral and passionate elements of our nature. Through education we can produce citizens who will resort to reason before passion, and who are at least moderately virtuous and other-regarding. Undoubtedly this education would require a particular content in order to engender such behaviour, because as will be seen below, other thinkers see the role of education as one which potentially exacerbates that which Bentham is trying to quell: disharmony, misunderstanding, and war.

Nationalism

It is significant that the discussion about Bentham's attempts to grapple with human nature end with his use of education as a bridge between peoples to increase understanding, engender cooperation and not separation, and minimize the chance of conflict. However, the very instrument upon which Bentham relies, education, is also considered a contributory element in the rise of nationalism.[45] The uses of education and the notion of self-determination are interesting factors to examine given the time in which Bentham wrote. The concept of the 'nation' was only just developing in the eighteenth century, little had been written on the topic of nations and nationalism, and the nineteenth century only produced the first phase in the history of nationalist movements which were 'purely cultural, literary and folkloric'.[46] Nevertheless, Bentham at the beginning of his career, was also writing concurrently with Immanuel Kant, with whom Bentham's work in international relations is often compared, and who played a pivotal role in the development of the notion of self-determination.[47]

What is the association between nationalism and human nature, if any, and why use the former concept to illustrate some of the challenges which Bentham's philosophy must face? Ernest Gellner claims that nationalism is not a result of human nature since '[O]ne may not invoke a general substrate to explain a specific phenomenon . . . This movement is the fruit neither of ideological aberration, nor of emotional excess.'[48] Rather states Gellner, nationalism is an 'external manifestation of a deep adjustment in the relationship between polity and culture which is quite unavoidable'.[49] That nationalism may be a purely external construct which has no bearing upon the nature of humanity may certainly be true, but this detached and external construct had, and still has, the potential to ignite a force within humanity. The massacre of Turks by Greeks at Tripolizza during the Greek struggle for independence may be taken as one grim example: (1821–7):

> As soon as the Greeks had entered the town in force, they [the Turks] sued for quarter, but in vain; the barbarians [the Greeks] went from house to house sparing neither age nor sex, and work of slaughter continued the whole night . . . The fires, shots, screams of agony and terror, and shouts of these monsters formed a night of dreadful horror . . . Never was a town so completely pillaged: . . . these wretches, as if not satisfied with the number of victims they had already devoted to most cruel deaths, determined on destroying those [women and children] that remained in the huts of the old camp. They stripped and drove them away intending to shoot them near a deep pit at some distance from Tripolitsa; but the thirst for blood was too great to enable them to wait so long, and they covered the road to the spot destined for their butchery with bodies of women clasping their infants to their bosoms and children clinging to their mother[50]

Elie Kedourie also sees nationalism as a spark for such flames:

> One feature, in particular, of Napoleonic policies is highly pertinent
> to the later spread of nationalism. While still a general, serving under
> the Directory, in 1796–97, Bonaparte invaded Italy and occupied
> Venice; the better to tame the Venetian Senate, he sent emissaries to
> the Ionian Islands, then under Venetian rule, among them a 'distin-
> guished man of letters' whose duty was to 'manufacture manifestoes'
> in order 'to stir up the shades of Sparta and Athens', to raise up the
> inhabitants against their masters by reminding them of the ancient
> glories of Greece, and exhorting them to resuscitate these glories.
> As Emperor, Napolean continued the same tactics.[51]

Nationalism may not equate with human nature, but perhaps it can be
considered a manifestation of an aspect of human nature, in this case the
desire or need to differentiate ourselves from the other even to the point
of gratuitous hostility. Of course, when defining nationalism the terror
which is often attendant on nationalist struggles is not necessarily the focus
of attention. Eric Hobsbawm uses Gellner's definition of nationalism
whereby it is 'primarily a principle which holds that the political and
national unit should be congruent.'[52] However, Hobsbawm goes further in
acknowledging that the politicial duty of the nationalist state focuses first
and foremost on those belonging to the group which articulated the nationalist rhetoric in the first instance.[53] Hobsbawm also recognizes the significance of examining the effects of such rhetoric on 'ordinary persons who
are the objects of [nationalist] action and propoganda'.[54] This recognition
goes beyond understanding nationalism as a historically-placed doctrine
which is primarily a manifestation of a 'particular stage of technological
and economic development'.[55] It makes the definition personal in that
action and reaction cannot be reduced to the point where human behaviour
and inclination are eliminated.

Examining Bentham's 'liberal' position against the concept of nationalism is a worthwhile exercise for two reasons: first in the comparison
between Bentham's understanding of human nature and nationalism and
the subsequent analysis; second, because of the tension which exists
between nationalism and liberalism, Bentham being a primary contributor
to the latter.

Broadly speaking, liberalism consists of the following distinguishing
characteristics: the units of analysis are primarily individuals, the system is that of the open market, international process is governed by some
sort of world society and interdependence, and leading norms consist of
freedom, human rights, cosmopolitanism, cooperation, and prosperity.[56]
Although 'liberalism' per se was not yet a formal theoretical position at
the time of Bentham's writing,[57] one can see that Bentham's ideas on the
emancipation of colonies, the dominance of the individual as a component

of society as well as being the unit for which the greatest-happiness principle functions, and certainly his concern for prosperity, are consistent with the theoretical position of liberalism.

How far does Bentham's thinking contribute to, or is at least consistent with, the doctrine of nationalism? In some respects his thinking resembles nationalist sentiments in that he more than once expressed the need for peoples to rule themselves when he called for the emancipation of colonies.[58] He strongly endorsed the actions of the French Revolution, at least in the beginning, as it was an expression of the people's will, and the French citizenry would no longer be dominated by the interests of the ruling few. These events even helped spur him on in the development of his theory of constitutional democracy.[59] As the violence grew however, Bentham quickly changed his mind: 'All France is become a great *Arena* – to exterminate or be exterminated is the question. To exterminate is at once the business and the amusement of life – Feigned tragedies are become insipid and produce no sensation – they must have real ones. All virtue is swallowed up in ferocity. The social virtues are become infamous.'[60] Even so, the French Revolution and what it originally stood for was probably close to what Bentham had in mind in terms of self-determination; the nationalism evident during this event possessed more of a civic than an ethnic orientation, so that all might be counted as equal citizens.

This civic nationalism can be seen in Bentham's idea of what constitutes the state or nation; Bentham followed in the footsteps of David Hume in seeing the nation as 'nothing but a collection of individuals'.[61] This individualism, which plays such an important part in liberalism as a whole, can certainly be found in Bentham's concept of the nation, which is simply one community among many:

> The interest of the community is one of the most general expression that can occur in the phraseology of morals: no wonder that the meaning of it is often lost. When it has a meaning, it is this. The community is a ficticious *body*, composed of the individual persons who are considered as constituting as it were its *members*. The interest of the community is, what? – the sum of the interests of the several members who compose it. It is vain to talk of the interest of the community, without understanding what is the interest of the individual.[62]

At best, any sort of nationalism which could be seen to be expressed in a nation composed as such is a civic nationalism, as little else binds these individuals other than the conveniences of such a community.

Immanuel Kant also recognized individualism such that only the individual could achieve, or move towards achieving, self-determination.[63] Elie Kedourie however sees Kant's view of individualism and resulting self-determination as being a crucial theoretical moment in the development of the doctrine of nationalism. Through the work of J. G. Fichte and

Adam Muller self-determination moved from the individual alone to the individual, self-determination being contingent on the state.[64] This is a move that Bentham would not make, regardless of the powers he would endow upon the legislator and government.

The result?

> Terrorism became the hallmark of purity: 'There is nothing', exclaimed St Just, 'which so much resembles virtue as a great crime.' It seemed, indeed as though great crimes were the only way to ensure justice: 'There is something terrible', St Just also said, 'in the sacred love of the fatherland; it is so exclusive as to sacrifice everything to the public interest, without pity, without fear, without respect for humanity ... What produces the general good is always terrible.' This style, spread and established by a successful revolution, found increasing favour in Europe after 1789.[65]

The above sentiments are very much like those expressed by Bentham but he was also desperate to curtail such excesses. The violent consequences of such doctrines as nationalism were contrary to what Bentham hoped to engender through the principle of utility, or greatest-happiness principle, but he certainly recognized their reality in his more somber moments when assessing human nature.

Even though by 1809 Bentham ultimately conceded defeat regarding the possibility of a virtuous component within human nature, he still felt compelled to structure his arguments and philosophy in such a way that positive and progressive results would follow. In this sense he was very much a product of his time: 'But the philosophy of the Enlightenment, which had discarded innate ideas and the orthodox religious account of the Creation, found it extremely difficult to make place for evil in its scheme, let alone to account for it.'[66] It is important to realize that Bentham struggled with his assumptions about human nature, and to recognize the extent to which his observations of his fellow human beings bore these assumptions out. But, as much as he saw evidence of carnage, he also saw progressive statesmanship, and chose to abide by the universalizing principle he developed throughout his lifetime. In the final analysis Bentham's approach is hard-pressed to allow or even account for the deplorable side of human nature which is so often exhibited, in his day as well as ours, as a consequence of nationalism.

Notes

1 Martin Wight, *International Theory: The Three Traditions*, ed. Gabriele Wight and Brian Porter (Leicester: Leicester University Press, 1991), p. 25.
2 Thucydides, *The Peloponnesian War*, translated by Richard Crawley, revised with an Introduction by T. E. Wick (New York: The Modern Library, 1982), Book Three, section 82, p. 199.

3 Christine Sylvester, *Feminist Theory and International Relations in a Post-modern Era* (Cambridge: Cambridge University Press, 1994), p. 7.

4 A. J. P. Taylor, *Rumours of Wars*, (London: Hamish Hamilton, 1952), p. 262; quoted in Wight, *International Theory: The Three Traditions*, p. 29.

5 I refer here to three, albeit not exclusive, but commonly recognized traditions of theorization within the field of international relations theory. See Wight, *International Theory: The Three Traditions*, and Chapter 4, for a discussion of these traditions.

6 Kenneth Waltz, *Man, the State, and War: A Theoretical Analysis* (New York: Columbia University Press, 1959), pp. 17–41.

7 Ibid., pp. 22–23. Some optimists, such as Marx or a number of feminist thinkers, think that humanity would not necessarily be so evil if it could escape the structural confines of influences such as class and gender. See Steven L. Schweizer, *Imagining World Politics* (New Jersey: Prentice Hall, 1997), pp. 21–22.

8 John Gray, *Berlin* (London: Fontana Press, 1995), pp. 4, 9, 10.

9 Incommensurables being those elements and values, which cannot be compared.

10 Ibid., p. 59.

11 Ibid., p. 58.

12 Gray, p. 59.

13 Ibid., pp. 20–21.

14 This point will be discussed further in Chapter 6 on international law.

15 J. E. Crimmins, 'Contending Interpretations of Bentham's Utilitarianism', *Canadian Journal of Political Science*, Vol. XXIX No. 4 (December 1996), pp. 751–77.

16 Crimmins, p. 751.

17 This kind of ambivalence in Bentham will be examined in subsequent chapters.

18 Crimmins, p. 777.

19 Bentham, *An Introduction to the Principles of Morals and Legislation* (New York: Hafner Publishing, 1948), p. 1.

20 See Hans J. Morgenthau, *Politics Among Nations: The Struggle for Power and Peace* (New Jersey: Alfred A. Knopf, 1949); F. Meinecke, *Machiavellism: The Doctrine of Raison d'Etat and its Place in Modern History* (New Haven: Yale University Press, 1957).

21 Don Jackson, 'Halevy Reconsidered: The Importance of Bentham's Psychological Epistemology in His "Conversion" to Democracy', (New Orleans: Fifth Congress of the International Society for Utilitarian Studies, 1997), pp. 14–18. As will be discussed below, the other-regarding factor is later dropped by Bentham.

22 See D. Lyons, *In the Interest of the Governed*, (Oxford: Clarendon Press 1973); and J. Dinwiddy, 'Bentham on Private Ethics and the Principle of Utility', *Revue Internationale de Philosophie* (1982), pp. 278–300. These examples have been provided by Don Jackson, 'Halevy Reconsidered', p. 30.

23 The principle of utility and the greatest-happiness principle are one and the same; however Bentham began to prefer the latter term as he found it to be a more accurate reflection of what he was trying to achieve. Since the former term is still the most widely known, both will be used interchangeably.

24 Jackson, p. 25.

25 Bentham, *Deontology*: Together with a Table of the Springs of Action; and the Article on Utilitariarism (1814) ed. Amnon Goldworth, Oxford: Clarendon Press, 1983.

26 Jackson, p. 17.

27 Ibid., pp. 24–25.

28 Stanley Hoffmann, *Duties Beyond Borders: On the Limits and Possibilities of Ethical International Politics* (Syracuse: Syracruse University Press, 1981) pp. 13, 41.

29 Ibid., p. 43.
30 F. Meinecke, *Machiavellism* pp. 3, 7.
31 See the general account of Bentham's international thinking in F. H. Hinsley, *Power and the Pursuit of Peace* (Cambridge: Cambridge University Press, 1963) pp. 81–91.
32 Even by Bentham's eighteenth-century standards, as in his writing about slaves, women and homosexuals. See Boralevi, *Bentham and the Oppressed* (1984).
33 See Boralevi, pp. 84–88.
34 Ibid., pp. 90–1.
35 The place of education to assist human beings in overcoming their prejudices and predispositions towards war is discussed below.
36 Jackson, p. 18.
37 UC XXV.32.
38 See Chapter 3, where Bentham's *Plan for a Universal and Perpetual Peace* is broken down into its original component essays of *Pacification and Emancipation*, *Colonies and Navy*, and *Cabinet No Secrecy*. This Chapter appeared in *The Journal for Bentham Studies*, 2001.
39 UC XXV.29, 33.
40 See Jackson, 'Halevy Reconsidered'.
41 Bentham cited this example from David Hume's *History of England* (1754–7), chronicling the negotiations between De Witte and Temple over the potential conquest of Spain and the Low countries by Louis XIV of France in 1668.
42 UC XXV.33–34.
43 The extent to which Bentham wished to be 'realistic' might be a matter for debate. Fred Rosen examines Bentham's philosophy in relation to the rise of Greek nationalism and the development of liberalism; Rosen describes the latter as ideological rather than philosophical. He therefore argues that although Bentham's theory did not translate well into practice, if at all, that was not the point. Bentham was intent on developing a philosophy; liberalism is an ideology of action, and therefore the practical and more 'realistic' programmes would fall under its umbrella. For a thorough discussion see Fred Rosen, *Bentham, Byron and Greece: Constitutionalism, Nationalism, and Early Liberal Political Thought* (Oxford: Clarendon Press 1992).
44 UC XXV.33.
45 See Ernest Gellner, *Nations and Nationalism* (Oxford: Oxford University Press, 1983) p. 35; E. J. Hobsbawm, *Nations and Nationalism Since 1780: Programme, Myth, Reality* (Cambridge: Cambridge University Press, 1990) p. 91.
46 Hobsbawm, pp. 3, 2, 12.
47 Elie Kedourie, *Nationalism* (Oxford: Blackwell Publishers, 1993) pp. 44–46.
48 Gellner, p. 35.
49 Ibid.
50 *W. H. Humphreys' First 'Journal of the Greek War of Independence'*, Sture Linner ed. (Stockholm: Almquist & Wiksell 1967), pp. 62–65. This example has been provided by F. Rosen, *Bentham, Byron and Greece: Constitutionalism, Nationalism, and Early Liberal Political Thought* (Oxford: Clarendon Press, 1992), pp. 139–40.
51 Kedourie, p. 89. Not only is this example useful as an illustration of how one could incite the masses on the basis of nationalist sentiment, but it is also an example which stems from Bentham's time and which he was able to observe. Bentham lived during a crucial phase of the development of these ideas and events.
52 Gellner, p. 1. Definition also provided by Hobsbawm, p. 9.
53 Hobsbawm, p. 9.

54 Ibid., p. 11.
55 Ibid., p. 10.
56 Barry Buzan, 'The timeless wisdom of realism?', in *International Theory: Positivism and Beyond.* Steve Smith, Den Booth and Marysia Zalewski eds. (Cambridge: Cambridge University Press, 1996), p. 57.
57 Fred Rosen, *Bentham, Byron and Greece:* pp. 292–3.
58 See *Pacification and Emancipation, Colonies and Navy, Emancipate Your Colonies.*
59 Rosen, pp. 50–8.
60 UC XLIV.2. Provided by Rosen, p. 58.
61 Kedourie, p. 6.
62 *Introduction to the Principles of Morals and Legislation*, p. 12.
63 Kedourie, pp. 12–43.
64 Ibid., p. 31.
65 Ibid., pp. 10–11.
66 Ibid., p. 44.

3 Bentham's International Manuscripts versus the Published *Works*[1]

Bentham has hitherto been one of the most neglected of the eighteenth century philosophers. His name is a household word; he is universally acknowledged to be one of the founders of modern utilitarianism, his body is preserved in a curious mummified form in a little glass cabin at University College, London. But hitherto his Works have been chiefly known through a notoriously bad collected edition made by a young protégé of his named Bowring – a knight, a general, a Christian (the author indeed of that famous Victorian hymn, In the Cross of Christ I Glory) – but not a utilitarian, not ever a scholar. Moreover, Bowring cut out from what he published anything that might offend Victorian sensibilities akin to his own.[2]

Until relatively recently, students and researchers of Bentham's vast work have primarily relied upon *The Works of Jeremy Bentham* edited in 1843 by John Bowring.[3] Apart from the original manuscripts, these edited works have been the primary source for Bentham's writings. The interpretation of Bentham's work has been heavily dependent upon the editing of this edition, resulting in the Bentham we currently know. This could not be more true for our understanding of his work in international relations, and especially the essay *A Plan for an Universal and Perpetual Peace*.

Unfortunately, it has been almost universally agreed that Bowring did not do justice to Bentham's work, and that the 1843 *Works* could not be considered reliable: 'at times the inadequacy of Bowring's editing stands clearly revealed',[4] and,

> For those seeking Bentham's own writings the principal resource has inevitably been the collected edition completed in 1843 under the super-vision of his executor, John Bowring. This has long been out of print; and even when accessible its eleven volumes of small type in daunting double columns (two volumes comprising what Leslie Stephen called 'one of the worst biographies in the language' – Bowring's *Memoirs of Bentham*) are defective in content as well as discouraging in form ... even now, despite the valuable work during the present century of such scholars as Elie Halevy, C. W. Everett, C. K. Ogden, and W. Stark, relatively little has been done to remedy these defects.[5]

The inadequacies of the Bowring edition stood out when subsequent editors attempted to re-decipher and reorganize Bentham's work. One such editor who undertook the challenge to rectify the disorder caused by Bowring and his editorial staff was Werner Stark. He noted:

> In the University College collection the papers designated Colonies and Navy are divided into two bundles: XVII, 50–57, and XXV, 36–49: the impression of the cataloguer was that the former set dealt with political economy, the latter with international law. Yet these are two aspects that, for Bentham, always formed one: and the simple fact of the matter is that we have to do with one manuscript. To date the one part 1786, the other 1790, is sheer nonsense: all was written at the same time, perhaps in one week, perhaps even on one day. The sequence in which the papers must be arranged in order to yield a coherent argument – and arranging them was like solving a jig-saw puzzle – clearly proves it. Here it is: XXV, 36–38 (39 is a footnote to 36); 44; XVII, 54; XXV, 45, 46; XVII, 55, 56; XXV, 41, 40, 47, 48; XVII, 57; XXV, 49, 42, 43.[6]

That the Bentham papers were, and still are, in such disarray can be attributed to the original editor's manner of categorizing and cataloguing the works, but also to a subsequent 1892 attempt by Thomas Whittaker.[7] Whittaker reported on the condition of the manuscripts and also noted that they were not 'treatises actually printed from or intended to be printed from', but that they were material of which the 'substantial equivalent' could be found in the published works.'[8] The manuscripts have remained essentially in the same order as Whittaker left them, albeit placed in more protective boxes, and the more obviously misplaced sheets have been re-catalogued.[9] In addition, because so many scholars have relied on, and cited from, the manuscripts in the original order in which they were catalogued, the organization of the Bentham papers remains somewhat haphazard.[10]

As Stark's efforts to organize *Colonies and Navy* illustrate, it is quite an exercise to arrive at a well constructed and accurate rendering of one of Bentham's essays. The same can be said for dismantling an essay found in the Bowring edition and determining the origins of the various components. When Stark explained why particular essays were constructed in the way that they were, he noted: 'The reason why the papers got so divided and disordered is not far to seek: the second volume of Bowring's *Works* gives the clue to the correct answer. Bowring arbitrarily selected some sheets for inclusion in his edition and as arbitrarily rejected others: the selected pages were XXV, 36–48 and formed the bulk of part IV of the *Principles of International Law* entitled: "A plan for a universal and perpetual peace,' not, however, without having been "corrected" and "improved".'[11] Yet, it is that very essay, *A Plan for an Universal and Perpetual Peace,*" on which international relations scholars rely when attempting to understand Jeremy Bentham's theory of international relations.[12]

Since the Bowring edition there has been a drive to present a more accurate understanding of Bentham's works, from his correspondence through to the many fragments and essays that lay hidden within the original manuscripts. What new editing has been achieved thus far is contained within the *Collected Works of Jeremy Bentham*.[13] Much has been done in this regard, but much work still remains. It is understood that if one wishes to study Bentham's work today one must examine the original manuscripts if the material is still not yet available through the *Collected Works* or Stark's *Jeremy Bentham's Economic Writings*. The greatest problem arises with the construction of *A Plan for an Universal and Perpetual Peace*; it distorts many of Bentham's ideas and raises questions as to whether Bentham himself wrote particular passages. Only a textual examination of *Plan* enables one to have a clear understanding of Bentham's work in international relations.

A Plan for an Universal and Perpetual Peace: the original manuscripts

As regards *A Plan for an Universal and Perpetual Peace* (1789), Stark was correct in noting that Bowring arbitrarily chose certain papers to include in this work. At least, he was correct in identifying many problems in the editing; one question arises, however, regarding the identity of the editor of this section. In the manuscripts themselves a document in handwriting other than Bentham's, but which is a reconstruction of Bentham's work in the Bowring edition, is credited as John Bowring's work.[14] In the published *Works*, credit for editing the *Principles of International Law* is given to Richard Smith, and not to the general editor, Bowring. Other than this small note, nothing more is known of Smith, although he has been credited with editing a number of sections of the Bowring edition.[15] It is likely that Richard Smith was the editor, although a comparison of the handwriting of the manuscript copy of the essay with John Bowring's handwriting could shed further light on the question.[16] Until such a comparison can be effected (and which I was not able to do), the question of editorship remains open. However, assuming Smith did edit *Principles of International Law*, he nevertheless did so under the supervision of Bowring, and apparently did not stray from Bowring's own questionable editorial style, identified by other scholars and noted earlier. Whether it was edited by Bowring, or under Bowring's general auspices, the section *Principles of International Law* aptly exemplifies the problems in relying on this presentation of Bentham's work and its subsequent interpretation. In this respect, Stark was still correct in charging the editor (if not the editorial staff) with negligence and arbitrary management.

Stark had already identified some of the manuscript papers in *Plan*. However, even more detective work was warranted, since, for example, the papers from UC XXV.36–48, although included in *Plan*, certainly did not constitute the bulk of the essay. In addition, there are segments of the work that come from the editor's original rendering of the essay,[17] but cannot be corroborated by the material written by Bentham. However, to edit Bentham's work is no easy task, and to some extent it is understandable that one might require some imagination to adequately present Bentham's essays in a clear manner, and this might partly explain the condition of the published *Works*.

When comparing the Bowring version of *A Plan for an Universal and Perpetual Peace* with the original manuscripts, one finds that *Plan* is actually a compilation of at least three essays found within the manuscripts, titled *Pacification and Emancipation*,[18] *Colonies and Navy*,[19] and *Cabinet No Secresy*.[20] In some cases these essays appear to be incomplete since these works do not always clearly introduce, conclude, or address all the issues they intend to cover. Although these pieces overlap with each other to a degree in terms of content, they can largely be viewed as being distinct by virtue of each essay's overall theme.

Within *Plan*, the essays *Pacification and Emancipation*, *Colonies and Navy*, and *Cabinet No Secresy* have been segmented and rearranged in a disconnected or piecemeal fashion. Perhaps Bentham intended this dissection and re-combination, but if this is not the case, the editor has deliberately presented scholars, and international relations scholars in particular, with a purposefully contrived and distorted picture of Bentham's writing in this area. The evidence in the original manuscripts suggests the latter.

Clues as to how the editor arrived at the final construction of *Plan* are found in the manuscripts. In addition to the fragmented essays, Bentham included a number of marginal 'summary sheets' or 'rudiment sheets',[21] listing the various sections and arguments he wished to make.[22] Only some of these sections are addressed in Bentham's essays, which might explain why it appears that these were used as guides in the editing of Bentham's work. The editor undoubtedly used one particular rudiment sheet showing, in the margin, that a title for the essay outlined should be 'Plan of universal and perpetual peace'.[23] This is the original rendering of the title that heads Bentham's most famous work in international relations. The rudiment sheet itself is titled *Pacification and Emancipation Ordo International*. In this and the other rudiments, Bentham refers to many of the themes that are addressed in *A Plan for an Universal and Perpetual Peace*. It is probable that the editor examined the various essays that covered these themes, and subsequently arranged them in an order that he thought to be consistent with the outline or rudiment sheets.

The connections between the rudiment sheets are, first, that they are all headed with the working title of *Pacification and Emancipation*, and second, that they tend to overlap in terms of content. The outlines which do not include *Plan*'s title are far more detailed; this could be due to their being redrafts of the first, simpler outline, or they are different outlines altogether. Based on the content of the resulting *Plan* essay, it seems possible that the former was assumed. The majority of the outlines, if not all of them, are only rudiments, and are not really indicative of the construction of any particular essay, either completed or in progress. However, it is fairly evident that the editor did use some of them as guides or indicators, at least with regard to editing *Plan*. Therefore these pages cannot be ignored when assessing the editing process of this essay.

A Plan for an Universal and Perpetual Peace: a figment of the imagination?

A Plan for an Universal and Perpetual Peace is a compilation of at least three separate essays contained within the collection of papers in box XXV. In the paragraph preceding the four essays collectively entitled *Principles of International Law*, the editor makes this note:

> The original MSS. from which these Essays are edited, consist of *Projet Matiere*, *Marginata*, and fragments. By the first of these terms, Bentham designated the contents of paragraphs he intended to write; by the second, the contents of the paragraphs he had written; – by means of these two sets of papers, the fragments have been arranged, and the connexion between them supplied: – but on this, as on every other occasion, the object of the Editor has been, without addition of his own, to show what Bentham has said upon each subject. This will account for the incompleteness of the Essays, and for the circumstance, that upon some points there are only indications of the subjects which Bentham has intended to discuss.[24]

The editor may have tried to be true to Bentham's work, but upon examining the final construction of *A Plan for an Universal and Perpetual Peace* it is difficult to imagine that Bentham wished his various arguments to be dismembered, reconfigured, and arbitrarily sewn together in the sort of 'Frankenstein' creation which resulted.

Although it has been acknowledged that Bentham's various works on international relations are not well organized within box XXV, each essay can be identified on the basis of its title, and is contained within one or two combinations of manuscript sheets. That they have been catalogued in this fashion does not reflect a consecutive order; Stark's experience in organizing *Colonies and Navy* is testimony to that. An examination of how *Plan* is organized shows that little consideration was made as to how the essays ought to be presented, either in terms of content or form.

Given the condition of the essays, it is necessary for any editor to rearrange some of the manuscript pages for clarity, thereby 'scrambling' the order of the catalogued pages; Stark's experience in editing *Colonies and Navy* shows us this. The reconfiguration of manuscript pages in *Plan* has been extensive and should provide a warning, flagging a concern about the accurate treatment of Bentham's work. The order of the manuscript pages chosen by the editor is as follows: UC XXV. 26, 34, 26, 34, 31, 36, 37, 38, 97*,[25] 38, 36 (rep.),[26] 84*, 39, 84*, 42, XVII. 55, XXV. 42, 43, 40, 41, 43, 28, 89*, 90*, 36 (rep.), 44, 45, 46, 47, 48, 49, 95*, 36 (rep.), 96*, 36 (rep.), 37 (rep.), 97* (rep.), 9, 132, 29, 30, 31, 32, 38 (rep.), 27, 32, 33, 34, 132, 104*, 35, 38 (rep.), 50–8. Additionally, not every line from each manuscript was used; although one can see that UC XXV.44–9 (*Colonies and Navy*) appears in the middle of the essay, not all of the text has been included.

It is plain that the rudiment sheet, UC XXV.119, was used to construct *Plan*, as the final essay loosely follows this design:

Pacif. & Emancip. Ordo InterNat.[27]

Title

Plan of universal & perpetual peace[28]

1. Mischiefs of extended empire
2. Motives that have given birth to the condition of extending empire
3. That the ancient motives subsist not at present
4. Encrease of [. . .?] encrease of security
5. Plan of general emancipation
6. Influence of that plan upon the interests of the several states
7. That such a plan is not visionary and that the world is ripe for it
8. Means of the plan of pacification – European Congress
9. Means of effectuating the adoption of the plan[29]

The three essays used to compose *Plan*, when combined, largely address most of the points on this rudiment sheet, but as each essay stands well on its own, the combination of the three makes the final result disjointed and often confusing. *Plan* is not a coherent and unified essay, and should not be the sole source from which Bentham's ideas are divined.[30]

Plan has been broken down into its manuscript components, illustrating the piecemeal fashion in which it was constructed. This is not illuminating, however, unless one is aware of the content as well. The example of the first paragraph of *Plan* is indicative of the whole treatment of the essay:

The object of the present Essay is to submit to the world a plan for an universal and perpetual peace. The globe is the field of dominion to which the author aspires, – the press the engine, and the only one he employs, – the cabinet of mankind the theatre of his intrigue.[31]

In the original manuscripts it is the first of these two sentences which opens the essay *Pacification and Emancipation*.[32] The second sentence is also a component of *Pacification and Emancipation* but it is included within the manuscripts a number of pages later.[33] Bentham's own opening words were unsatisfactory, or so it appears. If the combination of these two sentences seems more or less harmless, the result still raises the question of the editor's intent.

After this initial paragraph, *Plan* continues with the rest of *Pacification and Emancipation* as written by Bentham on UC XXV.26, proposing 'the reduction and fixation of the force of the several nations that compose the European system' and 'The emancipation of the distant dependencies of each state'.[34] The influence of the brief rudiment sheet discussed here earlier, especially point 7, 'that such a plan is not visionary and that the world is ripe for it',[35] becomes apparent. The editor follows Bentham's direction that the notion of 'visionaryness' be discussed at the beginning of the essay. The bulk of the text, however, can only be found in the editor's hand.[36]

Following what is at least the editor's contribution if not Bentham's, the essay leaps a few manuscript pages forward to plead to Christians for support,[37] and then jumps into *Colonies and Navy*.[38] *Colonies and Navy* and *Pacification and Emancipation* both speak to the emancipation of distant dependencies, perhaps justifying their merciless combination.[39] That point aside, other significant developments arise. *Colonies and Navy* contains thirteen propositions. *Plan* has fourteen. The likelihood that Bentham wrote thirteen of the propositions in one place and the fourteenth proposition in an entirely different location is not strong. The fourteenth proposition exists in the manuscripts, but it is an addition written in the editor's hand.

The fourteenth proposition (listed as proposition XII in *Plan*) makes an important claim: 'That for the maintenance of such a pacification, general and perpetual treaties might be formed, limiting the number of troops to be maintained.'[40] Bentham refers to arms reduction in earlier paragraphs, but not in the form of a proposition.[41] Assuming Bentham did not choose to highlight this point himself, it was probably for a good reason. When examining Bentham's manuscripts, arms reduction is clearly not as crucial as the emancipation of colonies.[42]

After introducing the fourteen propositions, the editor uses them as the foundation of *Plan*, repeating each proposition consecutively and following with fragments of the three identifiable essays that appear to explain the proposition. This 'cut and paste' approach continues; after a reiteration of the first proposition, for example, the editor introduces a discussion of it, and then looks to various pages of *Colonies and Navy*, *Pacification and Emancipation* and the editor's own apparent contributions to provide a further discussion.[43] This procedure is followed for all of the propositions discussed, for example, proposition IV, 'That it is not the interest of Great

Britain to keep up any naval force beyond what may be sufficient to defend its commerce against pirates',[44] is qualified by the statement that 'It is unnecessary, except for the defence of the colonies, or for the purposes of war, undertaken either for the compelling of trade or the formation of commercial treaties'.[45] The qualifying statement is, again, only to be found in the editor's hand.

There is frequent evidence that the editor relied upon the rudiment sheets, at least to some degree. For example, a footnote included by the editor in *Plan* discusses the inutility of maintaining colonies and refers to giving up Gibraltar. This idea is not addressed in any of Bentham's essays; it is touched upon in the rudiment sheets.[46] Is this yet another instance of the editor attempting to broaden the scope of examples from which one is to draw the required conclusions about colonies, or is this Bentham's work, as yet undiscovered? The former seems the more likely.

Some important themes in Bentham's work, colonial emancipation and a common tribunal, are unfortunately subject to misinterpretation, and have been influential in misconstruing Bentham's intentions in various interpretations of his work on international relations. Proposition XIII states 'That the maintenance of such a pacification might be considerably facilitated by the establishment of a common court of judicature, for the decision of differences between the several nations, although such court were not to be armed with any coercive powers.'[47] This proposition, emanating from *Colonies and Navy*, is subsequently supported by passages from *Pacification and Emancipation*. These passages address the need for a 'common tribunal', although only one page of manuscript in *Pacification and Emancipation* is explicitly devoted to such an institution.[48] The rest of the passages included do not specifically refer to a 'common tribunal', but have been erroneously used to support the notion:

> Can the arrangement proposed be justly styled visionary, when it has been proved of it – that
>
> 1. It is the interest of the parties concerned.
> 2. They are already sensible of that interest.
> 3. The situation it would place them in is no new one, nor any other than the original situation they set out from.
>
> Difficult and complicated conventions have been effectuated: for examples, we may mention, –
>
> 1. The armed neutrality.
> 2. The American confederation.
> 3. The German Diet.
> 4. The Swiss League[49]. Why should not the European fraternity subsist as well as the German Diet or the Swiss League? These latter have no ambitious views. Be it so; but is not this already become the case with the former?

How then shall we concentrate the approbation of the people, and obviate their prejudices?

One main object of the plan is to effectuate a reduction, and that a mighty one, in the contributions of the people. The amount of the reduction for each nation should be stipulated in the treaty; and even previous to the signature of it, laws for the purpose might be prepared in each nation, and presented to every other, ready to be enacted, as soon as the treaty should be ratified in each state.[50]

The manuscripts address an original proposal that is 'styled visionary'; it is not the notion of a common tribunal, but the 'emancipation of distant dependencies'.[51] This passage then moves from discussing an agreement for the emancipation of colonies, to the apparent construction of a multi-state 'league'; the focus is still at the treaty or agreement level, and the use of this passage makes it appear that the editor conflates the idea of treaties with the idea of a common tribunal. In actuality, the rest of the passages allegedly pertaining to proposition XIII discuss the propensity to which states are capable in coming to satisfactory agreements rather than convening at a common tribunal. The accuracy of these passages relating to proposition XIII must obviously come into question.

A Plan for an Universal and Perpetual Peace closes with a discussion of the final proposition, (XIV), which states, 'That secresy in the operations of the foreign department in England ought not to be endured, being altogether useless, and equally repugnant to the interests of liberty and peace.'[52] The editor injects Bentham's essay titled *Cabinet No Secresy* into *Plan* for the purpose of exploring the last proposition. This essay has retained its original construction to a greater extent than the other essays, but the few changes made are still worthy of note.

Cabinet No Secresy was probably one of the easier essays to incorporate into *Plan*. Bentham numbered each page, enabling one to follow the sequence of his argument. This essay also reads more clearly than the others; compared to the first essays, *Cabinet No Secresy* provides well-developed, lucid arguments, and each idea follows the next in a logical fashion. It is this portion of *Plan* that can unequivocally be said to be Bentham's work. For the most part the editor left the essay untouched except for occasionally rearranging sentences within a paragraph, or relegating part of the text to the status of a footnote;[53] for the most part such efforts make no difference to the argument being presented. Nevertheless, a couple of points need to be made.

When Bentham discusses the inutility of waging war to increase trade the example which follows states that 'The good people of England, along with the right of self-government, conquered prodigious right of trade.'[54] Bentham actually wrote 'The good people of Ireland'.[55] This cannot be a case of misjudgment or an error; uncommon though it is, in this case Bentham's handwriting is unmistakably clear. The assumption that this is a purposeful replacement of 'England' for 'Ireland' is corroborated a few paragraphs later when reference is again made to the example of Ireland. *Plan*'s version claims, 'The sylph so necessary elsewhere, was still more necessary to France';[56] yet in Bentham's manuscripts it reads: 'The Sylph so necessary to Ireland was still more necessary to France.'[57] The editor explicitly replaced the reference to Ireland, misconstruing the example that Bentham was trying to present.

The rest of the essay proceeds as Bentham wrote it in the manuscripts, until the very end. The concluding paragraph reads: 'In respect, therefore, of any benefit to be derived in the shape of conquest, or of trade – of opulence or of respect – no advantage can be reaped by the employment of the unnecessary, the mischievous, and unconstitutional system of clandestinity and secresy in negotiation.'[58] This paragraph is contained within Bentham's manuscripts and concludes the last page; however, it is not written in Bentham's hand but in the hand of the editor who included this last paragraph in his manuscript of *Plan*.

The first three essays in *Principles of International Law*

A Plan for an Universal and Perpetual Peace is not the only essay on international relations included in the Bowring edition. The section *Principles of International Law* begins with three additional essays: *Objects of International Law*, *Of Subjects, or of the Personal Extent of the Dominion of the Laws*, and *Of War, considered in respect of its Causes and Consequences*. These works also include passages that cannot be accounted for within Bentham's manuscripts. However, the passages in question are also not included in the Bowring manuscripts contained in box XXV. The same point can be made here as in *Plan*; there is no guarantee that Bentham did not write these passages, but then where are they? The presence of these questionable passages require scholars to be wary when using these essays too. Nevertheless, in this case each essay has been kept separate; one can find an essay in Bentham's manuscripts that corresponds to the bulk of the text within each of the essays that precede *Plan*.

How can we know and understand Bentham's work in international relations?

The fact that certain passages in *Plan* are not found in Bentham's hand does not unequivocally mean that these passages were not his. These passages are relatively consistent with what Bentham has written. But if Bentham did write these passages, why are they not included with the other sections of international text? Not only do they relate to previous points made by Bentham, but they attempt to summarize and conclude his thoughts. Examining *Plan* raises a number of additional questions: if Bentham did write those passages (thus far found only in the editor's hand), where have his corroborating manuscripts been catalogued? Why did the editor construct *Plan* using three separate essays?[59] Finally, what implications does this have for our understanding of Bentham's theory of international relations and his contribution to the discipline?

Apart from requiring an accurate presentation of Bentham's work in general, his writings on international relations would benefit from clearer presentation, and be better understood, if we came to know them as *Pacification and Emancipation*, *Colonies and Navy*, and *Cabinet No Secresy*. Taking these as separate pieces one can better detect themes that were important to Bentham. Instead of being confounded by the multiplicity of concepts poorly presented in *Plan*, Bentham's central ideas, such as the emancipation of colonies, become clearer and when understood through the individual essays.

Stark has already made it clear that *Colonies and Navy* can stand on its own. This can also be said for *Cabinet No Secresy* as this essay is remarkably clear and focused. The only essay that is not well-developed is *Pacification and Emancipation*. It is easy to see why the editor used this essay to frame *Plan*; almost all of the rudiment sheets are titled *Pacification and Emancipation* which suggests that this might have been a very general heading under which any or all ideas on the subject were kept.[60] But even as a less developed essay, *Pacification and Emancipation*, emphasizes and highlights many of the issues important to Bentham.

Ideally, every scholar interested in Bentham's work in international relations would have ready access to accurately edited essays. The Bentham Project at UCL is working hard to expand the *Collected Works*, but many of Bentham's manuscripts are still to be included; many scholars must still rely upon the Bowring edition. One cannot completely dismiss this source, but it is clear that the edition brings with it risks of inaccuracy and misunderstanding. Since *Plan* is somewhat consistent in theme, one might still insist on employing the Bowring edition. If using one of the preceding essays of *Principles of International Law*, that insistence might be justified. In the case of *A Plan for an Universal and Perpetual Peace* it is not, as *A Plan for an Universal and Perpetual Peace* does not exist.

Notes

1   This chapter first appeared in the *Journal of Bentham Studies*, Number 4 (2001); available at http://www.ucl.ac.uk/Bentham-Project/journal/jnl_2001.htm; Internet. It is reprinted here with permission.

2   Maurice Cranston, 'Forword,' in Lea Campos Boralevi, *Bentham and the Oppressed* (Berlin: Walter de Gruyter, 1984), p. vii. This view of John Bowring the editor of Bentham's work, is also controversial, and further exacerbates the problems of accessing Bentham's work in these initial volumes.

3   *Works of Jeremy Bentham*, ed. John Bowring, 11 vols (Edinburgh, 1843; reprint, New York: Russell & Russell, 1962). The volumes have been reprinted only once, in 1962. No additional editing was conducted in conjunction with the second printing (see opening pages of the 1962 edition: 'Published in 1962, in

a Limited Edition of Three Hundred and Fifty Sets Reproduced from the Bowring Edition of 1838–1843'). All citations from this collection will be noted with the editor's name, followed by the volume and page number: Bowring, Vol. II, p. 535. Citation of original manuscripts are presented as follows: location, box number (roman numerals), followed by page or folio number (Arabic numerals): UC (University College) XXV. 36.

4 'Introduction', *The Correspondence of Jeremy Bentham*, Vol. III, ed. I. R. Christie (London: Athlone Press, 1971), p. xvii.

5 'General Preface', *The Correspondence of Jeremy Bentham*, Vol. I, ed. T. L. S. Sprigge (London: Athlone Press, 1968), p. v.

6 *Jeremy Bentham's Economic Writings*, Vol. 1, ed. W. Stark (London: George Allen & Unwin, 1954), p. 46. Hereafter cited as 'Stark'.

7 Whittaker was 'entrusted with the task of reporting on the condition of the mass of papers and of compiling a catalogue, under the general supervision of Professors W. P. Ker and Croom Robertson.' (Taylor, A. Milne, ed., *Catalogue of the Manuscript of Jeremy Bentham in the Library of University College*, London (London: Athlone Press, 1962), p. v.)

8 Milne, p. v. These 'published works' refer to the Bowring edition.

9 Ibid., p. vi.

10 Ibid., p. ix. Another contemporary editor, Philip Schofield, states: 'The manuscripts have been left in a particularly confused and complex state.' Jeremy Bentham, *Colonies, Commerce, and Constitutional Law: Rid Yourselves of Ultramaria and Other Writings on Spain and Spanish America*, ed. Philip Schofield (Oxford: Clarendon Press, 1995), p. lviii.

11 Stark, Vol. Vol. I, p. 11. Stark credits Bowring himself with editing the *Principles of International Law*. The validity of this claim is discussed below.

12 Few scholars have focused on Bentham's theory of international relations. Of those who have tackled this subject, see Stephen Conway 'Bentham on Peace and War', *Utilitas* Vol. 1, No.1 (1969), pp. 82–101. David Baumgardt, *Bentham and the Ethics of Today* (Princeton: Princeton University Press, 1952); Georg Schwarzenberger, 'Bentham's Contribution to International Law and Organization', in *Jeremy Bentham and the Law*, ed. G. W. Keeton and G. Schwarzenberger (London: Stevens and Sons, 1948), pp. 152–84; and F. H. Hinsley, *Power and the Pursuit of Peace* (Cambridge: Cambridge University Press, 1963), pp. 81–91.

13 The *Collected Works of Jeremy Bentham*, general editors J. H. Burns and J. R. Dinwiddy, London, 1968–(in progress); subsequently cited as CW.

14 UC XXV.68–105.

15 Bowring, Vol. X, p. 548: '[The "Rationale of Punishment" was edited by] Mr. Richard Smith, of the Stamps and Taxes. He likewise prepared for the press, from the original MSS., the following works, published in the collected edition: "On the Promulgation of Laws." – "On the Influence of Time and Place in Matters of Legislation." – "Principles of the Civil Code." – "Principles of Penal Law." – "Political Tactics." – "Anarchical Fallacies." – "Principles of International Law." – "Manual of Political Economy." – "Annuity-Note Plan." – "Nomography." – "Pannomial Fragments." – "Logical Arrangements." – And "Introduction to the Rationale of Evidence."'

16 The fact that Richard Smith has been credited with editing so much of Bentham's work for the Bowring edition should sound alarm bells; his treatment of *A Plan for an Universal and Perpetual Peace* does not augur well for his treatment of the other essays.

17 Ibid.

18 UC XXV.26–35, 59; rudiment sheets UC XXV.60, 119–23.

19 UC XXV.36–49.

20 UC XXV.50–58, 61–63.

21 Occasionally these are also referred to as 'marginal outlines' in the catalogue of Bentham's manuscripts.
22 Rudiment sheets are indicated where appropriate. A number of current editors of Bentham's work, such as Philip Schofield and Fred Rosen, rely on the marginal summary sheets (if available) to determine the appropriate construction of an essay. See introductory editorial comments in *Colonies, Commerce, and Constitutional Law*, ed. Schofield. It is interesting to note the differences between the marginal summary sheets and the rudiments: "Bentham's habit . . . seems to have been to date the sheets and to write a sequence of several sheets of text, to read it over and make corrections, and then to write summaries of the content in the margin, The marginal summaries were written in the form of short paragraphs and numbered consecutively. These marginal summary paragraphs were then copied out onto separate sheets (marginal summary sheets) by an amanuensis . . . The marginal summary sheets also contain occasional additions and emendations in Bentham's hand. The marginal summary sheets are written on single sheets of foolscap ruled into four columns with a double line at the top for the date and the heading. Bentham did not add marginal summaries to all the text sheets which he wrote, while marginal summary sheets corresponding to some of the marginal summaries on the text sheets were either never made or have not survived. It should be noted that the marginal summary paragraphs were not intended for publication, unlike the marginal headings incorporated in some of the earlier works [see for instance *An Introduction to the Principles of Morals and Legislation*, ed. J. H. Burns and H. L. A. Hart, London, Athlone Press 1970], but rather seem to have been used by Bentham for purposes of reference. Additionally a few sheets containing 'Rudiments', or general statements or positions, and others containing plans, are written on double sheets of foolscap, each sheet again being ruled into four columns." *First Principles Preparatory to Constitutional Code*, ed. P. Schofield (Oxford: Clarendon Press, 1989), pp. XXXV–XXXVI.)
    On the basis of the above description of the marginal summary sheets and the rudiments, it is clear that the outlines included with Bentham's international work are rudiments. All the pages are distinctly in Bentham's handwriting and not that of an amanuensis, the text sheets have very occasional marginal notes or corrections but do not seem to be marginal summary paragraphs, none of the pages are double lined at the top for the date and heading, and the vast majority consist of double sheets of foolscap. Most importantly, these rudiments are not a concrete indication of what Bentham hoped to see as the final construction of his essays.
23 UC XXV.119.
24 Bowring, Vol. II, p. 536.
25 Each sheet which is marked with an asterisk comes from Bowring's re-working of the essay contained in UC XXV.68–105. These sections of text have not been corroborated by the presence of original manuscripts written in Bentham's hand. It is possible to conclusively identify three essays which do compose the bulk of *Plan*, but some of the paragraphs which are still difficult to identify can be found in Bowring's hand. It does not make sense that the original manuscripts for these missing paragraphs would be located in a place other than box XXV, and even that these paragraphs are not included in the essay, *Colonies and Navy*. Most of the unidentified writing discusses and qualifies the fourteen propositions presented at the beginning of the essay (taken from *Colonies and Navy*). That these explanatory paragraphs would be located elsewhere and yet specifically address the previous propositions is very unlikely. The only other possibility is that these qualifications were made by the editor for purposes of 'clarity' (which is not inconsistent with Stark's point about Bowring's 'improvements').

26 '(rep.)' indicates that this passage has been repeated from an earlier inclusion. Further discussion on this point will follow.

27 Working title that heads the entire summary.

28 This suggestion for a title is written in the upper, far left margin.

29 Written in the upper, far right margin is: 'Should not the defense against the charge of visionaryness come/stand/first.'

30 Not only is the construction of *Plan* haphazard, but some passages are difficult to associate with Bentham's manuscripts. Marginal summary sheets (see also n21) would be of great assistance, if they existed in this case.

31 Bowring, Vol. II, p. 546.

32 UC XXV.26.

33 UC XXV.34.

34 Bowring, Vol. II, p. 546.

35 UC XXV.119.

36 And Bentham had already discussed the question of 'visionary/not visionary' in the preceding paragraphs. If Bowring/Smith did contribute to the discussion here he just fleshed out Bentham's point contained within the rudiment sheet.

37 UC XXV.31.

38 UC XXV.36.

39 The editor re-ordered propositions 1–4, such that they read 1, 3, 4, 2. Otherwise it is Bentham's piece.

40 Bowring, Vol. II, p. 547.

41 This is referring to the UC XXV.26 passages of *Pacification and Emancipation* used at the beginning of *Plan*. Werner Stark, in editing *Colonies and Navy* for inclusion in *Jeremy Bentham's Economic Writings*, did not include this proposition.

42 Although Bentham makes note of the efficacy of arms reduction, it does not receive anything like the same consideration as do colonies, especially when each essay is examined separately.

43 Again a combination of sentences and paragraphs from both Bentham and Bowring are found here. It is possible, on the basis of the way the discussion is constructed, that the editor added a few of his own sentences to attempt to provide continuity between paragraphs and ideas. However, as mentioned before, there is no obvious indication from Bentham that the paragraphs were to be connected in the manner that they were and therefore, perhaps, no necessity for the editor's additions.

44 Ibid.

45 Ibid.

46 For example, UC XXV.132.

47 Bowring, Vol. II, p. 552.

48 UC XXV. 27.

49 "The Swiss League" is an example found only in the editor's manuscripts, not Bentham's.

50 Bowring, Vol. II, pp. 552–3.

51 UC XXV.32.

52 Bowring, Vol. II, p. 554.

53 Bowring, Vol. II, p. 555. The paragraph beginning, 'Sorry remedies these; add them both together, their efficacy is not worth a straw . . .' is a convoluted rendering of the original contained in UC XXV.50. Remarkably, however, the meaning has not really been changed, and it is understandable that the editor attempted to rework this paragraph as the original is almost incomprehensible. In addition, the footnote referring to the 'fate of Queen Anne's ministry' is actually part of the main text in Bentham's manuscripts. It is unclear why the editor decided to footnote this point as he retained many other examples within the

body of the text. Nevertheless, compared to previous uses of editorial licence, not much harm is done.

54 Bowring, Vol. II, p. 557.

55 UC XXV.54.

56 Bowring, Vol. II, p. 558. The initial paragraph beginning with the 'good people of England' continued as follows: 'The revolution was to produce for them not only the blessings of security and power, but immense and sudden wealth. Year has followed after year, and to their endless astonishment, the progress to wealth has gone on no faster than before. One piece of good fortune still wanting, they have never thought of: that on the day their shackles were knocked off, some kind sylph should have slipped a few thousand pounds into every man's pocket.' (Bowring, Vol. II, p. 557).

57 UC XXV.54.

58 Bowring, Vol. II, p. 560.

59 This is also keeping in mind that the only additional clues to any sort of intended construction are provided by rudiment sheets which, as mentioned previously, are really not to be used as explicit guides.

60 Many of the points mentioned in the rudiment sheets never made it past the conceptual stage, and certainly never made it into any of Bentham's main texts.

4 Bentham and the Traditions of International Relations Theory

There is a long-standing divergence between scholars of utilitarianism which centres on decidedly different interpretations of the thought of Jeremy Bentham (1748–1832). No doubt the sheer wealth of material that constitutes Bentham's corpus encourages contending views of his thought. However, in large measure these interpretations result from the emphases placed by commentators on different writings and on different elements within his utilitarianism. At the risk of disservice to particular commentators, the dispute over Bentham's thought can be reduced to two schools of analysis – here labelled 'authoritarian' and 'individualist.' . . . The 'authoritarian' school comprises commentators who stress illiberal tendencies in his thought. Modern individualist interpreters of Bentham explain the meaning and place of 'liberty' within his utilitarian theory in a manner quite different;[1]

References to Bentham . . . raise the question of whether utilitarianism is properly to be considered as a form of liberalism. There are grounds for seeing the two as being at odds with one another.[2]

Bentham's struggle over his desire for individual liberty and his need to contain human behaviour for the sake of order and security is often recognized in political theory, but not so in theories of international relations. Bentham is solidly placed within the rationalist or idealist traditions, or more broadly speaking, the liberal tradition.[3] While this book is predominantly engaged in presenting a broader and more accurate rendering of Bentham's work in international relations, questions of the interpretation and categorization of Bentham's contributions inevitably arise. Although Bentham's placement in the liberal tradition is often well-deserved, and his contribution to liberal international thinking quite obvious, the assumed strength of this position has led to a failure to thoroughly analyse Bentham's writings throughout. As much as Bentham's writing can be considered liberal in tone, there is also evidence of a realist side. Given the breadth of his work, it is an oversight to highlight only one tradition in order to understand Bentham's contributions to international relations.

The primary thesis of this book argues that Jeremy Bentham's preoccupation with security, especially the security of expectation, has been the source of much confusion when evaluating Bentham's contribution to work in international relations. Bentham's 'inconsistency' in his work is notable; some scholars argue that the application of the principle of utility can result in divergent outcomes, whereas others simply criticize Bentham for his ambivalence.[4] Nevertheless, although a few authors recognize that a dichotomy of views exists in Bentham's thought, this view is not widely shared in international relations theory, even though utilitarianism in general, and Bentham's work in particular, have received varying interpretations.

Where Bentham resides in the theoretical traditions depends on what elements of his writing become the focus of attention. Arnold Wolfers, among others, emphasizes the utopian features of Bentham's work, stating that Bentham, along with 'Sully, Kant, [and] Penn, . . . had proposed schemes of international organization for peace' and could thus be counted among the 'precursors of the new prophets'.[5] F. H. Hinsley recognizes that Bentham's work cannot be so easily summarized, but he includes Bentham in an analysis of contributions to internationalist thinking; these contributions include proposals to temper, if not eliminate altogether, the necessity for war, as well as explore, to varying degrees, the potential for a federation of states, or even a cosmopolis.[6] Other scholars who choose to emphasize the idealist component of Bentham's writing are Hans Morgenthau, E. H. Carr, Kenneth Waltz, and J. W. Burton, to name a few. In these interpretations Bentham is associated with others who look to public opinion, international federations, and unfettered commerce to bring peace to the world.

There are other scholars who focus less on federations and commerce, and more on Bentham's contributions to international law, such as Martin Wight, K. J. Holsti, Michael Donelan, and Brian Porter. The strength of Bentham's position within the liberal tradition lies with the rationalists, as the emphasis is not on his claims of the power of public opinion, but on a code of conduct between states that does not exclude the possibility of war. Rationalism does not hold that relations between sovereign states are inevitably and perpetually hostile; many instances exist where it would be prudent for states to cooperate rather than engage in combat. The moderate position of rationalism makes it an accessible category to utilize, and provides, again, the most compelling argument in favour of Bentham's liberalism.

Bentham has not been categorized a realist. *A Plan for an Universal and Perpetual Peace*, his best and often only-known, essay on international relations, has little bearing on the realist tradition. Any connection to a realist interpretation has come through some scholars' evaluation of utilitarianism in general, rather than Bentham's work in particular. As Bentham's work is one of the original contributions made to utilitarianism (he is considered the 'father' of utilitarianism), the observations made by the likes of Stanley Hoffmann and F. Meinecke shed a realist light on the subject. Stanley Hoffmann expresses discomfort with a theory that he finds cold, calculated, and merely a method of justification rather than a guide to moral development:

> Utilitarianism is better at giving one a good conscience than at providing a compass . . . The morality of international relations will simply have to be a mix of commands and of utilitarian calculations. The commands cannot be followed at any cost: 'Thou shalt not kill' or 'Thou shalt not lie' can never be pushed so far that the cost clearly becomes a massive disutility to the national interest.'[7]

To a degree, Hoffmann's evaluation of utilitarianism is not inconsistent with Lea Campos Boralevi's claim that the principle of utility produces a variety of results, from emancipating colonies in one instance, to retaining them in another.[8] She does not consider the varying applications of the principle of utility to be cold and calculating, but the application does not differ from Hoffmann's evaluation. F. Meineke provides a contrast between the idealist and utilitarian, stating: 'If he [the statesman] acts out of consideration for the well-being of the State – that is to say, from *raison d'état* – then there at once arises the very obscure question of how far he is guided in doing so by a utilitarian and how far by an idealistic point of view.'[9] He argues further,

> the advantage of the State is always at the same time blended too with the advantage of the rulers. So *raison d' état* is continually in danger of becoming a merely utilitarian instrument without ethical application, in danger of sinking back again from wisdom to mere cunning, and of restraining the superficial passions merely in order to satisfy passions and egoisms which lie deeper and are more completely hidden.[10]

Utilitarianism is dispassionate, useful and effective. Morality, at least that emanating from a source other than the state itself, is not relevant. That Bentham is not explicitly acknowledged in these passages can be an argument against including them in an analysis of his work; the utilitarianism mentioned here has no bearing upon the work of Bentham. It is possible that Hoffmann and Meineke speak to a utilitarianism that is only a by-product of what the founder of utilitarianism originally designed. As much as this may be the case, it is still inappropriate to divorce Bentham entirely from a theoretical perspective that is still fundamentally rooted in the assumptions that he laid down. Bentham's connection to the utilitarianism addressed by Hoffmann and Meineke is unavoidable.

International Relations Theory

Presenting a coherent and consistent elucidation of the many theories of international relations is an onerous task. Little agreement exists as to the delineation of the 'traditions' or 'paradigms', often making comparison of analyses problematic. Some of the difficulties in international relations theorizing emanate from the terminology used, especially among those perspectives offering alternative views to the power-politics paradigm of realism. These terms include rationalism, revolutionism, idealism, liberalism, Grotian or Kantian perspectives and cosmopolitanism. When Bentham wrote, he was not concerned with these classifications per se, but responded to his predecessors and contemporaries as if engaged in a dialogue with the ideas espoused by each. Nevertheless, these terms have subsequently been used when categorizing Bentham's thought. The chapters that follow make regular reference to either realism or liberalism. Liberalism spans a vast array of ideas, encompassing and combining works that would otherwise merit important distinctions. For this reason, it is useful to break this vast body of ideas down into rationalism and idealism, both indicating a particular stream of thought within the liberal tradition. 'Rationalism' is often the system of thought equated with liberalism, accounting for the arguments in favour of international law. Including 'idealism' as a concept within liberalism, however, reflects those ideas that originated in the works of eighteenth-and nineteenth-century writers and that were so influential during the inter-war years of the twentieth century, especially regarding the role of the individual and public opinion, and in promoting unfettered trade practices. Dividing liberalism into the two streams of rationalism and idealism makes us more aware of the vast array of ideas that currently reside within the overarching agenda of liberalism, and allow us to make finer distinctions between these ideas.

Certain distinctions in international relations thinking were discernible at the time Bentham wrote, as he periodically distinguished his work from the likes of Machiavelli, Vattel, and Abbé Saint-Pierre; according to Bentham, his work was unlike that of any of his predecessors. To provide a sense of the debates already in play at the time of his writing, some central features of the realist, idealist, and rationalist traditions are presented, focussing on the works that were either identified by Bentham, or have been associated with his work. Bentham did not delineate between thinkers through a notion of traditions, but he is nevertheless clear about fundamental distinctions between different writers. Machiavelli and Hobbes contribute to, and exemplify, crucial facets belonging to the realist tradition, Grotius and Vattel do the same for the rationalist tradition, and Kant and Abbé Saint-Pierre for the idealist.[11] Although these traditions are by no means limited to the works that follow, Machiavelli, Kant, and Grotius are chosen to represent some key components of realism, idealism, and rationalism respectively. These thinkers illustrate some of the more prominent debates that were current in Bentham's day and against which Bentham's work is often compared. It is against the backdrop of the ideas of these thinkers and their theoretical traditions that Bentham's work will be evaluated in the chapters to follow. The result should be a better understanding of how, or even if, Bentham may be situated accurately within one or other tradition or even if this is possible at all.

Realism

> If a man calculates badly, it is not arithmetic which is in fault; it is himself. If the charges which are alleged against Machiavel are well founded, his errors did not spring from having consulted the principle of utility, but from having applied it badly.[12]
>
> But it is in fact an essential part of the spirit of *raison d'état* that it must always be smearing itself by offending against ethics and law; if in no other way, then only by the very fact of war – a means which is apparently so indispensable to it, and which (despite all the legal forms in which it is dressed up) does signalize the breaking down of cultural standards and a re-establishing of the state of nature . . . the State – although it is the very guardian of law, and although it is just as dependent as any other kind of community on an absolute validity of ethics and law, is yet unable to abide by these in its own behaviour.[13]
>
> [T]he end justifies the means.[14]

In international relations, 'the end justifies the means' is taken to suggest that a state is free to pursue any action it deems necessary to ensure its survival. Unlike Hugo Grotius (1583–1645) or Immanuel Kant (1724–1804), who both identified a moral code, through natural law, that regulated state behaviour, Niccolò Machiavelli (1469–1527) did not acknowledge an abstract morality divorced from state interests.

If a moral code dictates state action, it is a morality of the state.[15] Realist thinking refuses to be contingent upon a moral code emanating from anything other than the tangible needs of the state. To do otherwise leaves the state vulnerable. To protect the state, Machiavelli defined common good modelled on the 'ancients', in that they 'honour and reward *virtù*; value good order and discipline in their armies, oblige citizens to love one another, to decline faction, and to prefer the good of the public to any private interest'.[16] The unchanging characteristics of human nature play a central role both in Machiavelli's and in realist reasoning:

> Wise men say, and not without reason, that whoever wishes to foresee the future must consult the past; for human events ever resemble those of preceding times. This arises from the fact that they are produced by men who have been, and ever will be, animated by the same passions, and thus they must necessarily have the same results.[17]

As a consequence, Machiavelli wanted to control human passion and engender *virtù* through an education of discipline.[18] This could be accomplished through a balance between two central human motivations: love and fear.[19] The sovereign could not be too beloved for fear of generating feelings of disrespect, but also could not be too harsh, for fear of incurring the hatred of the people and thereby destroying the state.

To protect the state, Machiavelli designed an armed force that works closely with the political interests of the state.[20] This force would be drawn from the people of the state, and would only be active during times of conflict, since no person should depend on war and aggression for a livelihood. Through order and discipline the common citizen becomes part of a unified and committed team, devoted to the preservation of the state:

> So that by establishing a good and well-ordered militia, divisions are extinguished, peace restored, and some people who were unarmed and dispirited, but united, continue in union and become warlike and courageous; others who were brave and had arms in their hands, but were previously given to faction and discord, become united and turn against the enemies of their country those arms and that courage which they used to exert against each other.[21]

An armed force remunerated to be always at the ready, in other words a standing army, is ill advised. The necessary passions of loyalty and devotion to the state, apparent in a militia, cannot exist in a force that is paid to go to war, where greed becomes the overriding force.

Discipline and order engender *virtù*, as do regular confrontations with other states, bringing each state back to its first principles. A 'community of states' is not plausible, according to Machiavelli, if a state intends to remain faithful to *virtù*; such a community encourages weakness and complacency within each member state. It is advisable, however to seek profitable alliances, and avoid neutrality.[22]

Not frightened by the prospect of war, Machiavelli still cautions against reckless behaviour, especially as regards expense. He debunks the notion that finances are the 'sinews of war'.[23] There is no advantage in engaging the enemy when relying solely on money, since 'gold alone will not procure good soldiers, but good soldiers will always procure gold'.[24] The progress of commerce dulls *virtù*, and if left unchecked could become a disease in the state. Though Machiavelli acknowledges the need for money and provisions during a conflict, the most important elements are men and arms.[25] Commerce breeds pacifism, leaving the militia and its *virtù* unattended, which is deterimental to the state.

State security ultimately relies upon the masses, and the sovereign must balance fear with judicious care for his people in order to inspire loyalty to the state.[26] To best gain the confidence of the people, sovereigns must behave with continence and justice, where 'the general must resort to such means as will expose him and his men to the least danger,' and discourage 'perfidy, which breaks pledged faith and treaties; for although states and kingdoms may at times be won by perfidy, yet will it ever bring dishonour with it'.[27] Machiavelli does not accommodate brutal tyrants, nor does he perceive the masses to be helpless and disposable; reckless behaviour as a sovereign inevitably leads to state insecurity. Machiavelli looks to the power of the masses, controlled by a strong military education, to secure the state. State power and survival dominate the Machiavellian scheme, where reliance upon community interests is unwise.[28] International relations is a realm dominated by a negative condition of anarchy and riddled with conflict.

Liberalism – *Idealism*

Immanuel Kant's *Perpetual Peace* is often used as the measure of idealist thinking, its defining features composed of Kant's preliminary and definitive articles: 1) concluding peace cannot include secretly harbouring the possibility of future wars; 2) prohibiting state acquisition through inheritance, exchange, purchase or donation; 3) eventual abolition of standing armies; 4) prohibition of national debt accumulation through external affairs; 5) mutual non-intervention; and 6) elimination of gratuitous violence during wartime to preserve future mutual confidence.[29] Peace must be guaranteed through law in the form of a concord among people.[30] To achieve this goal, each state must be republican, ensuring that all individuals live with freedom and equality. This places decision-making power, especially with regard to war, in the citizen's responsible hands.[31] While the individual seeks peace through the mechanisms of the republican state, each republican state is drawn to the other to constitute a federation, making firm the foundation for peace.

Through a covenant of peace it is hoped that war can be eliminated, not just postponed, or mitigated through laws of war. Republican states are inclined toward perpetual peace, and are most likely to form a federation, supported by international law. Because of the uniform republican values shared among the states, coercive law becomes unnecessary:

> For if by good fortune one powerful and enlightened nation can form a republic (which by its nature inclined to seek perpetual peace), this will provide a focal point for federal association among other states. These will join up with the first one, thus securing the freedom of each state in accordance with the idea of international right, and the whole will gradually spread further and further by a series of alliances of this kind.[32]

Safe travel, commerce, and open communication is encouraged by and facilitates good offices between states by bringing 'the human race nearer and nearer to a cosmopolitan constitution'.[33]

Kant considers union between republics possible since the fundamental and shared values are a reflection of the moral awareness achieved through nature and reason. Nature has placed human beings on a predetermined path shaped by historical process, making humanity increasingly morally aware and active over time, occuring regardless of human will.[34] War is also part, albeit a primitive stage, of this historical development.[35] As time progresses, 'Nature comes to the aid of the universal and rational human will' and 'irresistibly wills' human beings to place rights and morality a priori over evils.[36] States are naturally willed together as the principles among them blend, linguistic and religious, leading to mutual under-standing and peace.[37] The role of Nature is an important feature in Kant's perspective as it guides not only state action, but also individual action – both components are fundamental to the attainment of perpetual peace: 'The impulse for progress toward perpetual peace comes largely from the individual: from the moral outrage at the destructiveness of war, from the ability to learn from experience, and from the gradual moral improvement of mankind.'[38] This improvement of mankind allows Kant 'to dare to spec-ulate about (acknowledging pitfalls however) speculate about the utopian cosmopolis: 'And this encourages the hope that, after many revolutions, with all their transforming effects, the highest purpose of nature, a universal *cosmopolitan existence*, will at last be realized as the matrix within which all the original capacities of the human race may develop.'[39] Most scholars agree that Kant did not truly endorse the cosmopolis, but a debate still exists.[40] Whether Kant did or did not advocate the creation of the cos-mopolis, the fact that he was willing to entertain the notion, even fleetingly, illustrates the level of idealism that can be found in Kant's writings. The critical role of the individual, and the power of nature to compel states and people to band together in the name of peace, defines much about the character of idealism.

Liberalism – *Rationalism*

> There is a third way between Utopianism and despair. That is to take the world as it is and to improve it; to have faith without a creed, hope without illusions, love without God. The Western world is committed to the proposition that rational man will in the end prove stronger and more successful than irrational man.[41]
>
> Grotius seems to have been the first who attempted to give the world anything like a regular system of natural jurisprudence, and *De Jure Belli ac Pacis* with all its imperfections, is perhaps at this day the most complete work on the subject.[42]

Hugo Grotius argues that states predominantly follow the 'laws common to nations', in the interest of maintaining 'the bulwarks which safeguard its own future peace'.[43] Justice, too, inclines most states to abide by inter-national law, since such law cannot be enforced by coercion through a higher authority. The state ensures the well being and self-preservation of the individuals within it, but, Grotius argues, laws beyond the state are also necessary because a single state's own resources are sometimes not sufficient for its protection.[44] A community of states is an inevitable result of Grotius' assumptions, especially since there must be law connecting the whole human race: 'If no association of men can be maintained without law ... surely also that association which binds together the human race, or binds many nations together, has need of law'.[45] Among these laws are the laws of war.

While war is perceived by many realists as a degradation of all social norms and practices, the rationalists, exemplified in this case by Grotius, envision the possibility of war conducted 'within the bounds of law and good faith'.[46] A just war is not incompatible with civilized behaviour in that it abides by the laws of war and seeks to rectify any wrongs committed by transgressors. The laws by which just wars can be conducted are rooted in a combination of natural and positivist law or treaties made between states. That natural law allows for just war is plausible as '[I]t is not, then, contrary to the nature of society to look out for oneself and advance one's own interests, provided the rights of others are not infringed; and consequently the use of force which does not violate the rights of others is not unjust'.[47] Grotius does not deny a state the opportunity to protect itself and its interests as long as it can be shown that these interests are in jeopardy. If so, war is just.

Its foundations lying partially within the law of nature, international law plays a dominant role in the relations among states. The natural law of Grotius or the rationalists is not to be equated with that of Hobbes, since Grotian natural law is premised on the concept of social strength and cohesion, whereas Hobbes concentrates on anarchical liberty.[48] Natural law is 'the belief in a cosmic, moral constitution, appropriate to all created things including mankind; a system of eternal and immutable principles radiating from a source that transcends earthly power (either God or nature)'.[49] Natural law provides the motivation for human beings to act cordially in society and care for their fellow beings. Therefore treaties and compacts, which are conformable to natural law, are the logical course for international affairs.[50] As a result, rationalists place a heavy emphasis on the role of international law as it dictates the code of conduct between states and regulates international events, including war.

Preliminary comments on Bentham's place in the traditions

Kant, Grotius and Machiavelli illustrate the thinking that was prevalent during Bentham's time. He made frequent reference to Grotius and Machiavelli, although not to Kant. Kant's work is significant however as he and Bentham wrote at the same time, and Bentham's work in international relations has been often compared to the better-known work of

Kant, especially the latter's *Perpetual Peace*. In addition to providing a comprehensive presentation of Bentham's theory of international relations, the chapters that follow will continue to highlight areas in which Bentham is either a 'classic' liberal (rationalist or idealist), or indicate when he strays into the realist camp. Bentham appears to be most comfortable as a rationalist. Nevertheless he does not occupy this position exclusively. His work on international law and acceptance of 'necessary' wars makes Bentham's thought comparable to that of Grotius, but the latter's assumption that natural law and justice are at play in the international arena are flatly unacceptable in Bentham's framework:

> What is natural to man is sentiments of pleasure or pain, what are called inclinations. But to call these sentiments and these inclinations *laws*, is to introduce a false and dangerous idea. It is to set language in opposition to itself; for it is necessary to make *laws* precisely for the purpose of restraining these inclinations. Instead of regarding them as laws, they must be submitted to laws. It is against the strongest natural inclinations that it is necessary to have laws the most repressive. If there were a law of nature which directed all men towards their common good, laws would be useless; it would be employing a creeper to uphold an oak; it would be kindling a torch to add light to the sun.[51]

There is a significant difference between the fundamental assumptions proffered by the rationalist and idealist traditions as exemplified by Grotius and Kant, and the assumptions that underlie Bentham's beliefs about, and designs for, the international realm. Bentham's reliance on self-interest as opposed to justice and natural law detracts from assumptions of externally enforced moral behaviour, and moves Bentham closer to the realist tradition.

At other times Bentham is the obvious idealist; his initial enthusiasm for the force of public opinion surpasses even Kant's beliefs in the power of the individual. As will be seen in subsequent chapters, Bentham was not shy about presenting visionary proposals, even when he makes pains to argue that they are not visionary at all. Visionary though some of his ideas are, Bentham's place as an idealist, although plausible, is not very compelling when these same ideas are examined further. We could say, on the one hand, that because Bentham highlighted the significance of public opinion as a way to reduce the chance of war, he is an idealist. On the other hand we could say that Bentham looked to public opinion to temper war, but in the end he could not reconcile his desire for greater individual participation in international affairs with the interests and sovereignty of states. The latter conclusion reflects not only a deeper analysis of Bentham's work, but also the tension the Bentham experienced in trying to balance 'progressive' ideas against important security concerns.

Bentham's concerns about security becomes very important when trying to understand his apparently contradictory statements on issues about which we believe we know Bentham's views. Bentham is surprising in his less understood, but not insignificant, views in a realist vein. Primarily as a result of his need to meet security concerns, Bentham here is no less a utilitarian than those that Meineke speaks of, and no less a realist. Since this side of Bentham is rarely, if ever, explored, it is this aspect that requires proof to substantiate it. For example, Bentham's arguments for the emancipation of colonies are well-known, on the grounds that colonies are a burden to the mother country and oppressive to the peoples that are colonized. Less-known are his arguments to the contrary:

> This principle [of not permitting Governors to remain a long time in the same District] has a particular application to important commands in distant provinces, and especially those detached from the body of the empire.
> A governor armed with great power, if he is allowed time for it, may attempt to establish his independence . . . The disadvantage of rapid changes consists in removing a man from his employment so soon as he has acquired the knowledge and experience of affairs . . . This inconvenience would be palliated by the establishment of a subordinate and permanent council, which should keep up the course and routine of affairs. What you gain is the diminution of a power, which may be turned against yourself; what you risk is a diminution in the skill with which the office is executed. There is no parity between the dangers, when revolt is the evil apprehended.
> To avoid giving umbrage to individuals, this arrangement ought to be permanent . . . The want of a permanent arrangement of this sort, is plainly the cause of the continual revolutions to which the Turkish empire is subject; and nothing more evidently shows the stupidity of that barbarous court.
> If there is any European government which ought to adopt this policy, it is Spain in her American, and England in her East Indian establishments.[52]

For fear of revolt, strict control of the distant dependency is required, not emancipation, so much so that the colonizing sovereign does not even trust its own people to govern the colony – at least not for an extended period of time. Bentham's rationalization, in this example, is consistent with the 'cold and calculating' nature of utilitarianism, but is certainly the less familiar side of Bentham for international relations scholars.

This aspect is less well-known to those studying international relations, but not so to those arguing the 'authoritarian' versus the 'liberal' in Bentham's political theory as a whole.[53] Part of the analysis arguing for his authoritarianism is based on Bentham's contribution to the 'enlightenment

project to construct rationally grounded institutions and policies to education, condition and/or direct humankind to the end of optimizing personal
and public well-being'.[54] If this is the case, the authoritarian label can be
given to Kant as well as Bentham. Both design a scheme by which, through
education and legislation, a better political system results. A central difference, however, is that Bentham's scheme depends on interest, whereas
Kant's depends on nature. Nature inevitably leads humanity towards
progress, whereas interest, if defined by each individual, will not necessarily
do so. Bentham tries to direct human interest via legislation, attempting to
articulate the greatest happiness for the greatest number, and this inevitably
conflicts with and restricts individual interest.[55] Nevertheless, without the
'guarantee' that nature provides, Bentham's scheme does not always lead
'to progress'. Bentham's reliance upon the security of expectation can
explain this and the other inconsistencies in his writing on international
relations. These inconsistencies are frequent enough to warrant comment
from those studying Bentham's work, and are too significant to pass over
without comment. The inconsistencies do not negate Bentham's contributions to liberalism, either the rationalist or idealist stream, but they do
merit consideration, and a re-evaluation of the validity of understanding
Bentham's work when seen only from the liberal perspective.

Bentham's contribution to the theory of international relations has been
treated awkwardly at best. His work has not been ignored in international
relations literature; quite the opposite, as some of the most recent works,
such as Stephen Conway's articles on Bentham's writings on peace and war,
Michael W. Doyle's *Ways of War and Peace*, and Torbjørn L. Knutsen's
A History of International Relations Theory, pay homage to the important
ideas Bentham set forth in *A Plan for an Universal and Perpetual Peace*.[56]
Featured in all of these commentaries are the well-known arguments taken
from *Plan*. Doyle interprets Bentham's work as a completion of that of John
Locke, yet another contributor to the liberal view of international peace,
and states that 'Bentham ... effectively addresses ways to overcome the
"Inconveniences" that plagued Lockean international politics'.[57] Doyle
acknowledges Bentham's distance from Locke in relying on natural rights
as the explanatory tool, as well as the rationale, for moral conduct in the
international realm. Beyond that, however, Doyle claims that Bentham
recognized the same problems as did Locke, identifying that:

> (1) Ignorance and bias in information, (2) partiality and negligence in
> adjudication, and (3) weakness and fear in execution reflect and then
> shape all politics, but they are particularly prevalent in the interstate
> condition.[58]

Doyle, like Knutsen and Conway, then examines Bentham's celebrated
essay, *A Plan for an Universal and Perpetual Peace*, and highlights salient
details, especially as regards the maintenance of peace and the function of

disarmament and an international court as integral to peace. Though Doyle and Conway are alert to various contradictions in Bentham's writing on international affairs, neither views such contradictions as important enough to warrant further examination. As such, the current literature presents little evidence, and certainly no argument, that Bentham's contributions to liberal international relations theory are less solid than they have thus far appeared.

A different presentation of Bentham's work is offered here. Through each chapter the efficacy of the various theoretical traditions as they pertain to Bentham's work is shown to be tenuous. Bentham, for good or for bad, cannot be so easily categorized. The following chapters examine Bentham's theory of international relations, beginning with his views on sovereignty, which lays the foundation for the rest of Bentham's international writings. Where Bentham stands on the issue of sovereignty speaks to the sort of authority each state has in the international system, and how that authority is wielded. Although Bentham has moments where he envisions cooperation between states that suggests a disdain for sovereignty, he ultimately cannot relinquish the security found in the absolute sovereignty of each state. Security is inclusive, not exclusive. State and individual security are intertwined and interdependent.

Notes

1 James E. Crimmins, 'Contending Interpretations of Bentham's Utilitarianism', *Canadian Journal of Political Science*, XXIX:4 (1996), pp. 751, 754.
2 Anthony Arblaster, *The Rise and Decline of Western Liberalism* (Oxford: Basil Blackwell, 1987), p. 350.
3 The theoretical traditions are further discussed below.
4 For example, the contending interpretations of Bentham's work on colonies by Boralevi and Winch (see Chapter 7).
5 A. Wolfers and L. W. Martin, *The Anglo-American Tradition in Foreign Affairs* (New York: Yale University Press, 1956) in S. Hoffmann, *Contemporary Theory in International Relations* (New Jersey: Prentice Hall, 1960), p. 241.
6 F. H. Hinsley, *Power and the Pursuit of Peace* (Cambridge: Cambridge University Press, 1963), p. 81. Hinsley is very clear, however, that Bentham does not entertain the notion of a world state: 'For Bentham international integration was not so much unattainable and undesirable as utterly unnecessary'.
7 Stanley Hoffmann, *Duties Beyond Borders: On the Limits and Possibilities of Ethical International Politics* (Syracuse: Syracuse University Press, 1981), p. 43.
8 See Chapter 7 on colonies.
9 F. Meineke, *Machiavellism: The Doctrine of Raison d'État and its Place in Modern History* (New Haven, CT: Yale University Press, 1957), p. 3.
10 Ibid., p. 7.
11 Bentham does not make any mention of Kant, but Kant's work is often considered the definitive contribution to idealism in the later 1700s, so much so that the idealist tradition is also referred to as 'Kantian', and Bentham's work has likewise been compared to that of Kant.
12 Bentham, *The Theory of Legislation* (London: Kegan Paul, Trench, Trubner, 1931) p. 16.
13 Meinecke, pp. 12–13.

68   *Bentham and International Relations Theory*

14 Machiavelli, *The Prince and the Discourses* with an introduction by Max Lerner (New York: The Modern Library, 1950), p. 66.
15 Charles Beitz in *Political Theory and International Relations* (Princeton, NJ: Princeton University Press, 1979) argues against the notion of an 'alternative' morality, whereas Stanley Hoffmann acknowledges Machiavelli's position: 'Machavelli's whole work is based on the contrast between ordinary Christian ethics and the ethics of statecraft, which entails doing whatever is necessary for the good of the country – not an 'immoral' code of behaviour, except by Christian standards, but a different code of morality.' *Duties Beyond Borders: On the Limits and Possibilities of Ethical International Politics*, Syracuse: (Syracuse University Press, 1981), p. 23.
16 Machiavelli, *The Art of War* with an introduction by Neal Wood (New York: Da Capo Press, 1990), p. 12.
17 *Discourses*, III, 43, p. 530.
18 *Art of War*, p. 61.
19 *Discourses*, III, 21, p. 474.
20 *Art of War*, pp. 3–4.
21 *Art of War*, p. 41. Machiavelli also looks to religion as an effective tool for instilling order and discipline, but excludes the Christian Church in this regard, as Christianity encourages inward reflection and the life hereafter, as opposed to being concerned with worldly concerns of state preservation (*The Prince*, XXV, p. 91). Pagan religions possessed the qualities Machiavelli recognized would inspire the people to secure the state (*Discourses*, I, 14, p. 156). Religion gave the troops new hope when the old disappeared, united them to 'obey wholly one government', kept them disposed to any enterprise, and compelled the people to submit to the good laws, such that if they were not enforced properly, the governor could resort to invoking 'divine authority.' (*Discourses*, I, 11, p. 147; 12, p. 152; 13, p. 153).
22 Neither victor nor vanquished have cause to trust a sovereign who does not lend support. *Prince*, xxi, pp. 83–84.
23 *Discourses*, II, 10, p. 309.
24 Ibid., p. 310.
25 *Art of War*, p. 204.
26 And if they (the sovereigns) do need to use considerable violence, it should be applied as quickly as possible, and ensure that they are not saddled with the blame. *The Prince*, xix, pp. 69–70.
27 *Art of War*, pp. 95, 179; *Discourses,* III, 40, p. 526.
28 Thomas Hobbes mirrors some of these views, and is equally an influence in Bentham's international perspective. Seeking self-preservation and fearful of violent death resulting from the chaotic and anarchic state of nature, Hobbes finds refuge under the wing of an awe-inspiring and powerful sovereign: 'Hobbes's doctrine of the three great motives of war – gain, fear, and glory – is an amplification of the account given by Thucydides ... fear – not in the sense of an unreasoning emotion, but rather in the sense of the rational apprehension of future insecurity – [i]s the prime motive, a motive that affects not only some states some of the time, but all states all of the time ... that inclines mankind toward "a perpetual and restless desire of power after power, that ceaseth only in death."' (Hedley Bull, 'Hobbes and the International Anarchy', *Social Research*, Vol. 48 (1981), pp. 721–2). States interact with each other within a lawless condition; they behave according to the necessity to survive, in a manner consistent with such a condition. Individual self-preservation is addressed through enforced and coercive laws set by the sovereign, but relations between sovereigns are not regulated in the same way. The laws of nature are all that exist between sovereign states, where uninhibited liberty reigns, and where 'every man, ought to

endeavour peace, as far as he has hope of obtaining it; and when he cannot obtain it, that he may seek , and use, all helps, and advantages of war.' (Thomas Hobbes, *Leviathan* in *International Relations and Political Theory*, ed. Howard Williams *et al.*, (Vancouver: UBC Press, 1993), p. 95).

29 Kant, *Perpetual Peace*, in Hans Reiss, ed. *Kant: Political Writings* (Cambridge: Cambridge University Press, 1970), pp. 93–97.

30 Ibid., p. 108.

31 Ibid., p. 100. As Kant further elaborates, republicanism does not necessarily mean democracy. Democracy has the tendency to produce the evil of tyranny over the majority, whereas republicanism separates the executive power from the legislative. In actuality, monarchy is best suited for this system, since the fewer individuals in executive power the better.

32 Ibid., p. 104.

33 Ibid., p. 106.

34 Ibid., pp. 108, 110.

35 Ibid., pp. 110–12.

36 Ibid., p. 113.

37 Ibid., p. 114.

38 A. Hurrell, 'Kant and the Kantian Paradigm in International Relations', *Review of International Studies*, 16 (1990), p. 202.

39 *Idea for a Universal History*, ed. Reiss, p. 51.

40 Hurrell explores this debate in 'Kant and the Kantian Paradigm.

41 A. J. P. Taylor, *Rumours of Wars* (London: Hamish Hamilton, 1952), p. 262. In Wight, *International Theory*, p. 29.

42 Adam Smith, *Lectures on Justice, Police, Revenue and Arms* (c. 1762–3), ed. E. Cannan (Oxford: Oxford University Press, 1978), p. I, in Hedley Bull, Benedict Kingsbury and Adam Roberts, (eds), *Hugo Grotius and International Relations*, (Oxford: Oxford University Press, 1990) p. 3.

43 Hugo Grotius, *De Jure Belli ac Pacis Libre Tres*, (1625) in H. Williams, *International Relations*, pp. 81–82.

44 Ibid., p. 82.

45 Ibid., p. 83.

46 Ibid.

47 Ibid.

48 Martin Wight, *International Theory: The Three Traditions* (Leicester: Leicester University Press, 1991), p. 14.

49 Ibid.

50 Ibid., p. xxvii.

51 Bentham, *The Theory of Legislation*, p. 83.

52 Ibid., pp. 453–4.

53 The 'authoritarian' can be equated with realists in international relations as attention is given to the need to address security concerns above all else. Bentham becomes, according to this argument, no different from Hobbes.

54 Crimmins, p. 752.

55 Arblaster, p. 352.

56 See Stephen Conway, 'Bentham on Peace and War', *Utilitas*, Vol. 1, No.1 (1989), pp. 82–101; 'Bentham, the Benthamites and the Nineteenth-Century British Peace Movement', *Utilitas*, Vol. 2, No. 2, (1990) pp. 221–43, 'Bentham versus Pitt: Jeremy Bentham and British Foreign Policy 1789', *The Historical Journal*, Vol. 30, No.4 (1987), pp. 791–802.

57 Doyle, p. 226.

58 Ibid.

5　Bentham on Sovereignty

The emancipation of colonies, the Public Opinion Tribunal, international law – everything that Bentham wrote regarding international relations assumed the sovereign state to be fundamental. The state, and the power it wields, has been a source of controversy since its emergence, evidenced by the works of Bodin, Machiavelli, Hobbes, Rousseau, and others,[1] and Bentham is considered to be a contributor to the doctrine of sovereignty in his own right.[2] This chapter reviews previous critical discussions about Bentham's work on sovereignty, but also includes a hitherto neglected international essay, *Persons Subject* (published as *Of Subjects, or of the Personal Extent of the Dominion of the Laws*), expanding the analysis and shedding new light on Bentham's contributions. The inclusion of this essay reveals the importance of the security of expectation in the determination of sovereignty, its relationship to the individual, and offers an explanation regarding the current confusion surrounding Bentham's views on the subject. As there are varying interpretations of Bentham's view of sovereignty, there can likewise be varying conclusions about Bentham's design on the international realm. This chapter on sovereignty is intended to bring clarity to the issue, especially as sovereignty is fundamental to any discussion on Bentham's work on international relations.

Evidence of Bentham's earliest thoughts on sovereignty is found within *A Fragment on Government*, published in 1776.[3] According to J. H. Burns, this is the work that dictates Bentham's place in the traditional history of the idea of sovereignty.[4] In *Fragment*, Bentham argues against William Blackstone's use of the term 'society',[5] and although his intention is not to define sovereignty per se, Bentham nevertheless endows one type of society with sovereignty, but does not extend the same privilege to another. As a result, two very different 'societies' are distinguished from each other:

> In the one, SOCIETY, or a STATE of SOCIETY, is put *synonymous* to a STATE of NATURE; and stands *opposed* to GOVERNMENT, or a STATE OF GOVERNMENT: in this sense, it may be styled, as it commonly is, *natural* SOCIETY. In the other, it is put *synonymous* to GOVERNMENT, or a STATE OF GOVERNMENT; and stands

opposed to a STATE OF NATURE. In this sense it may be styled, as it commonly is, *political* SOCIETY. Of the difference between these two states, a tolerably distinct idea, I take it, may be given in a word or two.[6]

Bentham differentiates between 'natural' and 'political' society such that the former lacks government whereas the latter is synonymous with it, and he further differentiates between the two on the basis of a 'habit of obedience' versus a 'habit of conversancy':

> The idea of a natural society is a *negative* one. The idea of a political society is a *positive* one. 'Tis with the latter, therefore, we should begin.
>
> When a number of persons (whom we may style *subjects*) are supposed to be in the *habit* of paying *obedience* to a person, or an assemblage of persons, of a known and certain description (whom we may call *governor* or *governors*) such persons altogether (*subjects* and *governors*) are said to be in a state of *political* SOCIETY.
>
> The idea of a state of *natural* SOCIETY is, as we have said, a *negative* one. When a number of persons are supposed to be in the habit of *conversing* with each other, at the same time that they are not in any such habit as mentioned above, they are said to be in a state of *natural* SOCIETY.[7]

The political society has a governor dictating and enforcing law to the other members of the community, or the 'subject many'. The natural society lacks a governor, which removes the possibility of the members of that community being coerced into particular types of behaviour. However, natural society does not exclude the possibility of voluntary action, as Bentham's definition of 'habit' shows: 'A *habit* is but an assemblage of *acts*: under which name I would also include, for the present, *voluntary forbearances*.'[8] In a natural society, the members of the community cannot be coerced to behave in one manner as opposed to another, but they can voluntarily relinquish or assume responsibility as they see fit. That such action is voluntary presupposes a supreme authority, or sovereignty, residing within each member of the natural community, but at this early stage in Bentham's writings, this point is not explored.

Bentham also recognizes the possibility that a *governor* of one community can, at the same time, be part of the *governed* of another community. The result is a federation:

> In the same manner we may understand, how the same man, who is *governor* with respect to one man or set of men, may be *subject* with respect to another: how among governors some may be in a *perfect* state of *nature*, with respect to each other: as the KINGS of

FRANCE and SPAIN: others, again in state of *perfect subjection*, as
the HOSPODARS of WALACHIA and MOLDAVIA with respect
to the GRAND SIGNIOR: others, again, in a state of manifest but
imperfect subjection, as the GERMAN STATES with respect to the
EMPEROR: others, again, in such a state in which it may be difficult
to determine whether they are in a state of *imperfect subjection* or in
a *perfect* state of *nature*: as the KING of NAPLES with respect to the
POPE.[9]

Even though Bentham accounts for the possibility of federation, he does
not dismiss the relevance or importance of the supreme authority: 'The
authority of the supreme body cannot, *unless where limited by express
convention*, be said to have any assignable, any certain bounds.'[10] Bentham
argues against the notion that it is both the right and the duty of the supreme authority to make laws. He states that it is impossible for the supreme
authority to be duty-bound at all; if it were it would no longer be supreme.[11]
He argues that a supreme authority can be nothing short of absolute, not
unlike the Hobbesian position, but a difficulty exists if the supreme
authority is capable of relinquishing some power, as in the federal
example.[12] If Bentham qualifies his definition of sovereignty to include a
divide in supreme authority, how is this manifested on the international
stage?

In *Introduction to the Principles and Morals of Legislation* (1780)
Bentham's definition of sovereignty is still qualified; it cannot be universally applied as something inevitably and necessarily absolute.[13] In his
concurrent and subsequent writings, however, Bentham abandons his
concern over divided sovereignty. In *Theory of Legislation* (1782) Bentham
defines sovereignty in a similar manner as in *Introduction to the Principles
and Morals of Legislation*, but eliminates his qualifications that pertain to
the possibility of a federation. He states simply:

> We ordinarily give the collective name of government to the whole
> assemblage of persons charged with the different political functions.
> There is commonly in states *a person* or *a body of persons* who assign
> and distribute to the members of the government their several depart-
> ments, their several functions and prerogatives, and who have authority
> over them and over the whole. The person or the collection of persons
> which exercise this supreme power is called the *sovereign*.[14]

In this definition Bentham does not delineate between varying levels of
sovereignty as his primary concern is the security of the state vis-à-vis
offences against the sovereign. In *Of Laws in General* (1782), the definition becomes clearer as Bentham states that terms such as 'illegal' or 'void'
have no bearing upon the sovereign body or legislature.[15]

It follows that the mandate of the sovereign be it what it will, cannot be illegal; it may be cruel; it may be impolitic; it may even be unconstitutional ... but it would be perverting language and confounding ideas to call it *illegal*: for concessions of privileges are not mandates: they are neither commands nor countermands: in short they are not *laws*. They are only promises from the sovereign to the people that he will not issue any law, any mandate, any command or countermand but to such or such an effect, or perhaps with the concurrence of such or such persons. In this respect they are upon the footing of treaties with foreign powers. They are a sort of treaties with the people. It is not the people who are bound by it, it is not the people whose conduct is concerned in it, but the sovereign himself; in as far as a party can be bound who has the whole force of the political sanction at his disposal. The force then which these treaties have to depend upon for their efficacy is what other treaties have to depend upon, the force of the moral and religious sanctions.[16]

The power of the sovereign is absolute. The only way in which a sovereign can be bound by any covenant is if it chose to do so in the first place. In the event that one sovereign decides to take on certain obligations, its successor, according to Bentham, need not necessarily do the same. Sovereignty is determined through expectation; covenants are only binding on the new sovereign if it chooses, and only if the covenant has been present for an extended period of time will the expectation be that the new responsibilities will be assumed.[17] The same principle applies in the cases of treaties with foreign powers:

A treaty made by one sovereign with another is not itself a law; from which indeed it is plainly distinguished by the definition we set out with giving of the word *law*. It has an intimate connection however with the body of laws, in virtue of its being apt to be converted by construction into an actual law or set of laws, and at any rate from the expectation it affords of the establishment of express laws conformable to stipulations of which it is composed.[18]

The security of expectation plays the pivotal role in determining the extent and breadth of sovereign power. Expectation justifies the status quo, upon which Bentham relies. The object is to initiate reform through common practice, requiring such initiatives to be introduced well in advance of implementation so that those affected by the reform will not react adversely. Bentham uses a classically conservative methodology whereby all those affected must first become accustomed to the features of the covenants and agreements for the latter to achieve credibility and legitimacy.

Bentham's work on sovereignty has inspired an informative and insightful essay by H. L. A. Hart, in which he displays the depth of Bentham's arguments, indicating how and why Bentham tried to divide sovereign power in some instances but not in others, and acknowledges that Bentham's ideas can often be confusing and inconsistent.[19] In 'Bentham on Sovereignty', Hart examines Bentham's views, especially as they are often thought to have influenced John Austin.[20] Hart explains that, in some cases, Bentham was not so adamant about distinguishing a supreme authority, and that he argued it was possible to ensure that one position was not the source of ultimate power and authority in the state.

Hart shows that Bentham had difficulty with the idea of a sovereign endowed with absolute power; with such power, an authority stands to abuse those who are obliged to obey it. To safeguard against such abuse in the domestic setting, Bentham attempts to divide sovereign power, even recognizing the possibility of 'a constitution providing for two or more omnipotent or sovereign legislatures'.[21] Bentham refers to the Roman Republic, whereby 'two independent legislative bodies the *comitia centuriata* and the *comitia tributa* each possessed full and absolute authority'.[22] Although Hart alerts us to the fact that, for Bentham, the sovereignty of the state does not have to reside in one all-powerful entity, but can be limited (through the executive and judicial branches of government, for example), there still remains the difficulty of external sovereignty. Bentham attempts to mitigate the power of the sovereign with reference to 'the subject many' who are bound to obey it, but he alludes to a more finite, less fluid, definition that is ultimately required from the international vantage point. Upon the threat of external hostility, or even in the event of a national response, there is a power that speaks, in its entirety, for the state.

The difficulty of isolating Bentham's definition of sovereignty can be attributed to his concern for security. Bentham's 'limited' sovereignty appears to provide an alternative to the Hobbesian notion of absolute sovereignty, the same concept that Austin claims is missing from Bentham's work. Austin looks to Chapter I of *Fragment* for a definition and is dissatisfied when it is apparent that Bentham does not explicitly state that 'the superior generally obeyed by the bulk of generality of the members must not be habitually obedient to a certain individual or body'.[23] Although Hart reveals the complex and nuanced nature of sovereignty as Bentham saw it, he does not adequately address Austin's problem, nor that of the international relations scholar. The international realm presupposes that the 'habit of obedience', to use Bentham's phraseology, is finite and is not applicable beyond the state level. This does not eliminate the possibility of a 'habit of conversancy', but such a conversation is by no means binding, and certainly does not imply obedience in the same sense that obedience is required within the state by the subject many.

Neither Hart, nor J. H. Burns in his survey of Bentham's work, explored the notion of sovereignty in Bentham's international writings, but if they had, one of Bentham's 1786 essays, known as *Persons Subject*, could have contributed a different dimension to their research. Bentham not only provides a sense of what he means by sovereignty, but also offers a further explanation of the complexity of his view. *Persons Subject* distinguishes between dominion, or the supreme authority, and jurisdiction: 'correspondent to one field of dominion there may be many fields of jurisdiction'.[24] The dominion remains the purview of the sovereign whereas jurisdiction is the purview of the judge. Each jurisdiction has autonomous responsibilities, but overall is still contained within the dominion of one sovereign, hence the possibility of one dominion containing many fields of jurisdiction. The dominion embodies the supreme authority, and it is dominion that becomes important when understanding issues of international concern.

The purpose of *Persons Subject* is to determine the meaning and extent of dominion. Bentham's discussion of sovereignty more or less assumes supreme, boundless, authority without stating it outright. Bentham identifies the sovereign on the basis of his ability to cause harm to others who cannot do the same to him.

> A sovereign is stiled such in the first instance in respect of the persons whom he has the right or power to command. Now the right or legal power to command may be co-extensive with the physical power of giving force and effect to the command, that is by the physical power of hurting; the power of *hyper-physical* contrectation employed for the purpose of hurting. But by the possibility every sovereign may have the power of hurting any or every person whatsoever: and that not at different times only, but even at one and the same time. According to this criterion then, the sphere of possible jurisdiction is to every person the same. But the problem is to determine what persons ought to be considered as being under the dominion of one sovereign and what [others] under the dominion of another: in other words, what persons ought to be considered as the subjects of one sovereign, and what as the subjects of another.[25]

Bentham establishes the relationship between the individual and state, when and how the individual is obliged to pay obedience to one sovereign versus another, and over whom the sovereign has power: 'The question is to what sovereign a given individual is subject in a sense in which he is not subject to any other.'[26] Such a determination, Bentham notes, entails territorial dominion:

> The circumstance of territorial dominion, dominion over land, possesses the properties desired. It can seldom happen that two sovereigns can each of them with equal facility the other being unwilling

traverse the same extent of land. That sovereign then who has the physical power of occupying and traversing a given tract of land, insomuch that he can effectually and safely traverse it in any direction at pleasure at the same time that against his will another sovereign can not traverse the same land with equal facility and effect can be more certain of *coming at* the individual in question than such other sovereign can be, and may therefore be pronounced to have afflictive power over all such persons as are to be found upon that land; and that a higher afflictive power than any other sovereign can have. And hence the maxim, dominion over person depends upon dominion over land.[27]

Bentham makes clear that sovereignty consists of one supreme power having ultimate authority over a given piece of land, the persons residing upon that land, ruling out any possibility that another sovereign may lay equal claim upon either the same piece of land, people, or both. This contradicts earlier admissions that sovereignty can be divided, but Bentham's delineation between sovereignty and jurisdiction partially alleviates the problem. It is clear in *Persons Subject* that a supreme authority, residing in the state, must exist.

Persons Subject attempts to bridge the chasm between national and international law by determining who must abide by the laws of which sovereign, and also how sovereigns relate to each other, as well as to subjects who are not their own; a subject who is in the habit of obedience to one sovereign cannot be in a habit of obedience to another simultaneously. Bentham distinguishes between *standing* or *ordinary* subjects of the sovereign, and *occasional* or *extraordinary* subjects of the same. The difference between the types of subjects depends on the nature of their relationship to the state.

In every state, there are certain persons who are in all events, throughout their lives, and in all places, subject to the sovereign of that state; it is their obedience that constitutes the essence of his sovereignty these may be stiled the *standing* or *ordinary subjects* of the sovereign or the state, and the dominion he has over them may be stiled *fixed* or *regular*. There are others who are subject to him only in certain events, for a certain time while they are at a certain place: the obedience of these constitutes only an accidental appendage to his sovereignty: these may be termed his *occasional* or *extraordinary subjects*, or *subjects pro re nata*: and the dominion he has over them may be stiled *occasional*.[28]

Bentham defines citizenship through the habitual obedience of the subject. The event of a person's birth is relevant to the determination of sovereignty, although he recognizes that here too situations may arise that complicate the issue.[29] He attempts to construct a permanent but flexible methodology that would successfully determine how all people would be subject to one sovereign at any given time, no matter where they were.

The sovereign's ability to cause harm, his dominion over territory, and the subject's birthplace, determine the complicated issue of which sovereign commands power over whom. One central feature has yet to be addressed, and that is expectation. The fact that the sovereign expects to have dominion over certain persons, and that certain persons expect to pay obedience to a particular sovereign, is as important, if not more so, than the preceding features.

> Thus it is that dominion over the soil confers dominion *de facto* over the greater part of the natives its inhabitants: in such manner that such inhabitants are treated as owing a permanent allegiance to the sovereign of that soil. And in general there seems no reason why it should not be deemed to be so, even *de jure* judging upon the principle of utility. On the one hand, the sovereign on his part naturally expects to possess the obedience of persons who stand in this sort of relation to him: possessing it at first, he naturally expects to continue to possess it: he is accustomed to reckon upon it: were he to cease to possess it, it might be a disappointment to him. Any other sovereign having even begun to possess the allegiance of the same subject, has not the same cause for expecting to possess it; not entertaining any such expectation, the not possessing it is no disappointment: for subjects in as far as their obedience is a matter of private benefit to the sovereign, may without any real impropriety (*absit verbo invidia*) be considered as subjects of his property . . . On the other hand let us consider the state of mind and expectations of the subject. The subject having been accustomed from his birth to look upon the sovereign as his sovereign continues all along to look upon him in the same light: to be obedient is as natural as to be obedient to his father. He lives and has all along been accustomed to live under his laws. He has some intimation (I wish the universal negligence of sovereigns in the matter of promulgation would permit me to say any thing more than a very inaccurate and general intimation) some intimation he has however of the nature of them: when occasion happens, he is accustomed to obey them. He finds it no hardship to obey them, one at least in comparison with what it would be, were they alltogether new to him: whereas those of another sovereign were they in themselves more easy, (he might find harder on account of their being new to him) might merely on account of their novelty appear, and therefore be harder upon the whole.[30]

Sovereignty relies upon expectation. Even in these early writings, Bentham wishes to either instil a level of expectation to initiate reform, or, more importantly, respect the expectation that already exists. In the latter case, which becomes pre-eminent in Bentham's writings as time goes on, his reliance on expectation is no different from the fears expressed by Machiavelli with regard to innovation, and the need for people to have a system to rely on, even if a reprehensible one.[31]

Bentham's consistency in his definition of sovereignty appears contingent upon his ability to limit the power of the sovereign without reducing that power to the point where it becomes ineffectual. In the domestic sphere, such limitation is relevant for the purpose of protecting the 'subject many', but external sovereignty is not likewise limited: 'Legally speaking, declares Bentham, there is and can be no restraint on the power of the sovereign.'[32] This position is first suggested by Bentham's distinction between a natural and political society, and then explicitly stated in later writings. Bentham's natural society, although not dominated by a supreme authority, does not appear to be an anarchic war of all against all, as a 'habit of conversancy' is unlikely to exist under such conditions. Nevertheless, this also means that no supreme body exists in the natural society to ensure that conditions of 'conversancy' prevail. A division of sovereignty does not solve the problem without accepting empire as a result, but that is not Bentham's desire. Bentham's discrimination between dominion and jurisdiction explains, in part, the inconsistency of his ideas on divided and absolute sovereignty. The greatest determining factor, however, is expectation. Only expectation determines the extent to which sovereign power may be 'altered' such that a sovereign would consider himself bound by covenants. Bentham relies on expectation to enforce agreements upon sovereigns to limit the extent of their power, and this supports his place within the liberal tradition in international relations. More often than not, however, expectation acts as a prophylactic against innovation, and it is this function that can even explain Bentham's most visionary proposals, in that he often wishes things to return to how they used to be. When subjected to the measure of expectation, Bentham's definition of sovereignty reflects a Machiavellian concern in favour of constancy, and the resulting absolute nature of Bentham's sovereignty is read, by some, to be similar to the Hobbesian conception of unlimited power. It is this understanding of sovereignty that underpins Bentham's work on international relations.

Bentham therefore held the position that the power of the governing body, though practically capable of limitation through the operation of the causes which determine the degree of obedience, was theoretically beyond any limitation or restriction whatsoever.[33]

Notes

1 Ibid.; C. E. Merriam, *History of the Theory of Sovereignty Since Rousseau* (New York: Columbia University Press, 1900); F. H. Hinsley, *Sovereignty* (London: C. A. Watts, 1966).
2 Merriam, p. 131. Merriam claims that Bentham was a 'leader in the new movement' in defining sovereignty.

3 Bentham, *A Fragment on Government*, eds J. H. Burns and H. L. A. Hart, with an Introduction by Ross Harrison, (Cambridge: Cambridge University Press, 1988). Hereafter referred to as *Fragment*.

4 J. H. Burns, 'Bentham on Sovereignty: An Exploration', *Northern Ireland Legal Quarterly*, Vol. 24, No. 3, (Autumn 1973), p. 399.

5 Bentham's *Fragment* is meant to be a critical commentary on the legal commentaries of Sir William Blackstone, a prominent legal thinker of Bentham's era.

6 *Fragment*, pp. 39–40.

7 Ibid., p. 40.

8 Ibid., n. 1.

9 Ibid., p. 44.

10 Ibid., p. 98. Bentham states 'That to say there is any act they *cannot* do, – to speak of anything of theirs as being *illegal*, – as being *void*; – to speak of their exceeding their *authority* (whatever be the phrase) – their *power*, their *right*, – is, however common, an abuse of language.'

11 Ibid., p. 110.

12 Although the supreme power is divided, sovereignty still exists.

13 Bentham states 'the total assemblage of persons by whom the several political operations above mentioned come to be performed, we set out with applying the collective appellation of *the government*. Among these persons there *commonly** is some one person, or body of persons whose office it is to assign and distribute to the rest their several departments, to determine the conduct to be pursued by each in the performance of the particular set of operations that belongs to him, and even upon occasion to exercise his function in his stead. Where there is any such person, or body or persons, *he* or *it* may, according as the turn of the phrase requires, be termed *the sovereign*, or the *sovereignty*. (* I should have been afraid to have said *necessarily*. In the United Provinces, in the Helvetic, or even in the Germanic body, where is that one assembly in which an absolute power over the whole resides? where was there in the Roman Commonwealth? I would not undertake for certain to find an answer to all these questions.)' *An Introduction to the Principles and Morals of Legislation* (New York: Hafner Publishing, 1965), pp. 217–8.

14 Bentham, *The Theory of Legislation*, p. 243. Much later in his *Constitutional Code* Bentham states that 'the sovereignty is in *the people*. It is reserved by and to them. It is exercised, by the exercise of the Constitutive authority' (p. 25). Although sovereignty is placed in the people of the state, it is exercised on their behalf by the government, and supreme authority is still exercised.

15 Burns, p. 402.

16 *Of Laws in General*, ed. H. L. A. Hart, (London: Athlone Press, 1970), p. 65.

17 Ibid.

18 *OLG*, p. 16.

19 See H. L. A. Hart, 'Bentham on Sovereignty', *The Irish Jurist*, (1967). F. H. Hinsley noted that Bentham made important contributions to the idea of dividing sovereignty, but he still relied on the supreme authority of the state when looking to matters of international concern (Hinsley, p. 157). J. H. Burns has provided a survey of some of Bentham's most important ideas on sovereignty in his article, 'Bentham on Sovereignty: An Exploration'.

20 H. L. A. Hart, p. 399.

21 Hart, p. 329.

22 Ibid.

23 John Austin, *The Province of Jurisprudence Determined* (1832), p. 220; in Burns, pp. 400–1.

24 UC XXV.10; Bowring, Vol. II, p. 540.

25 UC XXV.10; Bowring, Vol. II, p. 540.

26 UC XXV.13; Bowring, Vol. II, p. 541.

27 UC XXV.13: Bowring, Vol. II, pp. 541–2.
28 UC XXV.12; Bowring, Vol. II, p. 541.
29 UC XXV.13; Bowring, Vol. II, p. 542 and UC XXV.14; Bowring, Vol. II, p. 543. Bentham briefly addresses the problems arising from situations in which persons are born in a territory that is not their fixed location of residence, or have emigrated.
30 UC XXV.14; Bowring, Vol. II, p. 542.
31 J. G. A. Pocock, *The Machiavellian Moment: Florentine Political Thought and the Atlantic Republican Tradition* (Princeton: Princeton University Press, 1975), pp. 153–4. See Chapter 6 for further discussion.
32 Merriam, p. 132.
33 Ibid.

6 Bentham on Peace

> As to the utility of such an universal and lasting peace, supposing a plan for that purpose practicable, and likely to be adopted, there can be but one voice. The objection, and the only objection to it, is the apparent impracticability of it; – that it is not only hopeless, but that to such a degree that any proposal to that effect deserves the name of visionary and ridiculous. This objection I shall endeavour in the first place to remove; for the removal of this prejudice may be necessary to procure for the plan a hearing.[1]
>
> Between the interests of nations, there is nowhere any real conflict: if they appear repugnant any where, it is only in proportion as they are misunderstood.[2]

The word 'international' first appeared in one of Bentham's earliest published works, *An Introduction to the Principles of Morals and Legislation*, and has subsequently become part of mainstream discourse. Bentham is best-known to international relations theorists for his contribution to the liberal tradition of international relations theory; this interpretation of his work stems primarily from *A Plan for an Universal and Perpetual Peace*.[3] On the foundation of the essays that compose *Plan* as well as his other international essays of the same period, the argument that Bentham is a liberal is very compelling. *Plan*'s origin, if not existence, is suspect, however, requiring a re-examination of Bentham's work in international relations. This chapter will identify the strengths and weaknesses of Bentham's liberal designation on the basis of his international essays written in the late 1780s. This evaluation will be both chronological and conceptual, considering the extent to which Bentham's ideas may have evolved over time, as well as isolating some of the key concepts that Bentham judged to be most significant. *Plan* and its companion essays bring to light a crucial period in Bentham's thought in view of the fact that he wrote on international relations in such a concentrated manner. Given his apparent sentiments during this period, they largely justify the description of 'liberal' with which Bentham has been endowed. Despite this argument, even Bentham's most idealistic moments are riddled with ambivalence and inconsistency, a fact not unnoticed by many who have studied his work.[4]

Bentham's reification within the liberal tradition is not entirely accurate, not for the reason that Bentham is, rather, a realist, but that the traditions in international relations theories do not serve to elucidate his work in the most accurate or useful way.

The vast proportion of Bentham's writings that focussed almost exclusively on international matters was written between 1786 and 1789. Most of these essays were published in the Bowring edition of Bentham's *Works*, under the heading *Principles of International Law*. Bentham did not concentrate on international matters again until the years 1827 to 1830, shortly before his death, when he revisited the subject of international law with the hopes of enlisting his acquaintance, Jabez Henry, in the task of drafting a code of international law.[5]

The 1786–89 essays, some of which contribute to *Plan*, consist of the following: *Pacification and Emancipation* (1786–89); *Colonies and Navy* (1786); *Persons Subject* (1786); *Cabinet No Secrecy* (1789); *Projet Matiere* (1786); *Gilbert* (1789); and *On War* (1789).[6] It is possible that these essays were eventually meant to constitute one, larger essay like *Plan*, but such a project is not clear. As they currently exist, each comprises its own distinct essay or fragment, and although the topics addressed in each are not entirely divorced from each other, they are best treated separately for clarity. We begin with an examination of *Plan* as it has been the most influential source of Bentham's work on international relations in the past, but the discussion will include some of Bentham's other international essays, both published and unpublished.

A Plan for An Universal and Perpetual Peace revisited

Plan is often visionary, even though Bentham tries to convince his readers that it is not. The material covered in *Plan* has two central themes; emancipation of colonies, and ridding the foreign department of secrecy. The force of public opinion and the possibility of arms control measures are also addressed, in support of these two main themes. The first half of *Plan* consists of *Colonies and Navy*, *Pacification and Emancipation*, and parts of *Projet Matiere*, with *Cabinet No Secrecy* completing the last half. Although the content of *Plan* is the subject of discussion, the individual essays that compose *Plan* that will be referred to, giving a sense of how Bentham chose to address the topics that concerned him, and how frequently he did so.

Colonies: troop reduction through emancipation

It is not coincidence that a substantial part of *Plan* is devoted to the argument against colonial possessions.[7] There can be no doubt about the extent of Bentham's contribution to, as well as interest in, this subject. Bentham's work on colonies should be considered one of the most, if not *the* most, significant contribution he has made to the study of international relations.[8]

The emancipation of the colonies is a central feature of Bentham's plan for peace, and is a point he repeats wherever possible within the 1786–89 manuscripts.

In *Colonies and Navy*, reducing a state's reliance upon a naval force is among the many arguments Bentham offers in favour of emancipating the colonies. Upon releasing distant dependencies, the navy's only obligation would be in warding off any pirates attacking vessels of commerce.[9] Additionally, a reduction in the naval force eliminates the need for regulations such as a Navigation Act and other 'nurseries for seamen'.[10] Bentham's call for a reduction in naval forces does not receive further explanation in *Colonies and Navy*. He does take up the matter in *Projet Matiere* however, when he explores the possibility of a treaty for arms control:

> An agreement of this kind would not be dishonourable. If the covenant were on one side only, it might be so. If it regard both parties together, the reciprocity takes away the acerbity. By the treaty which put an end to the first Punic war, the number of vessels that the Carthaginians might maintain was limited. This condition was it not humiliating? It might be: but if it were, it must have been because there was nothing correspondent to it on the side of the Romans. A treaty which placed all the security on one side, what course could it have had for its source? It could only have had one – that is the avowed superiority of the party thus incontestably secured, – such a condition could only have been a law dictated by the conqueror to the party conquered. The law of the strongest. None but a conqueror could have dictated it; none but the conquered would have accepted it.[11]

Bentham favours 'honourable' treaties only because they already exist; beyond that he has difficulty following through on his ideas. It is clear that security is the motivating factor behind the success of such an initiative. Security is established through reciprocity, and must exist on all sides if an arms control agreement is to have any merit. Although Bentham entertains notions of arms control, subsequent passages in *Projet Matiere* are decidedly more sceptical about the possibilities:

> Whilst as to naval forces, if it concerned Europe only, the difficulty might perhaps not be very considerable. To consider France, Spain and Holland, as making together a counterpoise to the power of Britain, – perhaps on account of the disadvantages which accompany the concert between three separate nations, to say nothing of the tardiness and publicity of procedures under the Dutch Constitution, – perhaps England might allow to all together a united force equal to half or more than its own.[12]

Bentham's argument supports his cause but is still hesitant. His treaty for arms control relies upon a balance-of-power argument; the combined weakness and ineptitude of three European states are no match for Britain's power, therefore this treaty would not be a threat. He does not explore the implications of reducing the naval force beyond stating, once again, 'take away the colonies, what use would there be for a single vessel, more than the few necessary in the Mediterranean to curb the pirates'.[13] The rest of Bentham's commentary does not hold out much hope for the initiative.

Bentham provides additional but weak support for his arms control argument in a marginal outline titled *International Economy* where he makes note of precedents such as the

> 1. Convention of disarmament between France and Britain in 1787. –This [is] a precedent of the measure or stipulation itself. 2. Armed Neutrality-Code – This [is] a precedent of the *mode* of bringing about the measure: and may serve to disprove the impossibility of a general convention among nations. 3. Treaty limiting the Russian forces to be sent to the Mediterranean. Does not exist. 4. Treaty forbidding the fortifying of Dunkirk.[14]

Even though Bentham notes an instance where one such treaty does not exist, it is clear that he strives to prove that treaties of arms control can be concluded with success. He speculates about the possibility of reducing more than just the navy, but again, he is sceptical:

> If the simple relation of a single nation with a single other nation be considered, perhaps the matter would not be very difficult. The misfortune is, that almost everywhere compound relations are found. On the subject of troops, – France says to England, Yes I would voluntarily make with you a treaty of disarming, if there were only you: but it is necessary for me to have troops to defend me from the Austrians. Austria might say the same to France; but it is necessary to guard against Prussia, Russia, and the Porte. And the like allegation might be made by Prussia with regard to Russia.[15]

Bentham does not solve the dilemma of 'compound relations'; rather, his words offer no optimism and no direction out of this predicament. Bentham considers a reduction of the naval force, but this is owing to the fact that he considers the navy to be a relatively insignificant asset.[16] A reduction in the army, or land force, receives little or no support.

Additional consideration of treaties in *Pacification and Emancipation* is devoted to emancipating colonies, and the rhetoric is nothing short of visionary: 'Whatsoever nation got the start of the other in making the proposal [to emancipate colonies] would crown itself with immortal honour. The risk would be nothing – the gain certain. This gain would be, the giving an incontrovertible demonstration of its own disposition to peace, and of the opposite disposition in the other nation in case of its rejecting the proposal.'[17] The nation taking the lead in colony emancipation undertakes the most honourable and glorifying project available to a state. The process should be conducted in public, 'sound the heart of the nation addressed', and 'discover its intentions, and proclaim them to the world'.[18] Relinquishing claims to colonial possessions eliminates the motivating factor behind nations engaging in war. The possession of colonies leads to expense, not revenue, and only makes a nation more vulnerable to attack.

The essay *Pacification and Emancipation* completes the remaining first half of *Plan*, full of hope that the ills of humankind can be remedied with a degree of education and information, yet lamenting the fact that humanity is jealous, prejudiced, and malevolent. Although many of Bentham's ideas in *Plan* are visionary, and suited to idealist categories, the fact that these ideas are also shot through with scepticism has largely been overlooked. Surrounding his recommendations to emancipate colonies and use the force of public opinion are statements that contradict his initiatives:

> But, as I have observed, men have not yet learned to tune their feelings in unison with the voice of morality on these points. They will feel more pride at being accounted strong, than resentment at being called unjust; or rather the imputation of injustice will appear flattering rather than otherwise, when coupled with the consideration of its cause. I feel it in my own experience. But if I, listed as I am in the professed and hitherto only advocate in my own country, in the cause of Justice, set a less value on Justice then is its due, what can I expect from the general run of men?[19]

The fact that Bentham makes this and similar statements throughout *Plan* is important to our understanding of Bentham's strategies and his fears about those strategies. These doubts articulate his paramount concern: the degree to which men's habits might be changed so that they will expect and applaud certain initiatives over others. The only way Bentham foresees his plan gaining acceptance is if he couches the benefits of his suggestions in terms of self-interest:

> Can the arrangement proposed be justly stiled visionary if it has been shown
> 1. That it is in the interest of the parties concerned
> 2. That they are already sensible of that interest
> 3. That the situation it would place them in is no new one nor any thing more than the original situation they set out from.[20]

Bentham not only makes clear that emancipating colonies is in the interest of all the states involved, but that emancipation does not run contrary to expectation. Eliminating colonial possessions only returns international conditions to their prior state. The outcome of Bentham's initiative would be nothing new, and agreements such as these have occurred in the past. There have been other 'complicated and difficult conventions effectuated' such as the Armed Neutrality, the American Confederation, and the German Diet: 'Why should not the European fraternity subsist as well as the Swiss or German League?'[21] Bentham's argument relies on three assumptions: that he has accurately articulated the interests of the state, that a return to conditions of the past is desirable, and that it is possible to effect such an agreement between states. Bentham uses conservative methods to engender a community of states; he argues that what he proposes is nothing less than a manifestation of the interests of the states, and nothing more than a return to a familiar way of life.

When Bentham next speaks of a 'reduction', it is not in arms, as was presented by his editor (see Chapter 3), but in the 'contributions of the people'.[22] He does not explain his intention in proposing this reduction, leaving one to speculate. It is nevertheless clear that his intention is to make 'the subject many' aware of his proposal and what it offers so that they may realize that this plan is in their interest and therefore support it. Immediate publication of this initiative is imperative, according to Bentham, since the 'mass of the people' are otherwise 'most exposed to be led away by prejudices'.[23] Bentham's defence against the ignorance and malevolence of men is freedom of the press and public opinion. While the press informs, public opinion responds, and together they might be able to effect positive change on the international landscape.

Public opinion and the tribunal

Bentham argued for the creation of a forum for public opinion through a 'common tribunal'. It is one of his best-known contributions to liberal internationalist thinking.[24] Bentham sought the application of the moral sanction to inspire state action through the tribunal, which would otherwise have no legal or political authority.[25] Apart from the emancipation of colonies, the tribunal appears to be uppermost in the minds of those who read Bentham's *Plan*. His ideas are often cited as an influence in the construction of a twentieth-century international institution: 'The influence of social thinkers like Locke and Bentham is most apparent in the idea of a League of Nations.'[26] As a result, Bentham's tribunal presents a complicated problem; his influence on this or related institutions is apparent, but although the concept may be a focal point for many scholars, it is also giving credit where it is probably not due. In this case Bentham's undoubted influence is built on a tenuous foundation. A closer examination of what Bentham said about the tribunal will reveal a distinct lack of clarity and little confidence in the concept. Bentham may have planted the seed, but he did little to ensure that it would take root.

The notion of a tribunal, or formal organization designed for the expression of public opinion, receives only sporadic attention from Bentham.[27] He presents the idea of a tribunal in *Pacification and Emancipation* as a means to alleviate conflict through negotiation and arbitration:

> It is an observation of somebody's, that no nation ought to yield any evident point of justice to another. This must mean evident in the eyes of the nation that is to judge – evident in the eyes of the nation called upon to yield. What does this amount to? – that no nation is to give up any thing of what it looks upon as its right – no nation is to make any concessions. – Wherever there is any difference of opinion between the negotiators of two nations, war is to be the consequence.
>
> Without a common tribunal, something might be said for this. Concession to notorious injustice invites fresh injustice.
>
> Establish a common tribunal, the necessity of war no longer follows from difference of opinion – Just or unjust the decision of the arbiters will save the credit, the honour of the conceding party.[28]

Bentham's tribunal provides an alternative to war, offers the opportunity to determine justice openly, and more importantly, allows arbiters to take responsibility for decisions made, thereby reducing the 'shame' that would otherwise affect the obliging party. Arbitration also suggests that the tribunal has the capacity to dictate, if not enforce, judgements upon any offending party. Bentham does not explain how less shame and better compliance will result when the tribunal dictates state action; he assumes that decisions from a body of states are more palatable than from the 'winner' of the conflict alone.

In *Colonies and Navy* Bentham makes fleeting reference to a 'court of judicature', where he explores the possibility of publicly advertising all government activity and decision-making in foreign relations. In *International Economy*, a marginal outline, Bentham speaks of a 'Congress or Diet', to be constituted in the following manner:

> Each power to send two: one principal with an occasional substitute.
> Form of proceedings Public.
> Powers
> 1. Power of reporting opinion only
> 2. Power of causing the report to be circulated in the dominions of each state
> 3. After a certain time – putting the refractory state under the Ban of Europe.[29]

The most important role of Bentham's tribunal – whether it is termed a court, congress, or diet – is for the expression and publication of opinion pertaining to the conflict. The conclusion that the court, tribunal, congress or diet are one and the same such that the terms are interchangeable, is a plausible, but not certain conclusion to draw. The court of judicature has the power to dictate solutions to the affairs between states, although this power is not coercive. The 'Ban of Europe', the tool available to the Congress, might constitute one such solution, but it appears to encompass far less latitude than that given to the court. The tribunal is empowered with an arbitration function, which appears similar to the powers of the court, but again, this is not clear. Only much later does Bentham bring some clarity to the issue in his unpublished manuscripts of 1827–30 when he more effectively distinguishes between a Congress, a Judicatory, and a tribunal, the latter serving only as an appeal of last resort, as an institution to decide on an international matter.[30] Nevertheless, in these later papers Bentham addresses the functions of at least four different international bodies: a Confederacy, a Congress, a Judicatory, and a Public Opinion Tribunal. The Confederacy and Congress appear to be the same instrument as both are fora for the member state's opinions.[31] There is no indication that the Congress has any function beyond the expression of opinion. The apparatus of paramount importance is a separate body that Bentham calls the Judicatory, endowed with the capacity to administer international law, and this body receives most of Bentham's attention. The only mention Bentham makes of a Public Opinion Tribunal is in relation to the Judicatory, where it does not receive pride of place: 'The Judicatory in dernier resort, should in effect be the Public Opinion Tribunal, composed of all the several individuals belonging to all the several states.'[32] It is not clear how the Congress and Tribunal differ, other than in Bentham's explicit lack of confidence in the latter.

The main point to make here is that Bentham wished to see an international body in place to help mitigate conflict. Bentham clearly had difficulty expressing what form this body was to take. He pursued the notion of a tribunal because he thought a formal institution bringing states together was warranted. On this basis it makes sense that Bentham's contribution to the concept, even to a 'League of Nations', should be acknowledged. What needs to be equally acknowledged, however, is the difficulty Bentham found in articulating this concept, in part due to the conflict between sovereignty and community that inevitably ensues.[33] If Bentham holds a prominent place in the history of such an institution, it must be recognized that he did not contribute a solid foundation. Bentham seeks to increase communication between states in order to enable contesting parties to avoid war. He recognizes that he must overcome the many vices of humanity, but if prejudice could be replaced by knowledge, ambition by honour, and jealousy by confidence, his hopes have a chance of realization.[34] The rest of *Plan* is devoted to ensuring that the people who are most affected – the masses – have ready access to information and education so as to enable them to express their views on international affairs, especially those affairs that would call them to war. For Bentham, a significant part of the problem lies in the secret diplomacy of the foreign department, committing 'the subject many' – the people – to fight in wars that are of no interest to them, but only to the sinister few – the elite.

Secrecy in the foreign department

Bentham's views on secrecy in foreign departments are best known from *Plan*. *Cabinet No Secrecy* comprises the last half of *Plan*, easily the most complete and cohesive essay of the 1786–89 set. This essay is devoted to exposing the sinister nature of secrecy in foreign affairs, but Bentham's continued emphasis on the economic implications, especially as regards foreign dependencies, is unmistakable. This is logical given Bentham's belief that one of the most fundamental, if not the primary cause of war, is the possession of distant dependencies, and the unscrupulous trade practices that result. It is Bentham's contention that empire requires secrecy to maintain control, but by eliminating distant dependencies, reliance upon secrecy is no longer necessary, and can be eliminated as well. Bentham's proposal is simple:

> I lay down two propositions
> 1. That in no negotiation and at no period of any negotiation ought the negotiations of the Cabinet in this country to be kept secret from the public at large: much less from Parliament, and after enquiry made in Parliament.
> 2. That whatever may be the case with preliminary negotiations, such secrecy ought never be maintained with regard to treaties actually concluded.[35]

Throughout this essay Bentham sustains his unqualified demands for the elimination of secrecy in the foreign department, but for one small comment inserted in the margin of the manuscript, beside the first of his propositions: 'It lies upon the other side at least to find a case in which want of secrecy may produce a specific mischief.'[36] In other words, if there is an argument to be made to retain secrecy, it can be legitimately introduced by the other parties involved. Bentham does not acknowledge this possibility again in this essay, but the suggestion appears influential in his future treatment of the subject.

Treaties increase the propensity to war when they are negotiated in secret. Secrecy is the method by which ministers may, without regard for the people who must endure the fight, plunge the nation into war for the illusory goals of enhanced wealth and power. Bentham decries the feeble methods used to halt wars already in progress, belittles the ineffective and

improbable punishments that can be imposed upon the offending ministers, and disparages the assumption that the power of the state is dependent
upon secret diplomacy.[37] Secrecy's only benefit is to allow government
action to take place in the most unabashed and gratuitous manner, without
any check against it. The product of secrecy, says Bentham, is war.

Bentham's arguments against secrecy are directed toward Britain, a
'civilized' nation and great power. If her circumstances were otherwise,
an argument could be made whereby secrecy is acceptable, and where war
is necessary and desirable. Bentham argues that Britain has no choice
but to eliminate secrecy from her foreign affairs because she is powerful
and has nothing to fear from other nations. As a result Britain has no need
to 'conceal' its foreign agenda. Other nations, on the other hand, may still
require secrecy and even be justified in making conquest.

> Conquests made by New Zealanders have some sense in them. While
> the conquered fry, the conquerors fatten. Conquests made by the pol
> ished nations of antiquity, conquests made by Greeks and Romans, had
> some sense in them. Lands, moveables, inhabitants, every thing went
> into pocket. War Invasions of France in the days of the Edwards and
> the Henrys had a rational object. Prisoners were taken and the country
> was stripped to pay their ransom. The ransom of a single prisoner a
> Duke of Orleans exceeded 2/3 of the revenue of England. Conquests
> made by a modern despot of the continent have still some sense in
> them. His new property, being contiguous, is laid on to his old property:
> the inhabitants men as many as he thinks fit to squeeze from them,
> goes into his purse. Conquests made by the British nation would be
> violations of common sense, were there no such thing as justice. They
> are nothing but confirmed blindness and stupidity that can prompt us
> to go on mimicking Alexander and Caesar and the New Zealanders,
> and Catherine and Frederic, without the motive.[38]

It is not entirely clear why Britain does not profit when New Zealand does,
given that the benefits of contiguous land are irrelevant to both. Additionally, Bentham argues only paragraphs earlier that for the costs that go into
conquest, the benefits of extracting the resources, whatever they are,
amount to nothing. For despots, however, profit still appears to be possible.

'Oh, but you mistake! ... We do not now make war for conquests, but for trade.'[39]

In anticipation of the claim that war must be made for increased trade,
Bentham repeats his often repeated argument that trade is not possible
without capital (see Chapters 8 and 9). In some respects, the substance
of *Cabinet No Secrecy* often appears tangential to the theme of secrecy
itself. War depletes capital so trade cannot be the result.[40] Since secrecy is

considered necessary to trade, Bentham declares that trade can only be accomplished by 'forcing independent nations to let you trade with them, and conquering nations, or pieces of nations, to make them trade with you'.[41] Britain in particular falls prey to Bentham's attack; as such a powerful nation she does not need such poor excuses for war. Bentham bemoans the decisions made in British foreign affairs and the lack of action in Parliament: 'Being asked in the House of Lords about secret articles, the Minister for foreign affairs refuses to answer. I do not blame him. Subsisting rules, it seems to be agreed, forbid him. They throw a general veil of secrecy over the transactions of the Cabinet with foreign powers.'[42] According to Bentham, Britain has no justification for endorsing secrecy, especially as this practice is repugnant to its constitution and people:

> What, then, is the true use and effect of secrecy? That the prerogatives of the place may furnish an aliment to petty vanity: that petty vanity may draw an aliment from the prerogatives of place: that the members of the *Circulation* may have a newspaper to themselves: that under favour of monopoly, ignorance and incapacity may put on airs of wisdom: that a man, unable to write or speak what is fit to put into a newspaper may toss his head and say I don't read newspapers: as if a Parent were to say, I don't trouble my head about school-masters: and that a Minister, secure from scrutiny in that quarter may have the convenience upon occasion of filling the posts with obsequious cyphers instead of effective men. Any thing will do to make a Minister whose writing may be written for him, and whose duty in speaking consists in silence.[43]

Secrecy perpetuates ignorance, on the part of both the ministers of state and the masses. Britain should not engage in secrecy since her vast power does not necessitate it; she need not fear any one nation, or even two, her power is so great.

> Oh but if every thing were written were published, were liable to be made public, who would treat with you abroad? – Just the same persons as treat with you at present: negotiations, for fear of misrepresentation would perhaps be committed somewhat more to writing than at present – and where would be the harm: Your King and his Ministers might not have quite such copious accounts, true or false, of the tittle-tattle of each court: or he must put into different hands the tittle-tattle and the real business: . . . And suppose our head-servants were not so minutely acquainted with the Mistresses and Buffoons of Kings and their Ministers, what matters it to you as a nation, who have no intrigues to carry on, no petty points to gain?[44]

Bentham suggests that if Britain is not, by definition, a war-mongering state, then it must do away with secrecy in the foreign department. If Britain claims that these wars are made in the name of trade, 'with equal justice might they look upon the loss of a leg as a cause of swiftness'.[45] Whether secrecy enabled Britain to become a great power is not addressed by Bentham. His only conclusion is that Britain does herself a disservice in utilizing secrecy now, and that war is an expense that can never result in prosperity.[46]

In accord with his other international essays, *Cabinet No Secrecy* speaks to the issue of security. While persuading his readers that war is absurd, Bentham anticipates the argument that war, and the perceived opulence and prosperity it brings, encourages Britain's neighbours and potential aggressors to 'respect' Britain's position in world politics. Bentham claims that this is not respect but fear, and 'fear is much more adverse to security than favourable'.[47] He further states:

> So many as fear you, join against you till they think they are too strong for you, and then they are afraid of you no longer. Mean time they all hate you and jointly and severally they do you as much mischief as they can. You on your part are not behind hand with them. Conscious or not conscious of your own bad intentions, you suspect theirs to be still worse. Their notion of your intentions is the same. Each does his endeavours to begin for fear of being forestalled. Measures of mere self-defence are naturally taken for projects of aggression. The same causes produce both sides the same effect: Each makes haste to begin for fear of being forestalled. In this state of things if on either side there happens to be a minister, or a would-be minister who has a fancy for war, the stroke is struck, and the tinder catches fire.[48]

Not unlike Machiavelli, Bentham recognizes the disadvantages of fear. Machiavelli's balance between fear and loyalty, love and disrespect, is different to Bentham's, but in general their point is the same; too much fear will work against those who try to instil it. Where Machiavelli and Bentham most certainly differ, however, is in their subsequent treatment of the problem. Machiavelli's concern about fear lies primarily with the citizens of the state and their support of their sovereign, thereby recommending a balance of fear and loyalty and often fostering loyalty by means of religion. Bentham expresses a distaste for the use of fear in any context, and believes that fear can be overcome through education. The more we know, the less we fear. Fear escalates due to perceived interests, not known interests; in trade, the perceived interests dictate that war increases opulence, if not 'splendor, greatness, [and] glory'.[49] Bentham's foremost concern is trade and the road to prosperity. War can only produce ill-gotten gains, and in the end, these are not gains at all.

In *Cabinet No Secrecy* the strength of Bentham's convictions is readily apparent – there are no circumstances under which secrecy in the foreign cabinet can be justified. When the people are regularly apprised of the decisions being made on their behalf by the ruling few, then the ruling few would be adequately kept in check. But recall that Bentham allowed for the possibility that, under certain circumstances, in particular identified by other parties in the negotiation, a lack of secrecy could do more harm than good. *Cabinet No Secrecy* argues that secrecy is entirely unnecessary for an advanced and powerful state such as Britain, but in subsequent works Bentham does not sustain this position.

In later works, security concerns prevent Bentham from advocating 'publicity' – in the sense of complete openness in government, and least of all in the foreign department. Publicity is important, but only if it can be assured that no harm will come of it:

> Exceptions excepted, – in every Subdepartment and Department, and in every Office belonging to each Subdepartment and Department, publicity will at all times be maximized … Where, in this or that particular case, in addition to the evil of *expense*, if any, the evil of the publicity would, in the instance of this or that particular person or class of persons, be preponderant over the good … Subdepartments in which this preponderance is most apt to have place, examples are the following:
>
> 1. The *Constitutive Department*: to wit, in respect of the evil that would result from its being known which way the several voters, or any of them, gave their votes …
> 2. The *Army Bis-subdepartment*: to wit, by making known to the enemy of the State the strong and the weak points of its means of defence.
> 3. The *Navy Bis-subdepartment*: the two together constituting the *Defensive Force Subdepartment*: to wit, by information given as above.
> 4. The *Preventive Service Subdepartment*: to wit, in respect of the like information given to delinquents.
> 5. The *Health Subdepartment*: to wit, in respect of any such evil as may be liable to result from its being known who the persons are who have been labouring under any disease to which disrepute is attached.
> 6. The *Foreign Relation Subdepartment*: to wit, by information given, to those, who at any time are *liable* to become *enemies*, and who are at all times, *in one way or other, rivals*.[50]

Bentham reflects realist concerns here. Contrary to his earlier advice, he separates three sub-departments from his broader mandate against secrecy. These three departments are critical to the state's international position, and include Foreign Relations and the Defensive Force (Army and Navy). Bentham articulates classic security concerns, recognizing the chance that open and public relations could result in a weaker defence, and therefore weaken state security. Unlike *Cabinet No Secrecy*, Bentham appreciates that publicity could leave the state vulnerable and exposed to threats from others. As such, Bentham allows for and accommodates a reversal of his original commitment that should otherwise guide government.

In a climate of openness, secrecy prevails only as long as the legislature requires: 'Then is the regular time for divulgation. But if the cause for secrecy subsists, divulgation may be referred to the same Legislature on some succeeding day of that year, or to the next succeeding Legislature; and so on from Legislature to Legislature.'[51] In the Defensive Force sub-department and the Foreign Relation sub-department secrecy is acceptable, if not entirely necessary. In an attempt to maintain the guise of open and transparent governance, Bentham allows the Prime Minister the opportunity to inform the Legislature of various instances in which the 'demand for secrecy has, in his opinion, ceased, [and] that divulgation may be made accordingly'.[52] For some, the fact that after 1809 Bentham embraced broader, democratic principles, contesting the status quo and so designating him a radical, had significant implications in his writing, especially in that his 'Tory' side becomes less apparent. As far as secrecy is concerned, however, Bentham's thinking reflects an opposite trend, where security and maintenance of expectation dilute his idealistic notions of the 1780s. The fact that Bentham hoped for publicity to be maximized is meaningful only if one can accept his exceptions.[53] The radical in Bentham is very cautious, and state security must be protected at all times, if not at all costs.[54]

Bentham's *Plan* encapsulates his ideal measures, and it is understandable that most readers assume Bentham to be firmly entrenched within the liberal paradigm if *Plan* is the only source available to them. He reserves his most powerful arguments for the emancipation of colonies and the elimination of secrecy from the foreign cabinet. The main objective of these initiatives is to increase peace and *prosperity* in Britain, if not the rest of the 'civilized' world. Bentham's arguments for the tribunal are more tenuous, even though it relates to his interest in international law, and the difficulty in enforcing international law is exemplified by Bentham's reluctance to commit to this institution he created.

Bentham's other essays: international law

Bentham's definition of sovereignty is fundamental to any understanding of his work in international law. It is on the basis of sovereignty that the latitude and expression of international law is determined. Bentham's contribution to international law in his 1786–89 writings is not extensive: he includes a list of possible scenarios emanating from the relations between subjects of foreign states in *Persons Subject*, and sets the stage for a potential international legal code in *Projet Matiere*. In the latter he considers what sort of offences ought to be included under international law, who constitutes the offenders, and possible preventive measures. Like many of Bentham's essays, *Projet* is vague, possibly incomplete, and poses more questions than it answers, but the points that it does raise are still intriguing, especially as to the ways in which Bentham tries to connect the principle of utility to the institution of international law.

The principle of utility was barely discussed in Bentham's 1786–89 international writings. He made more frequent mention of expectation, and how expectation ought to guide action in the international realm. It is no different in this next essay – expectation, again, plays a crucial role, but as was indicated in the introductory chapter, the security of expectation (later articulated as the disappointment-prevention principle) and the principle of utility are inextricably linked, with the former guiding the latter. This is apparent in Bentham's opening statements of *Projet Matiere*:

> If a citizen of the world had to prepare an universal international code, what would he propose to himself as his object? It would be the common and equal utility of all nations . . . Whatever he may think upon these questions-- how small soever may be the regard which it may be wished that he should have for the common utility, it will not be the less necessary for him to understand it. This will be necessary for him on two accounts: In the first place, that he may follow this object in so far as his particular object is comprised in it;-- secondly, that he may frame according to it, the expectations that he ought to entertain, the demands he ought to make upon other nations. For, in conclusion, the line of common utility once drawn, this would be the direction towards which the conduct of all nations would tend--in which their common efforts would find least resistance--in which they would operate with the greatest force--and in which the equilibrium once established, would be maintained with the least difficulty.[55]

By maintaining the expectations of his own and other nations, legislators, or sovereigns, abide by the dictates of the 'citizen of the world', with the result that each state follows a course of action that effects the 'least resistance'. This easier and presumably more 'natural' course of action would enhance peace between states, and alleviate the misperceptions and misunderstandings that would lead to war. Expectation determines utility, and utility results in peace – but Bentham does not explain what the expectations of his own, and other nations, are. From other essays we can be certain that the security of the state is an expectation. Bentham is not clear as to how expectation would be likely to lead to peace, especially as history suggests that it has more often led to war. To Bentham, however, this is merely a matter of correctly determining the greatest happiness for the greatest number.

The sovereign who endeavours to maximize the greatest happiness for the greatest number can do so in two possible ways; he seeks happiness for his own subjects alone, or, he seeks happiness for all people of the world. The former is the course that has been pursued in the past, such that his own subjects were the sovereign's pre-eminent concern, and foreigners were treated no better than beasts: "as all the models of virtue in antiquity, as all the nations with whose history we are acquainted, employed them"[56] In declaring 'c'est le but que determine les moyens',[57] Bentham agrees with Machiavelli that the end justifies the means, but he claims that the end has changed, and that the sovereign can no longer look out for the interests of his subjects alone. To ensure the least resistance for the attainment of the greatest happiness for the greatest number, each sovereign would be wise to consider the interests of all peoples. This interest would be best established through a code of international law.

The objects of international law are both positive and negative; negative in that no injury ought to be caused to any nation, by any nation, and positive in that each nation ought to receive from, and bestow upon, every other nation the greatest good.[58] This criterion enables Bentham to distinguish between positive and negative crimes, such that wrongs committed against other nations are positive crimes, and negligence to act resulting in a wrong, is a negative crime.[59] The objects of international law are qualified, however, in that they, and the prevention of positive and negative offences, can only prevail as long as the security of any state is not in jeopardy.[60] If state security is threatened and war is the only option available to it, one additional object of international law must be considered: in the event of war, care should be taken that the least possible evil occurs, commensurate with the desired end.[61] Bentham does not explore definitions of state security in this essay, nor does he recognize that his qualification provides a great deal of latitude for state action. Bentham looks to international law effectively to curtail the need for states to resort to war, but only through the moral imposition that it makes upon state behaviour.

The notion of sovereignty is crucial to this discussion. State security dictates the extent to which international law has any force, and it is ultimately left up to the state, as a sovereign entity, to determine the course of international affairs. The fact that the highest authority rests with each state is illustrated in Bentham's treatment of the subject. Whether he condemns or applauds the actions of a sovereign, it is always clear that the fullest extent of power resides within the sovereign. The sovereign is the only actor subject to international law, and it is the sovereign who must be kept in check through international legislation:[62]

But however dishonest the intention of their chiefs may be, the subjects are always honest. The nation once bound – and it is the chief which binds it – however criminal the aggression may be, there is

properly no other criminal than the chief: – individuals are only his innocent and unfortunate instruments. The extenuation which is drawn from
the weight of authority, rises here to the level of an entire exemption.

The weight of responsibility for the actions of war rests solely upon the
shoulders of the sovereign. Citizens are innocent instruments, an argument
that would have been welcomed by those facing judgement at Nuremburg.
Bentham also sympathizes with the sovereign, however; 'so much has
been said of the injustice of sovereigns, that I could wish a little consideration were given to the still more common injustice of their detractors;
who, whilst they preserve their concealment, revenge themselves upon the
species in general, for the adulation which in public they lavish upon individuals.'[64] On the one hand, the sovereign is responsible for taking innocent
civilians to war, and on the other hand the sovereign is responsible for the
reprehensible behaviour of its citizens – in either case, the sovereign is
the only relevant actor in international relations. The fact that the sovereign possesses absolute authority is uncontested. International law does not
mitigate, or even qualify, the strength of sovereignty, unless the sovereign
chooses.

Projet concludes with a list of the causes of war, citing the right of succession, troubles in neighbouring states, uncertainty over the limits of new
discoveries, religious hatred, and disputes of any kind.[65] Bentham's suggestions for safeguards against war consist of ratifying already existing
customary law, designing new international laws for those points as yet
unascertained, and perfecting the style of laws, both national and international.[66] Contrary to many of his predecessors, Bentham does not base
international law on 'natural law'. He criticizes the tendency of 'the
pretended law of nature,' to lack distinction between the *is* and *ought* of
international law, blurring reality and falling prey to methodological errors.[67]

> The ambiguous connotations of the phrase '*natural law*' suggest that
> something contrary to nature cannot physically take place. But that
> will hardly do in a political context where, as Bentham noted, the main
> *complaint* is that the 'impossible' (in whatever sense is meant here)
> *has* been and *is* being done, and that violations of natural law *are*
> being committed . . . committing oneself to general principles as funda-
> mental laws *in advance* of a detailed investigation – is so contrary to
> reason, Bentham suggests, as to betray much darker motives than any
> genuine concern for human welfare.[68]

Alternatively, Bentham distinguishes between complete law, 'that is to say,
which possess[es] everything necessary to give [it] effect, to put [it] into
execution,' and incomplete law, which does not carry the force of sovereignty and coercion.[69] International law is incomplete law, and is defective

as a result. 'The happiness of the human race would be fixed, if it were possible to raise these two classes [defective and incomplete] of laws to the rank of complete and organized law.'[70] Although international law comes closer to perfection by becoming complete law, Bentham does not take the next step to design a coercive authority to enforce international law. Bentham claims that an international code ought to be adopted by all states as such action is consistent with the principle of utility and will effect the least resistance. The objectives of international law endeavour to keep the peace among nations, as long as it is in each nation's interest to do so.

Forty years later when he was almost eighty years old, Bentham again addressed the issue of international law, in the hope that his acquaintance, Jabez Henry, would construct a code of international law under his guidance. These papers from 1827 and 1830 have not yet been published, even though this work is uncharacteristically brief and coherent. Bentham constructs a draft of guiding articles regarding relations between states, their obligations as well as privileges:

Art 1.   The [Political] States concurring in the establishment of the present all-comprehensive International Code are those which follow.

Here enumerate them in alphabetical order to avoid the assumption of superiority from precedence in the order of enumeration.

Art 2.   The equality of all is hereby recognized by all.

Art 3.   Each has its own form of government – each respects the form of government of every other.

Art 4.   Each has its own opinions and enactments on the subject of religion: each respects that of every other.

Art 5.   Each has its own manners, customs, and opinions –, each respects the manners, customs, and opinions of every other.

Art 6.   This Confederation with the Code of International Law approved, adopted, and sanctioned by it has for its objects or say ends in view the preservation not only of peace, (in the sense in which by peace is meant absence of war, but of mutual good will and consequent mutual good offices between all the several members of this Confederacy.)

Art 7.   The means by which it aims at the attainment of this so desirable end – and the effectuation of this universally desirable purpose – is, the adjustment and preappointed definition of all rights and obligations that present themselves as liable and likely to come into question: to do this at a time when no State having any interest in the question more than any other has, the several points may be adjusted by common consent of all, without any such feeling as that of disappointment, humiliation, or sacrifice on the part of supposed to have place, no such cause of antisocial affection in any of the breasts concerned *will have place.*

Art 8.   Of each of these several confederating States the Government can do no otherwise than desire to be regarded as persuaded that its own form of Government is in its nature in a higher degree than any other conducive to the greatest happiness of the whole number of the members of the community of which it is the Government: and by this declaration it means not to pass condemnation on the fitness of any other for governing in the community in which it bears rule.[71]

In these, his final comments on international law, Bentham is both innovative and cautious; innovative for his suggestion that a confederacy be entered into on the basis of international law, and cautious in that each state's sovereignty and style of governance cannot be subject to any interference from any other state. Bentham designed a constitutional code with the hopes that it would be adopted by interested states, but the adoption of his recommended style and method of governance is not a precondition to developing a community of states. Unlike Kant, Bentham does not insist that participating states assume republican, or any other, ideals. This being the case, however, the ability to enforce international law is reduced when state values, priorities, and agendas are potentially so different. This difficulty is supposed to be mitigated through the use of the principle of utility, but the universalization of this principle is less likely without the cohesion of similar values among states.

The rest of the unpublished 1827 manuscript discusses the mandate of the international Judicatory, and its relationship to the Congress, or Confederacy of states, that Bentham envisioned:

The Congress itself might form a sort of Apellate Judicatory.

The Immediate Judicatory might be constituted of a single judge elected by the Congress.

By this Judge should be exercised all the elementary functions of Judicature, with the exception of the Imperative.

Under a system of International Law, the Imperative could not be exercised by any authority: not even by the International Congress.

The admission of the faculty of issuing Imperative Decrees with power for giving execution and effect to them, would have the effect of an attempt to establish an Universal Republic, inconsistent with the sovereignty of the several sovereigns, within their respective dominions.[72]

Respect for sovereignty overrides any consideration of enforcing international law. If a state deems it necessary to breach international law, little can be done. The Judiciary, in actual fact, has very little power to enforce its own decrees. The only way in which decisions from the Judiciary could have any effect is if those decisions were rooted in 'argumentation universally notorious, [and] would possess a probability of experiencing general if not universal deference'.[73] The issues over which the Judiciary prevails are similar, if not identical, to the many issues Bentham delineates in his *Persons Subject* manuscript, although he did not refer to a judicial body in this earlier essay. In both works Bentham is preoccupied with procedure, and how to determine who has sovereignty over whom, under what conditions, and why. In response to the potential criticism that his agenda is idealistic and impracticable, Bentham states:

> Even suppose no such Congress and Judicatory established, a work grounded on the greatest happiness principle, viz. a work such as is here attempted would, if the plan and execution be more moral and intellectual than Vattal's, possess a probability of superceding it, and being referred to in preference.
>
> From the impracticability of the Abbé de St. Pierre's *Projet de paix perpetuelle*, no just inference can be drawn, affecting the impracticability of the system here proposed.[74]

Bentham's argument in favour of his own plan relies on refuting his predecessors: the greatest happiness principle make the logic of his plan self-explanatory, but as mentioned previously, the adoption of the greatest happiness principle, or principle of utility, by all states is questionable. Nevertheless, the 1827 manuscript clarifies, reiterates, and develops the points over which Bentham is most concerned. Communication between states is desirable, if not necessary, for the prevention of war; mechanisms such as the Judiciary, the Congress, and international law, all serve to facilitate communication between states.

Identifying the strengths and weaknesses of liberalism's claim over Bentham and his international work is extremely difficult. On the surface, the claim is justified, as Bentham argues for the emancipation of colonies, open diplomacy, international law, and even international institutions for the expression of public opinion. These demands cannot be ignored or undervalued for the purpose of denying Bentham's place in the liberal paradigm, but as has also been shown, his status there is sometimes questionable. Beyond his hesitations and misgivings, however, his undeniable reliance upon expectation to justify his lofty peace plans, and his willingness to concede defeat, are striking. Expectation also has a profound influence on Bentham's views on war. Expectation guides Bentham's pen no matter what the argument, and it is this feature of his work that causes such difficulty for international relations theorists trying to accurately assess Bentham's contribution to their discipline.

Notes

1 UC XXV.26; Bowring, Vol. II, p. 546. Where applicable, the original manuscript citation will be followed by the published citation in Bentham's *Works* edited by John Bowring.
2 UC XXV.57; Bowring, Vol. II, p. 559.
3 UC XXV.26–58; Bowring, Vol. II, pp. 546–60. Hereafter referred to as *Plan*.
4 See Winch, Schwarzenberger, Conway, and Boralevi, for examples.
5 Discussed further below.
6 Bowring also used material from Bentham's marginal outlines to construct *Plan*. The essay *On War* is discussed in Chapter 7, 'Bentham on War'.
7 In *Plan*, a large part of the discussion on colonies comes from the essay *Colonies and Navy*.
8 The subject of colonies is of paramount importance in Bentham's work, and will be discussed in Chapter 8.
9 UC XXV.36; Bowring, Vol. II, p. 546.
10 UC XXV.37; Bowring, Vol. II, p. 546.
11 UC XXV.9; Bowring, Vol. II, pp. 550–1.
12 UC XXV.9; Bowring, Vol. II, p. 550. The original manuscript is written in French but is illegible. The above translation is courtesy of the Bowring edition of Bentham's *Works*.
13 UC XXV.29; Bowring, Vol. II, p. 551.
14 UC XXV.132; Bowring, Vol. II, p. 550. Bowring did not include #3 in the published version of this manuscript.
15 UC XXV.9; Bowring, Vol. II, p. 550.
16 See discussion on the Defensive Force in Chapter 6.
17 UC XXV.29; Bowring, Vol. II, p. 551. The Bowring edition incorrectly states that this proposal is intended to 'reduce and fix the amount of its armed force', but in truth, Bentham only speaks of a proposal to emancipate colonies.
18 Ibid.
19 UC XXV.32; Bowring, Vol. II, p. 552.
20 Ibid.
21 UC XXV.32; Bowring, Vol. II, p. 553.
22 Ibid.
23 UCxxv.33; Bowring, Vol. II, p. 553.
24 UC XXV.27; Bowring, Vol. ii, 552. E. H. Carr, F. H. Hinsley, K. J. Holsti, to name a few, all make reference to the tribunal.
25 Bentham conceived of various *sanctions* as motives that determined interest and inspired action.
26 Torbjørn Knutsen, *A History of International Relations Theory* (Manchester: Manchester University Press, 1997), p. 215. E. H. Carr does not state that Bentham's thinking was directly related to the idea of the League, but he acknowledges Bentham's contributions to nineteenth-century thinking that spurred on American incentives, especially those of Woodrow Wilson, to design such an international organization: 'Just as Bentham, a century earlier, had taken the eighteenth-century doctrine of reason and refashioned it to the needs of a coming age, so now Woodrow Wilson, the impassioned admirer of Bright and Gladstone, transplanted the nineteenth-century rationalist faith to the almost virgin soil of international politics ... The most important of all the institutions affected by this one-sided intellectualism of international politics was the League of Nations.' E. H. Carr, *The Twenty Years' Crisis 1919–1939: An Introduction to the Study of International Relations* (New York: Macmillan, 1966), pp. 27–28.
27 One of the difficulties in understanding Bentham's intentions with regard to the tribunal is that his terminology varies, and as a result his subject matter is not

always clear. Additionally, the assumption has subsequently been that an international tribunal is the equivalent of the 'Public Opinion Tribunal' of which Bentham makes mention in his *Constitutional Code*, and further complicates the interpretation of the role of the international body.

28 UC XXV.27; Bowring, Vol. II, p. 552.

29 UC XXV.132; Bowring, Vol. II, p. 554. Bentham contemplates a number of options to 'enforce the decrees of the court', including 'regulating as a last resource the contingent to be furnished by the several states'. Better yet, he advocates the use of a 'clause guaranteeing the liberty of the press in every state to its decrees and to every paper whatever it might think proper to sanction with its signature the most extensive and unlimited circulation'. UC XXV.35; Bowring, Vol. II, p. 554.

30 Additionally, the international tribunal has often been conflated with the notion of Bentham's 'Public Opinion Tribunal' in the national context. The lion's share of discussion on the Public Opinion Tribunal takes place in Bentham's *Constitutional Code* and *Securities Against Misrule*, and, as Fred Rosen points out, the concept lacks clarity: 'Admittedly, Bentham's conception of the Public Opinion Tribunal, on which reform depends, is not altogether clear. He might have explained more fully how he conceived of the Public Opinion Tribunal as a judicial body ... An even greater difficulty arises with his argument that the Public Opinion Tribunal in some way expresses the public interest. The Public Opinion Tribunal expresses itself in many different forms and seems composed of disparate elements ... But how can these differing sources of public opinion be considered fused in a single body called the Public Opinion Tribunal? And how can the voice of the Public Opinion Tribunal be more than a confused outpouring of conflicting and disparate voices? Bentham does not seem to have resolved these problems, but his failure does not extent to an over-optimistic view of the power of the people to rule ... he rejects claims on behalf of the people to rule or to take important decisions on policy. For Bentham, the people can have security and accountability through the constitutional system. They can share in politics to an extent by voting.' Fred Rosen, *Jeremy Bentham and Representative Democracy* (Oxford: Clarendon Press, 1983), p. 39.

31 BL Add. MS 30151.

32 Ibid. Bentham has been both lauded and chastised for his vision of a tribunal that would have some sort of an effect in international relations. E. H. Carr makes note of Bentham's tribunal, but his evaluation is misguided. Carr's definition of the tribunal is taken from *Securities Against Misrule*, which discusses the concept in a domestic setting, but does not address the international context. (Carr, p. 24.) Knutsen goes so far as to discuss Bentham's 'Congress of States', which is not only a term that Bentham never used himself, but a concept by no means explored to the extent that Knutsen's analysis would suggest (Knutsen, pp. 152–53.). F. H. Hinsley treats the subject most accurately by acknowledging that the tribunal receives a 'subsidiary role' in comparison to emancipating colonies or secrecy in government.

33 The importance of sovereignty is explored in the section 'International Law' below.

34 For example, Bentham praises the virtuous negotiating power of De Witt and Temple (see chapter 8).

35 UC XXV.50; Bowring, Vol. II, p. 554.

36 Ibid. Bowring includes this comment as a footnote in the published *Works*.

37 'If bribe-taking, oppression, peculation, duplicity, treachery, every crime that can be committed by statesmen sinning against conscience produce no desire to punish, with what dependence can be placed in punishment in a case where the mischief may so easily happen without any ground for punishment? Mankind is

not yet arrived to that stage in the track of civilization.' (UC XXV.51; Bowring, Vol. II, p. 555.)

38 UC XXV.53; Bowring, Vol. II, p. 557.
39 UC XXV.54; Bowring, Vol. II, p. 557.
40 This argument will be further elaborated in Chapters 6 and 7, on colonies and international political economy.
41 Ibid.
42 UC XXV.50; Bowring, Vol. II, p. 554. The occasion Bentham speaks of took place 22 May 1789.
43 UC XXV.56; Bowring, Vol. II, p. 558.
44 Ibid.
45 UC XXV.57; Bowring, Vol. II, p. 559.
46 Again he does concede that prosperity can result from war if a state is despotic. His rationale is unclear.
47 Ibid.
48 Ibid.
49 UC XXV.58; Bowring, Vol. II, p. 559.
50 Bentham, *Constitutional Code*, pp. 163–4.
51 Ibid., p. 57.
52 Ibid., p. 167.
53 A leading justification for secrecy, according to Bentham, is 'war, existing or supposed impending'. (*Constitutional Code*, pp. 408, 426). The security of the state, under these circumstances, has carte blanche with regard to the various activities it considers necessary for state preservation.
54 Bentham's obvious and increased concern for state security also reflects his view of sovereignty; the 1786–89 essays predominantly envision a strong community of states, but his later writings foresee the need to maintain explicit sovereign power over a state's domain.
55 UC XXV.1; Bowring, Vol. II, p. 537. The text has been left in the original French, with no editorial changes.
56 UC XXV.5; Bowring, Vol. II, p. 537.
57 Ibid.
58 UC XXV.5; Bowring, Vol. II, p. 538.
59 UC XXV.2; Bowring, Vol. II, p. 538.
60 UC XXV.5; Bowring, Vol. II, p. 538. In either upholding the objects of international law or preventing various offences, 'sauf les egards qui il lui convient d'avoir a son propre bien-etre.' No offence can be considered within the confines of international law if the well-being of the state is threatened.
61 Ibid.
62 In *Persons Subject* Bentham lists a number of situations in which offences may be committed by nationals or foreigners, but his purpose is to identify which sovereign these individuals are bound to obey.
63 UC XXV.4; Bowring, Vol. II, p. 539.
64 Ibid.
65 UC XXV.4; Bowring, Vol. II, pp. 539–40.
66 Ibid.
67 *Fragment*, p. 94.
68 Jeremy Waldron, ed. *Nonsense Upon Stilts: Bentham, Burke, and Marx on the Rights of Man* (London: Meuthen, 1987), p. 38.
69 Bowring, Vol. III, p. 162.
70 Ibid.
71 BL Add. MS 30151.
72 Ibid.
73 Ibid.
74 Ibid.

7   Bentham on War

> The first passion of every man is the desire of his own preservation, and
> . . . courage is more or less a factitious quality, a social virtue which owes
> its birth and growth to the public esteem more than to every other cause.
> A momentary ardour may be kindled by anger, but a courage, tranquil and
> sustained, is only formed and ripened under the happy influences of honour
> . . . The external security of the state against its rivals depends upon the
> courage of its soldiers; the internal security of a state against those very
> soldiers depends upon the courage of the mass of citizens. In one word,
> courage is the public soul, the tutelary genius, the sacred palladium by which
> alone we can be protected against all the miseries of servitude, remain in
> the condition of men, or escape falling beneath the very brutes.[1]

In general, Bentham's work in international relations addressed the various
means by which a state could prevent war; Bentham's writings were predominantly occupied with issues of peace maintenance, not warfare. What
Bentham wrote about war was relatively limited, which in part explains
the lack of attention these ideas have received from international relations
scholars. Nevertheless scholars have often neglected his essay *On War*,
found in the broader section of international writings that John Bowring
designated as *Principles of International Law*, and that also included *A
Plan for an Universal and Perpetual Peace*. To present Bentham's views
on war I examine the brief essay *On War*, and introduce another previously ignored work, *The Defensive Force*, from Bentham's *Constitutional
Code*.

Bentham designed a fascinating and illuminating structure of defence
for a state that aptly illustrated his thoughts and concerns about war. This
design involved an intricate collage of ideas that often reflected – though
not necessarily derived from – the works of his predecessors, Niccolò
Machiavelli and Adam Smith. By reflecting both the ideas of the liberal
in Smith and the realist in Machiavelli, Bentham's defensive force provides
an excellent example of the complexity, and sometimes awkwardness, that
was intrinsic to his thinking. After exploring some of the ideas contained
in *On War* to serve as a foundation for Bentham's arguments, I examine

some of the central tenets of Smith and Machiavelli's work on defence, and follow with a detailed analysis of Bentham's ideas. As in his other work in international relations, Bentham did not sustain a predominantly liberal outlook. His work on the defensive force, which has not been examined by international relations scholars, provides more insights into our understanding of Bentham's ideas and his place in the theoretical traditions of international relations.

On War

Among Bentham's papers of the 1780s there was one essay, *On War*, that exclusively addressed that topic. This is easily the smallest essay among the collection comprising Bentham's work on international relations. In many respects Bentham addressed the same theme in all of his essays at this time, focusing on the understanding and the prevention of conflict. However, of the essays written in the 1780s, including *A Plan for an Universal and Perpetual Peace*,[2] *On War* is the only one which contains a discussion of the causes of, and justifications for, war.

At the forefront of Bentham's analysis in the essay is the state and property. In his writings in international relations more generally, Bentham emphasized, to a degree not seen before, the extent to which the individual was capable of altering or affecting international circumstances. This emphasis emanates, in part, from his views on the possible efficacy of public opinion and the public opinion tribunal. As the previous chapters have illustrated however, Bentham's confidence in individual and public influence on the international realm was considerably less than usually assumed by today's international relations scholars. Bentham expressed a hope to see a world where individual influence could bear on international politics, but the realization of his hope relied greatly on the actions of enlightened states – a point he maintains in both his early writings such as *On War*, as well as in his much later constitutional writings in *The Defensive Force*.

Bentham was clear that war was within the purview of the state, and could only be successfully evaluated with a state-centred analysis. He asserted that any parallels made between the state and the individual could only be taken so far, such that 'tracing the process from the original source to the ultimate effect a variety of intermediate considerations will present themselves in the instance of war which have no place in the quarrels of individuals'.[3] This argument was further sustained by the fact that the state may not have 'persons distinct from the persons of individuals: but they have property which is the property of the state, and not of any individuals'.[4] This is meaningful for two reasons: the first is that the state is the prime, if not sole, actor in the event of war; the second is that 'property' is central to the cause of war.

Security of property did not however justify conquest. Offensive action for the purpose of conquest was more likely to place one's own territory in jeopardy rather than promote the maintenance or increase of security. It was also not in every case, when a threat to a state's property or territory existed, that war should be the outcome:

> In all these cases the utility with regard to the state which looks upon itself as aggrieved, the reasonableness in a word of going to war with the aggressor depends partly upon his relative force, partly upon what appears to have been the state of his mind with relation to the injury. If it is evident there was no *mala fides* on his part, it can never in that case for the aggrieved state to have recourse to war, whether it be stronger or weaker than the aggressor, and that in whatever degree. In that case be the injury what it will it may be pronounced that the value of it should ever amount to the expense of war, be it ever so short and carried on upon ever so frugal a scale.[5]

If no malicious intent was present then war should not be an option; the breach of security or threat must be dealt with by other means, although those means were not clearly presented in this essay. Bentham did not offer an illustration of the above scenario, in part suggesting that although it was an appropriate guide to action, it might also have been a scenario that was rare.

The other scenario, where *mala fides* were present, and for which Bentham did give examples, provided Bentham's justification for war.

> In case of *mala fides*, whether even then it shall be worth while to have recourse to war will depend upon circumstances. If it appear that the injury in question is but a prelude to others, and that it proceeds from a disposition which nothing less than entire destruction can satisfy, and war presents any tolerable chance of success how small soever, reason may join with passion in prescribing war as the only remedy to so desperate a disease.[6]

If the aggressor appeared to have no other intent than the destruction of the victim state and its property, then war was justified. This makes sense if one takes the position that a state has nothing to lose in entertaining such an endeavour. Bentham appears to advocate war if the state deems this aggression to be a prelude to others, and total destruction is considered the only solution, no matter how small the chance of success. This statement is open to a great deal of interpretation and, although the argument assumes it is a relatively enlightened state, if not yet a 'constitutional democracy' that is deciding on action, this could amount to a carte blanche to go to war on the basis of any presumed aggression. In addition:

> Though in case of perseverance on the part of the assailant, successful resistance may appear impossible, yet resistance such as can be

opposed, may be gaining time, give room for some unexpected incident to arise, and may at any rate by the inconvenience it occasions to the assailant contribute more or less to weaken the mass of inducements which prompt him to similar enterprises.[7]

War may also be thought of as an option for the purpose of wearing out the assailant. In this way the aggressor would be dissuaded from pursuing similar attacks elsewhere, if not on the state in question. As an example Bentham referred to the Spartans at Thermopylae where they 'finished to a man', but the sacrifice was not without its use.[8] The instance where war may not be advisable, even if *mala fides* motivate the action, is in the event that the action has for its object a limited goal, and that under some situations allowing that goal would be more advantageous, for both the people and their finances. This distinction could have merited more attention since otherwise war appears to be an open option in earlier statements. If the aggressor's goal is 'limited', without Bentham clearly defining what this would mean, war is not recommended. But how would Bentham determine this? He does not say.

In addition to this essay, Bentham made a number of notes regarding the causes of war but did not explore them in depth.[9] In these Bentham indicated the causes of war, followed by methods of prevention:

Guerre – Causes

I.

Debits reals ou pretendre des citoyens d'un état envers les citoyens d'un autre. Causes par les interets des sujets.

1. Injures en general
2. Injures occasionments par la rivalité de commerce – Interception de droits de propriété

Guerre – Preventifs

I.

1. Liquidation des pretensions de chaque souverain a l'egard des sujets de chaque autre souverain
2. Liberté generale de commerce
   – par les interets des souverains.
1. Disputes par les droits de succession.
2. Disputes par les [boundaries][10]

It is unfortunate that Bentham did not seek to explore these points in depth. However it should not be forgotten that these were merely notations, and not explicitly intended for a more well-developed essay. Bentham examined some of the above causes of war in his other writings, especially with regard to colonies and commerce, but the fact of war became, although still very important, tangential to that he provided. The rest of his essays from the 1780s focused on how to engender better relations between states, the object being the avoidance of any conflict that manifested itself through dialogue, court action, and moral and economic sanctions, as well as war. The central feature of *On War* was his emphasis on the state and its role in war. This foundation was maintained in his subsequent work on conflict.

The Defensive Force

Over forty years passed before Bentham spoke explicitly to the issue of war again, this time through his work on the defensive force. Bentham wrote very little about such a force in his papers of the 1780s, except for one or two comments regarding standing armies. In these earlier works Bentham did not see the worth of standing armies, as these were only to be found in a state that desired war. Bentham's later position on the composition of a defensive force still reflected this fear, but through a unique and complicated structure, and explicitly limited by the demands of a constitutional democracy. Nevertheless, given those limitations Bentham ensured that the State had as much power as possible to decide its fate as regarded war. To best understand this structure I have chosen to discuss the ideas of Smith and Machiavelli on the subject of defence and war, and in my view Bentham's work on the defensive force accomplished a remarkable feat by attending to concerns similar to those expressed in the ideas of Smith and Machiavelli but which was designed to protect a civilized and constitutionally democratic society.

Previous thought on a defensive force: Smith and Machiavelli

Bentham's strategy on defence could be considered to be a unique combination of theory from Machiavelli and Smith, resulting in a synthesis that respected the security concerns of the realist while aspiring to the civilized, modest defence concerns of the liberal, especially as these concerns were limited as far as possible within the consitutional code Bentham developed.

Bentham's brief evaluation of the development of defence was similar to Smith's. Smith noted that in primitive societies all members must participate in war, 'even the women',[11] but as society evolved and became more civilized, the necessity for all members of the community to participate was reduced. Agriculture was the key to determining the extent to which the members of a society were able to go to war; once a society relied on agriculture it must be settled rather than nomadic, and the habitation must be tended at all times, even during periods of war. In this case, Smith said, consideration had to be given to the time taken away from harvest, and the costs involved in keeping members of the community from the source of their subsistence for the purpose of war.[12] Societies advanced beyond an economy based in agriculture had yet other concerns. According to Smith, agriculture was predominantly reliant upon natural forces (such as climate and harvests) and therefore not solely dependent upon human power for its continuance; those societies making use of manufactures could not rely on the processes of nature to pick up the slack; the work of the artisan lay dormant until the return of the individual upon which the manufacture relies: 'A shepherd has a great deal of leisure; a husbandman, in the rude state of husbandry, has some; an artificer or manufacturer has none at all.'[13] Likewise, with the progress of civilization came the complexities of the war machine. War was no longer a matter of taking up a weapon and heading off to battle; particular training was required for the more intricate devices and complicated strategies employed in conflict.

The more advanced and the wealthier a state became, the greater the likelihood that it would be attacked. Smith suggested that there were two defensive options for the advanced state: first, conscription, whereby each citizen was required to train in military exercises regardless of inclination, interest and aptitude as in a militia; or second, employ a small, permanent, and paid military force composed of those individuals in society so inclined to the military profession (a standing army).[14] The latter approach was seen to be more consonant with the civilized state, and reflected the advanced and progressive evolution of the division of labour. In a complex society, members divided themselves into specialized areas of labour, honing their particular skills for exchange with other community members, rather than managing numerous professions with less time and ability. This division applied to the military as well. Society became so advanced as to require the specialization of military activity as a profession in its own right.

Smith supported his case for a specialized military force based not only on the complexity of advanced society, but also on the complexity of the armaments. With civilization came the advent of the firearm, introducing the 'great equalizer'. Physical skill and ability were indispensable for war between what Smith considered 'the more barbarous societies', these being attributes which the hunter and shepherd brought to the field. Physical prowess became less significant, although by no means irrelevant, as it was necessary to 'regularity, order, and prompt obedience',[15] through large-scale, vigorous training and exercise. Smith illustrated his point by providing multiple examples of how militias had failed when opposed to standing armies. The irregularity and inconsistency of training that was a defining element of the militia resulted in a product 'effeminate and ill-exercised'.[16] The only way in which a militia had any potential to become an effective force in war was if it met regularly on the battlefield, thereby forcing those who would normally be casual and occasional warriors to become professionals by default.[17] In this way the militia became strong and, to all intents and purposes, a standing army.

The standing army not only benefited the defence of the civilized state, but it also ensured that civilization was introduced, in the case of a conquered barbarous nation, and maintained within the civilized state itself.[18] The standing army prevailed on all accounts as far as Smith was concerned. However, he was not insensitive to the criticisms provided by 'men of republican principles,' that the standing army was a potential threat to liberty.[19] Smith noted that the existence of a standing army must, at all times, be consistent with the general interests of the public and the constitution of the state.[20]

> But where the sovereign is himself the general, and the principal nobility and gentry of the country the chief officers of the army; where the military force is placed under the command of those who have the greatest interest in the support of the civil authority, because they have themselves the greatest share of that authority, a standing army can never be dangerous to liberty.[21]

With the loyalty of the standing army, the sovereign, and by extension the public, would feel secure.

Smith also addressed the expense of the military project, especially as the maintenance of a standing army dictated some sort of expenditure on the part of the state. A concern of Bentham's, it was also a concern for Smith, albeit for different reasons. Bentham wished to reduce the expense as much as possible. Smith, on the other hand, merely acknowledged the existence of the increased expense; military expenditure was unavoidable in a civilized community.

> In modern war, the great expense of fire-arms gives an evident advantage to the nation which can best afford that expense; and consequently to an opulent and civilised, over a poor and barbarous nation. In ancient times, the opulent and civilised found it difficult to defend themselves against the poor and barbarous nations. In modern times, the poor and barbarous find it difficult to defend themselves against the opulent and civilised. The invention of fire-arms, an invention which at first sight appears to be so pernicious, is certainly favourable both to the permanency and to the extension of civilisation.[22]

Not only was the expense acknowledged, it was condoned. It was the price a state paid for civilisation.

Niccolò Machiavelli was a man of 'republican principles', and unlike Smith argued in favour of a citizen militia. The idea of an armed force composed of native troops was one of the most important contributions Machiavelli made to international political thought. The design of a militia, composed of citizens of the state,[23] was a response to the problems Machiavelli saw occurring in the Italian states' military system.[24]

These states often hired professional armies rather than using the human resources available to them within their own territory: '[A] wise and well-governed republic ought never to keep such commanders in constant pay; rather, it should employ its own citizens in time of war and subsequently dismiss them to pursue their former occupations'.[25] Machiavelli was not sympathetic to fallen regimes, since he attributed such failures solely to imprudence, laziness and the desire for luxury, as well as their failure to depend upon themselves and their own state's ability to preserve security.[26] He feared the very results he observed when the many princes of Italy made use of foreign troops:

> I understand by auxiliary troops such as a prince or a republic sends to your aid, but which are paid, and the commander of which is appointed by the prince or republic . . .
>
> I repeat, then, that of all kinds of troops, auxiliaries are the most dangerous; for the prince or republic that calls them to their assistance has no control or authority whatever over them, as that remains entirely with him who sends them; for, as I have said, auxiliary troops that are sent you by any prince are under officers appointed by him, under his banner, and are paid by him . . .
>
> A prince or republic, then, should adopt any other course rather than bring auxiliaries into their state for its defence, especially when their reliance is wholly upon them; for any treaty or convention with the enemy, however hard the conditions, will be less hard to bear than the danger from auxiliaries.[27]

The sovereign ought to control as much as possible; in doing so the acts of *fortuna* are more likely to be held at bay and the state has a greater likelihood of directing the outcome. If a victory is dependent upon the armed forces used to attain it, then the state requires a great deal of control over those very forces. Machiavelli reiterated this point frequently throughout *The Prince*, *The Discourses* and *The Art of War*.

In keeping with his conception of the common good of the state, Machiavelli advocated the use of a citizen's militia that would be available during times of war, but would not exist during times of peace. Machiavelli was vehemently opposed to a professional army:

> since war is not an occupation by which a man can at all times make an honourable living, it ought not to be followed as business by anyone but a prince or a governor of a commonwealth; and if he is a wise man, he will not allow any of his subjects or citizens to make that his only profession . . . War will not maintain them in time of peace, and thus they are under a necessity either of endeavouring to prevent a peace or of taking all means to make such provisions for themselves in time of war so that they may not lack sustenance when it is over. *But neither of these courses is consistent with the common good.*[28]

The militia would function only during times of conflict and training; the rest of the time the citizens who composed the militia would sustain themselves with typical civilian professions. Mercenaries on the other hand, whose only occupation was the waging of war for a fee, illustrated everything that Machiavelli believed to be wrong with military organization. There was no incentive other than money for mercenaries to carry out the wishes of the sovereigns who hired them. Machiavelli preferred to create and develop a more honourable and loyal soldier by controlling and disciplining the human passions.

> A soldier who is nothing but a soldier is a menace to all other social activities and very little good at his own . . . because his *arte* [of war] is to exercise the means of coercion and destruction . . . it is important 'to restrict the practice of this art to the commonwealth.' . . . This *arte*, more than any other, must be a public monopoly; only citizens may practise it, only magistrates may lead it, and only under public authority and at the public command may it be exercised at all.[29]

Like Machiavelli, Bentham distrusted the motives and intentions of a fully employed but idle group of people knowledgeable in the ways of war. It is to Bentham's ideas on the defensive force that we now turn.

Bentham's Defensive Force

Bentham's extensive chapter in his *Constitutional Code*, *The Defensive Force*, is one of the most overlooked but illuminating works he produced on the issue of state defence and war. In this piece written in the late 1820s Bentham broadly addressed the subject, reviewing topics as various as the compensation one might receive for the loss of a limb during service, through to how many subordinates ought to fall under the command of a superior. Here we are given an excellent view of Bentham's mature thought on the subject of defence. Although he did not oppose conquest outright, by the late 1820s he clearly felt that notions of conquest were no longer relevant to the modern state. This principal idea was clearly laid out in the *Constitutional Code*, first in the inaugural declaration of the legislator, and then in the chapter on the defensive force. Since conquest was no longer a part of the agenda, an offensively trained force would be inappropriate. A defensive force was still a very necessary instrument however. Although a state no longer needed to conquer its neighbours, it still needed to defend itself if neighbours saw fit to conquer it.

It must first be made clear that the defensive force Bentham designed was to function within the context of his *Consitutional Code*. As such, the legislator who determined state action on behalf of the people was restricted by the constitution, as the people were sovereign according to Bentham's *Code*. The design of the constitution was meant to ensure that the legislator would 'genuinely seek to promote the general interest of his constituents for he knew that if they came to believe he was not acting in their interest, they would refuse to re-elect him at the next election'.[30] Within a relationship between subordinates and 'superordinates', as Bentham termed them (inferiors and superiors within the government ministerial divisions), legislators and their support staff could only work within the parameters allowed to them by the constitution. When a subordinate did not function within the parameters of the powers endowed to him, the superordinate could take measures to correct or dismiss him. If the superordinate did not take such measures, his superordinate would have the power to do so. This prerogative operated through to the apex of the command structure, with the Prime Minister taking full responsibility and power on behalf of the sovereign people: 'In a representative democracy, the electorate, what Bentham termed the constitutive power, was therefore superordinate or supreme in relation to the Legislature or the legislative power.'[31] This framework of subordination was intended to secure the 'appropriate aptitude of government officials', and provided the security that was most likely to be introduced in a constitutional democracy.[32] In this respect, the public opinion tribunal appeared to play a somewhat more concrete role than that envisioned by Bentham in his international relations writings. Through publicity and the public opinion tribunal, to which 'potentially everyone belonged', anyone who was capable of doing so could, and indeed was obliged to take notice of the subjects at hand at the legislature, including 'the inhabitants not only of the territory of the political state in question, but of every other territory on the earth's surface'.[33] Within this structure the power of the government was without limit apart from the 'checks' established 'in the form of the securities for appropriate aptitude'.[34] The subordination system in conjunction with the accountability of legislative representatives to the electorate (who keep watch on the legislature as members of the public opinion tribunal) is the method by which unlimited governmental power is kept in check. It is important to keep this process in mind in respect of the allowed powers of government with regard to war. If the ultimate method by which legislators can be kept in check is through the public opinion tribunal, what of those decisions which could be legitimately withheld from the public eye, such as matters of defence?

Bentham's defensive force was designed to be available in times when there was an 'efficient cause' of necessity, the cause consisting of 'the need of contribution in any shape, to the supply in every shape, which happens to have been provided for the purpose of national defence; and note that, 1. For the purpose of national *defence*, it may at any time happen that operations of an *offensive* nature may be necessary'.[35] Bentham's definition of defence was broadly based, reflecting the fact that state security was paramount, and even justified a type of 'pre-emptive strike' in addition to defence against overt attack.

The defensive force was endowed with both positive and negative ends to ensure the defence of the state. The positive end worked toward the preservation of the state from external, hostile, forces. The negative ends worked to 'minimize the danger to the supreme authority, and thence to the whole community, from the quantity of force lodged in an authority intended to be subordinate', as well as 'minimizing the amount of the attendant evil in all shapes', including the minimizing of any expenses involved in creating and maintaining the defensive force.[36] Overall, Bentham's design of the defensive force attempted to maintain a fine line between defending the state from without, and defending it within. Defending it from external forces was fairly straightforward – when a state was attacked, it had to make sure it could defend itself. But Bentham wanted to ensure that a defensive force would not constitute a threat to the people at large, and also that the people at large would not constitute a threat to the state. Bentham needed to prevent threats, therefore, from both, inside and outside the state. How did he set out to accomplish this?

The defensive force had to be subject to a military discipline that would result in the optimum security for the state and its people. The sort of military discipline that Bentham required reflected his concern for protection of the state from hostilities that could originate from within, as well as from without:

> Of military discipline, the objects are these:-
> 1. The *good of the service*: that is to say, making the species of the force in question, on each occasion, effectual to the purpose of national defence; and, to this purpose, securing to superordinates obedience at the hands of subordinates.
> 2. Securing subordinates against oppression by superordinates.
> 3. Securing the members of the community at large from oppression and wrong, at the hands of these their military functionaries and intended defenders.
>
> Primary object, the first: secondary objects, the two others. Of these antagonizing objects, in time of war or imminent danger of war, the first will have the superior claim to regard: in time of undisturbed peace, the two others.[37]

If the defensive force must not only secure the state from external pressures, but also from the state's 'military functionaries and intended defenders', in other words, from the defensive force itself, the force must be designed in such a way that such internal policing can succeed. The notion of internal policing is pivotal to Bentham's design and as such will be continuously monitored through evaluation of the defensive force. The need to police the state's own security force becomes immediately apparent in this chapter of the *Constitutional Code*. What also becomes immediately apparent is that even though this policing might exist, Bentham could not help but release ultimate authority to just one body, resulting in a definite weakening of the system he tried so hard to construct.[38]

Bentham apparently thought that he had effected a balanced design for a defensive force, but he set himself up to accomplish the most difficult of tasks, since he granted virtually absolute power to the same functionaries whom he wished to defend himself against:

> Annexed, of necessity, to power of military command, in the instance of every person to whom it is given, – are the eventual power of *suspension* and the eventual power of *arrestation*; both powers being exercisible on the spot, over every person in relation to whom the power of command having by the superordinate as per Arts. 2, 3, been exercised, the exercise thereof has been followed by *disobedience* or say noncompliance, or want of sufficiently and practically prompt compliance.
>
> In the exercise of such power of arrestation, whatever physical force is necessary to subdue resistance may be lawfully employed: of such modes as are effective, the least afflictive being always employed in preference.[39]

This clause is vitally significant since it allowed supreme authority to fall into the hands of the superordinates. It illustrated Bentham's inability to rely on his own mechanisms that were designed to make sure that the subordinates, and 'the subject many', prevail. Bentham deferred to the above procedure in the event of a question about superior orders. He initially declared that no subordinate was obligated to obey a command that required the subordinate to 'inflict wrong in any shape, on the person or property of any individual at large'.[40] A command that dictated an action of wrongdoing on public property might be required, and even considered acceptable, if the circumstances warranted it, but Bentham stated that this did not hold true in the case of private individuals and their property. The above clause, however, allowed for the power of *arrestation* that could render void any effort to keep the civilian population and private property out of the fray of war. But perhaps things are not as bleak as they appear. Bentham's design might nevertheless have kept the power granted to the military command in check with a division of the forces, between the 'stipendiary' and the 'radical' force, as Bentham called them.

Bentham's defensive force consisted of a land-service (army) and sea-service (navy), both subsequently broken down into the stipendiary and the radical forces. These two types of force distinguished between those who were permanent and paid members of the defensive force (the stipendiary) and those who were not (the radical). Bentham's justification for the presence of a paid portion of the force, not unlike that of Smith, was the 'progress made in the career of civilization'.[41] In the 'early and immature state of society' everyone, even 'the weaker sex', was made to participate in the preservation of the security of the state at a moment's notice.[42] At that time, according to Bentham, society was not sufficiently organized to have established functionaries charged with the sole duty of ensuring survival and security. However, with the progress of time a 'small portion [of individuals is] withdrawn from the care of producing the matter of subsistence and abundance, the whole remainder of the population is left exclusively in maximizing the aggregate mass of the matter on which life and prosperity depend'.[43] Although society's increasing sophistication allowed for the presence of a paid, stipendiary force, Bentham acknowledged that such a force ought not to grow too large, and that the bulk of the defensive force ought to be contained within the radical, unpaid force. The radical force also ensured security against the stipendiary force, in the event of the latter turning against the state; the radical force was the only source of security against the stipendiary force.[44]

Bentham was aware of the difficulties of having a paid military force available during times of peace, and he mirrored many of the concerns of Machiavelli. For that reason he explored options for making the most productive use of the paid personnels' time when not occupied with training for, or participating in, a war. There was no fearing the possibility of idle hands in the radical branch as those serving in that branch were first and foremost devoted to their various domestic and civil occupations. Those, however, who depended upon the military life for their livelihood, needed to be occupied during peacetime.[45] The vast proportion of the stipendiaries' time was spent in training, but as 'the whole of the disposable portion of the four-and-twenty hours will not be filled up',[46] Bentham suggested what sort of time-occupying endeavours ought to fill the spare time. He included activities that enhanced one's comfort, such as recreation and regular exercise, but especially activities that would, at the same time, promote the development of military aptitude. Each individual was allowed to decide for himself how his time should be occupied, but within certain parameters:

> Lest by the idea of obligation and coercion, an occupation which would otherwise be *acceptable*, should by the circumstance of its appearing to be prescribed by government, be rendered *unacceptable*, – let the choice of it, although antecedently made in a general way by the government, be on each individual occasion felt, and by each individual person understood, to be made by himself.[47]

Ideally each individual had the opportunity to choose how to occupy his time, but to ensure that such choices did not conflict with the interests of the state, the state was provided with the ability to control those choices.

The balance achieved between the paid and unpaid forces also dictated the roles assigned to each. The stipendiary force was first and foremost responsible for all hostilities emanating from outside the state, and secondly responsible for responding to hostilities initiated from within; alternatively, the radical force had to pay particular attention to internal discontents, and secondly address hostilities from without.[48] It is clear that the internal security question was generated from a fear of insurrection on the part of the stipendiary force, and that the radical force existed to ensure that the stipendiary force would not be allowed to cause harm to the state or its people. Bentham made this fear plain when he discussed the composition of each force, in that the stipendiary force had to be minimized and the radical force maximized:

> *Reasons.* 1. Minimization of danger to the constitution from insub-ordination on the part of these [stipendiary] functionaries, and from resistance to, or even forced ascendancy over, their respective super-ordinate authorities, whether in the military line or the non-military; to wit, the army minister, the navy minister, the prime minister, and the legislature.
>
> 2. Minimization of expense, – of the quantity of the expense bestowed upon the service of this compound subdepartment.
>
> 3. Minimization of power and disposition, on the part of the govern-ment, to engage in offensive aggression against other states, and thence to involve this state in needless and internally pernicious warfare . . .
>
> Reasons for the maximization [of the radical force.]
>
> 1. Maximization of security, and sense of security, against danger of insubordination and ascendancy on the part of the stipendiary force.
> 2. Giving increase to the chance and facility of affording, without expense of bounty or enlistment, or at less expense, as well as without compulsion, increase in case of need, to the stipendiary force.[49]

The fear that the stipendiary force could turn against the state also dictated the size each force was to take; the principle to be applied was to mini-mize, to the extent that potential external hostilities would allow, the stipendiary force, and relative to that number, make the radical force proportionately greater in size. Bentham did not state how much greater in size the radical force ought to be, just that by being the larger force it would be capable of dealing with any wayward stipendiary force. It is difficult to understand, however, how Bentham thought that such a design could be successfully achieved. Bentham himself did not give the radical force much credit in its historical foundation and training, and he was ambiguous when determining the actual size of the force. The balance would be difficult to maintain if one was to follow Bentham to the letter.

The stipendiary force, as will also be seen below, was too heavily relied upon for both external and internal security issues.[50]

Confusion dominates Bentham's balance between the two types of forces he has designed. It becomes unclear how the radical force would be a check upon the stipendiary force given the training each force receives. The stipendiary force must be trained in the 'manipulationary and evolutionary movements with small arms, but moreover other branches of physical art and science, wide in extent and variety; mechanical and chemical for example – through the medium of fortification and artillery exercise'.[51] The radical force need only be trained in the 'small arms exercises, as above, ... with which the members in general will naturally be apt to content themselves'.[52] Apart from numbers, the radical force does not appear to be much of a threat to anyone. This is clear when Bentham reiterated that the stipendiary force was an effective product of civilization. The radical force was the product of an 'inferior culture', and 'has everywhere pined or withered under the shade of it'.[53] Even though Bentham did not appear to take the radical force very seriously in terms of its military might, he relied upon it to ensure the 'greater the security against all enterprises, to the temptation of engaging in which the members of the stipendiary force stand exposed'.[54]

The radical force was trained by personnel from the stipendiary force, but the material that the radical force had to train with was of a lower calibre, and they were to be trained with less: 'The appropriate *material* instruments will be the least expensive of those which will suffice for the exercises: for articles no otherwise employed than by being instantaneously consumed – powder and ball, for example – no absolute need will, for this species of service, have place'.[55] The only required field of service would be infantry, as this was also the least costly. The legislature would decide whether or not cavalry, common artillery, and horse-artillery service would be included in the radical branch, as these more expensive services would have to be paid for by the government.[56] Bentham liberally applied what he referred to as the 'expense-minimizing' principle where the radical branch was concerned. The stipendiary force was the one that must be primed and ready for any hostile eventuality, thereby justifying various government expenses to ensure that the stipendiary branch was well-trained and prepared. The radical branch did not receive as favourable a treatment, and the only result could be a less- if not ill-prepared force, in comparison with their paid colleagues.

Although the general objectives that Bentham wished to achieve are relatively clear, he managed to confound those objectives with his details. His arguments became circular and confusing, especially where the radical force was concerned. Bentham, for example, declared that the radical force ought not to be compared to what many would think of as a 'militia', since his radical force is supposed to be something quite different:

To an English or English-bred mind, the idea of an aggregate body, the individuals of which are brought together by compulsion, with a view to land-army service, – and which is distinguished from an army by its comparative unserviceableness for the purposes for which both are intended, – presents the word *militia*. As to the *existence* of this institution, in England, and in the Anglo-American United States, it is unquestionable. To find for it anything like *a use*, must be the work of imagination. Two, and no more than two, uses, does this instrument (it is believed) ever bring to mind.

1. Supposable Use the first. *Nursery for the army*: this phrase may serve to give expression to one. – 2. Supposable Use the second. *Protection against* the army, and those who have the command of it: this phrase may serve for the other.

As to the benefit derivable from the keeping up, at *all* times, – by pay, and compulsion to boot, a large body of ineffective men, with no better prospect than that of a *chance* of being able, *with*, or though it were even *without*, compulsion, at one time or other, to aggregate a small portion of it to the effective army, instead of aggregating to that body, on each occasion, at the minimum of expense, the number actually wanted and no more, – this first imaginable use has just been held up to view.

[...]

Remains, the protection imagined to be afforded or affordable by the militia *against* the army: against the army, and thence against those who have the command of this last-mentioned instrument, the force and formidableness of which are not open to dispute.[57]

Bentham has himself provided an adequate critique against a militia, but it is difficult to see how the militia differed from his radical force. The radical force was designed to keep a better trained, more able and advanced defensive force in check, but only its force of numbers appeared to be the radical's advantage. In large part, what Bentham created in the radical force is precisely that which he criticized in the same breath. Bentham noted that the militia as utilized by England and the United States was the only military force available to those states. Bentham, of course, advocated the institution of a permanent force, in addition to the radical force which could still be styled a militia. For the sake of efficacy, however, Bentham's radical force did not appear to be any more efficient or effective than that which he criticized. Although Bentham did frequently pay homage to the idea of the 'people' having the last word and the ability to exercise power – his continued criticisms of the British and American militias and the fact that they were controlled by the ruling few is an example – ultimately his own organization ensured that the state machinery retained final authority.

The advanced and 'civilized' stipendiary force was necessary since the state required a force constantly prepared for any instabilities that might occur, externally or internally. The inferior radical force had to be able, with little training and only a relatively larger number of troops, to combat the stipendiary force that would, more than likely, rebel against the state and cause it harm. But assuming that the radical force, inferior though it was, was still capable of its delegated functions, Bentham had to ensure that it had the numbers required to do so.

Bentham initially appeared to be in favour of only voluntary service, but his position was flexible. His discussion focused on recruitment for the stipendiary force, but he did not ignore some important issues about the radical force.[58] With 'exceptions excepted', the radical force was open to those who 'being apt with respect to the performance of the appropriate exercise, are willing to join therein; none who are not willing'.[59] In addition, and for the purposes of reducing expense as much as possible, candidates would not be solicited from anywhere other than urban areas. This would reduce the cost of transportation to and from the location of the military exercises, and would not impose such an expense upon those individuals unable to endure it.[60] If enough people voluntarily enlisted in the radical force, then all was satisfactory. However, how could the required number (which must be relatively larger than the stipendiary force) be obtained with certainty, if not through compulsion?

Bentham attempted to address this very question, and stated that compulsion, 'for this service men in sufficient number . . . would not be needed'.[61] He assumed that a number of principles applied in the acquisition of a radical force, and that they revealed how compulsion was not only unnecessary, but also detrimental to its creation. To begin with, it was assumed that those with a relish for the military service would likewise have a particular aptitude for it; those with less relish, less aptitude. Therefore the radical branch was available for those who found the service appealing and were more suited to the task, and no one who felt otherwise should be forced to take part. Compulsion would be detrimental in that efficiency would remain the same at best, and at worst, be reduced. Discontent would increase, resulting in members avoiding service or deserting. Many would suffer at the hands of those few in the leading ranks, and the expense of pursuing, catching and convicting deserters did not justify the practice.[62] Apart from the suffering that was endured by those individuals compelled into service through enlistment, such a practice was costly in application.

The radical force relied on the willingness of its participants to be there. Willingness was facilitated in two ways; through time and distance.[63] A man must not be made to sacrifice whatever time was required for generating an income to provide for himself and his family; the time devoted to the radical force must be convenient and not disruptive. The distance to training facilities must also be minimal. Bentham advised that participants should come from towns and cities of relatively dense population.

This not only ensured a short travel time to and from the site of training, but also ensured that the service attracted people of intellect.[64] Such were Bentham's reasons to recruit only on a voluntary basis, and they provide the sole answer to the question of generating enough troops for the radical force. It is true that troops would probably be generated, but would they be enough? Bentham required that the radical force be relatively larger than the stipendiary force; the security of the state was vested in the radical force as it was the only viable remedy against a wayward stipendiary force.

Bentham did not address the problem of enlistment in the radical force any further. It appears that he ultimately hoped to have an adequately sized radical force. The stipendiary force receives more attention however. If short on stipendiary personnel, Bentham offered a solution: conscription. 'Obligatorily located, if any, are those, whom in a time of extreme peril, through inability to procure a sufficient number voluntarily serving, the Legislature shall have ordered to be thus located.'[65] Having already provided lengthy arguments against, Bentham still conceded that '[i]n all branches of the Defensive Force service, *involuntary*, or say *compulsorily-enforced* enlistment may, to an unlimited amount, be but too indispensably necessary.'[66] There is not much question that Bentham considered conscription to be undesirable, but as in many other circumstances, he provided an option such that the state was not bound by particular ideals. As much as it would be best that all enlistment occur voluntarily, it was possible that the state would find it necessary to compulsorily enlist recruits. Conscription was only to take place under conditions of necessity, but since these conditions 'consist in the need of contribution in any shape, to the supply in every shape, which happens to have been provided for the purpose of national defence',[67] the state was able to determine with particular latitude whether conditions warranted conscription or not.

The extent of this latitude was apparent when Bentham spoke of desertion, and what measures should be taken to prevent or curtail it. He admitted that desertion would not be a concern if recruitment was strictly voluntary, but there were two conditions where the status of volunteer no longer applied: in war, and 'in a state of peace, if the number of those desirous to quit should be so great, that by the substitution of that same number of recruits to veterans, the deterioration to the strength of the aggregate of the force in the branch in question would be perceptible'.[68] There is no indication as to how this deterioration would be determined, leaving one to assume that this determination was left up to the state. Although the state was confined to action on the basis that '[E]xaction of services of a military nature is, for the time that the course of the operation lasts, *compulsory enlistment*; enlistment, for a *time* corresponding in duration to the emergency',[69] and '[C]onsistently with this constitution, – only in the case of invasion, or imminent danger of invasion, or civil war, can any such compulsory recruitment have place',[70] there was still ample room for the state to manoeuvre.

Bentham's design for the defensive force was an intricate balancing act between the interests of the people, the state, and the defensive force itself. Ideally the state deferred to the people, and the defensive force deferred to the state. Ultimately, however, the state was authorized to exact necessary evils and was granted significant powers through the constitution to carry out actions of necessity. These acts were understood to be those by 'military necessity, the necessity of giving by law to military functionaries authority to produce, on each occasion, in any shape whatsoever, whatsoever evil may be at the same time sufficient and *necessary* to the exclusion of greater evil.'[71] Allowing for such 'evil' to take place must be legislated; Bentham noted that many societies (he did not state which ones) prohibit any evils to take place; Bentham argued however that it was better to legislate these actions rather than prohibit them altogether:

> That which you prohibit, you cannot regulate . . .
>
> If you *prohibit* the production of the supposed necessary evil, – the prohibition will include in it the effect of an order for *concealment*: and, under favour of this concealment, the supposed agent stands exposed by you to the temptation of producing, over and above the evil necessary to the exclusion of the supposed greater evil, evil in whatsoever shape and quantity may afford a present gratification in any manner to himself.[72]

For the purposes of security Bentham allowed extensive legislative and state control. His methods were not arbitrary, and he distinguished between conditions of peace and war when determining the sort of measures that ought to be pursued,[73] but there was no question as to the power granted the state when it was threatened:

> Regulations which, in a civil case, would be established with a view to *justice*, are accordingly, in this or that military case, made to give way to others, which are regarded as most conducive to the *maximum of efficiency* on the part of the national force. This sort of conflict being admitted, – follows the observation – that in time of *war*, the demand for corroboration of *power* is at its *maximum*; the demand for *justice* at its *minimum*; in time of peace the demand for *justice* is at its *maximum*; the demand for corroboration of *power* at its *minimum*.[74]

The state was required to play the dominant role in times of crisis, or where there was a perceived threat to the state's security.

Most of what has just been discussed applied primarily to the land-service of the defensive force. As mentioned earlier, Bentham also envisioned the inclusion of a sea-service, but only for those states that had access to water routes. The land-service took precedence over the sea-service as far as necessity was concerned, as not every political community was situated in such a way as to require a sea-service, whereas all need a land-service. Bentham had a romantic respect for the sea-service, and he claimed that the sea-service prevailed over the land-service in terms of dignity; so far as 'dignity is proportioned to quantity of demand for appropriate intellectual and active aptitude'.[75] A littoral state would have a navy, but Bentham gave no impression that a state received any particular benefit from it.[76] If a sea-service was required, the state needed not fear from the potential risks of an employed defensive sea force.

Unlike the land-service, there was no need to check the dangerous inclinations of a paid sea-service. Although the sea-service was also broken down into the stipendiary and radical divisions, the stipendiary naval force was no threat:

> In the stipendiaries belonging to the sea-service branch, no such source of danger is perceptible. The element on which they act keeps them in a state of comparative separatedness; and at the same time mostly at an uninfluential distance from the seat of the legislature ... But as, in comparison with the danger from the land stipendiary force, the danger to a constitution from the sea stipendiary force is inconsiderable; – so, on the other hand, is the use of it, in the character of a check, as above, correspondently inconsiderable; in its serving as a source of constantly applicable supply, consists its principal use.[77]

Since the state was capable of supplying itself otherwise, a check against the sea-service (as a source of supply) was not necessary in the event the sea-service turned against the state. The role of the sea-force was not pivotal to the survival of the state, it just supplemented the efforts of the land-service. The radical arm of the sea-service was also conveniently ready and able with little to no training needed. It was 'in its own way, trained, (unarmed or armed as it may happen,) and thus kept in a state of comparative preparedness for eventual military sea-service.'[78] All in all, if a state had a sea, it almost inevitably required a sea-service.

But again, it was the land-service that was most crucial to a state's survival, and it was the state that was in question. Bentham's emphasis on the state and its pre-eminence rings more true of the realist perspective than the liberal. As such, and in keeping with Machiavelli's fears of a paid military, the stipendiary, or professional armed force had to be kept in check. The stipendiary land force was only a small component of the defensive force, but because they were kept in a constant position of preparedness they were capable of threatening, as well as defending, the state. This threat could manifest itself in two ways – under the command of the 'commander in chief', or under the command of any 'subordinate leader'.[79] Since there was always a force ready for action, it was possible for the leader of the state, or anyone else who would have power over the force, to usurp the legitimate authority endowed by the people. Bentham offered one hopeful suggestion, however, that would ultimately balance these difficulties out and result in a successful 'liberal' conclusion.

The fear that a state's own armed forces might turn against it could be present in any political system. This fear is reduced somewhat, however, if the state happens to be a representative democracy where the 'governors and governed are to the greatest possible extent the same individuals'.[80] Although it was still possible that the stipendiary division of the defensive force could turn against the state, it was less likely because those who would guide the defensive force were 'the subject many'. This was the only remedy to the fear, but once achieved it appeared that the defensive force could be safely and efficaciously utilized in a variety of ways:

> the principal and sole constant use of a body of stipendiaries is – that which consists in their serving as an instrument of security against aggression by *foreign* adversaries, actual and eventual. But, moreover, a collateral and highly useful, though but eventual and occasional use, is – the affording aid to the *justice minister* and the *preventive-service minister* respectively, in the application of remedies, suppressive or preventive, against delinquency in various shapes, when operating upon a large scale: – that is to say, upon a scale too large to admit of the mischief's being suppressed or prevented, by the personal force constantly at the command of the directing functionaries at the head of the above-mentioned non-military departments and subdepartments; and capable of being, with adequate promptitude, brought to bear by them respectively upon the place in which the mischief has its seat.
>
> A casualty to which a democratic constitution, like any other, stands perpetually exposed, is – that of giving birth to a knot of malefactors, who, acting in manifest opposition to the ordinary official establishment of the government, constitute thereby a sort of temporary government of their own formation, monarchical or aristocratical as the case may be, waging war upon the government established by law: in which case, although no such prospect should be entertained by them as that of subverting the government which they find established, yet were it not for a body of well-trained military men in readiness to act for their suppression, no limit might be assignable to the quantity of the mischief which, before an end could be put to it, might be produced by them.[81]

Assuming that a representative democracy was in question (and Bentham's *Constitutional Code* was designed primarily for, if not itself a design for, such a political regime), the risk of maintaining a paid military force was outweighed by the benefit of the same force being immediately deployed to suppress insurrection. Bentham acknowledged that the radical force was capable of achieving the same effect, eventually, but that the stipendiary force was able to act more rapidly as it was constantly prepared.[82]

The further a state moved from democratic principles, the more that a stipendiary force posed a threat to the security of the state. In a federative democracy, for example, which Bentham considered to be somewhat removed from the representative democracy, a stipendiary force could still be recommended if a safe balance was maintained; there ought to be enough troops available to suppress any 'disobedience to the general will' by any one member of the federation, but not so many troops that they could wield power over the majority of the population belonging to the entire federation.[83] This argument claimed that the further the people of the state were from governing themselves, the greater the insecurity from any paid, military force. Additionally, the radical branch of the defensive force could only have true efficacy in a republic as it is only in a republic that the people feel they have something they wish to preserve and make secure; in a monarchy or aristocracy the members of the community who would constitute the radical force would have nothing to lose if the state were threatened, whereas they would have much to lose, according to Bentham, if their republic was threatened.[84] This logic drew Bentham to conclude that '[I]n none but a republic or a mixed government, therefore, can there be either security or care about security.'[85] Bentham did not explicitly explore the fact that in a monarchy or aristocracy, participants in the military force might be compelled to ensure state security, either through coercion or allegiance to the state or head of state.

Bentham acknowledged that progress through civilization required a form of defence other than a militia. His stipendiary force was designed to become fully competent in the ways of modern warfare, just as Smith required, given the development of armaments. Bentham, too, was willing to pay a price for the permanent and well-trained military force, although, typically, he still tried to make most effective use of those costs. Beyond these similarities, however, Bentham was not a disciple of Adam Smith. A concern for security lingered within Bentham's thinking that could not be tempered by relying solely upon a professional military force. Those who made a career out of warfare were dangerous to the state and its citizens. Bentham sought a design for a defensive force that could alleviate his fears about the standing army. Here his ideas appeared to turn to Machiavelli.

Bentham's ideas mirrored the thoughts of Machiavelli in the evaluation of 'evil doing' for the sake of the state, and in the security of a republic. Both Machiavelli and Bentham advised that the most secure political regime was a republic; both agreed that the more citizen involvement existed, the more secure the state was likely to be since the citizens had a vested interest in that security. These sentiments were not directed at reducing or taking away authority from the state, but instead supported the notion that the more loyalty that could be engendered through the people toward the state, the more secure it would be. When it was time for war, a state had to be prepared to defend itself. Sometimes this meant defence to the limits. This was the greatest 'end' which 'justifies the means'. When no other recourse was available, the state had to be defended, even by unsavory means:

> for the purpose of saving the country no propositions ought to be rejected . . . it ought to be saved at any price; . . . the defence of their country was always good, no matter whether effected by honourable or ignominious means . . . For where the very safety of the country depends upon the resolution to be taken, no considerations of justice or injustice, humanity or cruelty, nor of glory or of shame, should be allowed to prevail . . . the only question should be, What course will save the life and liberty of the country?[86]

In the last analysis, if it depended on the survival of the state, any means to ensure survival had to prevail. Would Bentham go so far? He was not as explicit, but as has been seen above, some situations dictated the use of necessary evils, and the security of the state was one such situation. Neither Machiavelli nor Bentham would have endorsed the use of gratuitous violence, that which goes beyond whatever is deemed necessary to ensure control and order, but both recognised its utility.

Bentham wanted the efficiency and expertise of the standing army together with the security, won through loyalty, of the militia. Bentham's respect for the sea-service, and resigned acknowledgement of the necessity for the land-service, spoke to his conception of both. To possess a land-service was imperative, but it was also a source of danger. Here arose some of Bentham's difficulties in balancing defence concerns with the freedom of the individuals composing that society. A small group of people could justifiably be supported by the society to meet security needs, but that same small group was also a source of insecurity for the state. Instead of ensuring, as Machiavelli does, that no paid defence force exists for fear of their being idle (given the fact that their livelihood is dependent upon war), Bentham attempted to balance the fears of having a permanent defence that stood idle against the benefit and convenience of a force constantly at the ready. This balance became the determining element in establishing the defensive force.

Bentham was not a realist or Machiavellian, but in certain respects he followed Machiavelli quite closely. Quite unlike Bentham, Machiavelli had an intense distrust of the motives and methods of commerce, finding the commercial life to have a debilitating effect on the *virtù* of the citizenry. He also thought that regular visits to the field of war were advantageous for the maintenance and development of *virtù*, a practice that would never have been endorsed by Bentham. Nevertheless, the similarities of the two thinkers cannot be overlooked, and although Bentham may not be a Machiavellian, he still drew his security expectations from the tradition that Machiavelli inspired. At the same time, Bentham's insistence on retaining a paid military force established his connection to the progress-oriented, liberal thinking of Smith.

Bentham's thoughts on war, and his design of the defensive force, revealed the depth of understanding he had of world politics. Understanding world politics cannot be confined to one theoretical perspective, just as Bentham could not confine himself to one theoretical perspective. In Bentham's work, the complexity of international politics was sometimes manifested in confusing and contradictory attempts to balance concerns of state security with notions of progress and international well-being. Nevertheless, his work provided an important illustration of the challenges confronting state leaders, especially in today's world where sovereignty is still just as important as international commerce. Bentham's writings on war pave the way for an overall understanding of his work in international relations. Realizing the conditions under which a state must react violently, and the conditions when it must not, we can further consider how the various states of the world were advised to make sure that any and all unnecessary conflict could be prevented. Although there are circumstances which a state must consider having recourse to war, such occasions are few, and Bentham would have a state explore alternative options before sending the citizens off to encounter 'mischief upon the largest scale'.[87]

Notes

1 Bentham, *The Theory of Legislation* (New York: Havcourt Brace, 1931), p. 303.
2 Subsequently referred to as *Plan*.
3 UC XXV.22.
4 UC XXV.23.
5 UC XXV.25.
6 Ibid.
7 Ibid.
8 Ibid.
9 This sheet of notes was one of the many marginal outlines Bentham constructed while apparently thinking through the many themes he could address in his essays. The Bowring edition of Bentham's *Works* includes some of the content of this marginal outline within the essay *On War*, but this did not appear to be Bentham's intention.
10 UC XXV.124.
11 Adam Smith, *An Inquiry into the Nature and Causes of the Wealth of Nations* (London: Ward, Locke and Tyler, 1812), p. 312.
12 Ibid.
13 Ibid., p. 314.
14 Ibid.
15 Ibid., p. 315.
16 Ibid., p. 316.
17 Additionally, the militia of less-civilized nations, being led by the chieftains who are habitually obeyed in times of peace and war, are more effective than those that are led by less familiar authority figures. This inherent allegiance evident in barbarous militias makes the militia of the civilized nation even more vulnerable, as the latter is not capable of engendering the strength of loyalty found in the former (ibid., p. 318). Such a situation strengthened the argument for a standing army.

18 Ibid.
19 Ibid.
20 Ibid.
21 Ibid.
22 Ibid., p. 319.
23 There is a distinction between the military community and the civil community in Machiavelli's work, but they are closely linked. See Neal Wood, p. lxxviii.
24 In chastising the many princes of Italy who had been using foreign troops or mercenaries, Machiavelli claimed the failure to use native troops was not due to the lack of capable citizens or subjects available, but solely the fault of the prince, who did not have the sagacity to lead those citizens (*Discourses*, I, 21, p. 175.
25 *Art of War*, p. 23.
26 *The Prince*, XXIV, p. 90.
27 *Discourses*, II, 20, pp. 349 and 350.
28 *Art of War*, p. 15. See also pp. 16–19.
29 J. G. A. Pocock, *The Machiavellian Moment: Florentine Political Thought and the Atlantic Republican Tradition* (Princeton: Princeton University Press, 1975), pp. 199–200.
30 Bowring, Vol. IX, p. 384.
31 Ibid., p. 336.
32 Philip Schofield, 'The Constitutional Code of Jeremy Bentham', *King's College Law Journal*, 2 (1991–92), p. 50.
33 Ibid., p. 51.
34 Ibid., p. 52.
35 Ibid., p. 54.
36 Ibid., p. 60.
37 Bowring, Vol. IX, p. 366.
38 Bentham argues that power ultimately resides with the state (Schofield, p. 36). On any occasion deemed appropriate by the Legislature, can the Legislature effect the use of the defensive force. The only time that a subordinate can exercise power without order from a superordinate is in time of great military need, usually linked to that individual's self-preservation. This power would be exercised over others in the military or over the population in general, especially during war time (Schofiled, p. 394.). Likewise, the judicatory is granted immense power for purposes of punishment during times of war for such things as desertion or disobedience of orders. This power is reduced in peacetime; however, the point is made that when the state suffers a condition of threatened security, it is allowed great latitudes (Bowring, Vol. IX, p. 394).
39 Ibid., p. 366.
40 Ibid., p. 367.
41 Ibid., p. 334. Bentham believes that the stipendiary force is the pre-eminent force of any political society. It is the most efficient and 'is the only one that suits that which is everywhere the *actual* end of government; namely, the prosperity of those by whom the powers of government are possessed'(ibid., p. 337). The radical force is the product of an 'inferior culture,' hence Bentham's justification for having a paid military force; it is the product of civilization. A military force emanating from the public at large, such as a militia, is reflective of more primitive cultures.
42 Ibid.
43 Ibid.
44 Ibid., p. 338.
45 Ibid., p. 341.
46 Ibid.
47 Ibid., p. 342.

48 Ibid., p. 338
49 Ibid., p. 339.
50 In later passages Bentham claims that fears about the stipendiary force rebelling against the state are mitigated by the type of political regime that is in place.
51 Ibid., p. 339.
52 Ibid.
53 Ibid., p. 337.
54 Ibid., p. 339.
55 Ibid., p. 343.
56 Ibid.
57 Ibid., pp. 345–6.
58 Bentham notes the possibility of the use of compulsion to generate an adequate radical force, but this point is neither explored nor explained. Ibid., p. 340.
59 Ibid., p. 343.
60 Ibid., p. 344.
61 Ibid., p. 344.
62 Ibid. Some of these costs are deflected with the funds obtained from those who pay a price for their exemption from the service; an untenable suggestion for anyone concerned with even the most minimal of egalitarian practices. Not only does this work against those who cannot afford to pay, but those at the very top of the social scales rarely, if ever, pay for their exemptions while receiving them all the while. Ibid., p. 345.
63 Ibid., p. 345.
64 Ibid. 'in the seat of the densest, not in that of the thinnest population, – has the nature of man, in unison with the nature of things, placed the seat of the most intellectual public.'
65 Ibid., p. 351.
66 Ibid., p. 353. Bentham further states that the constitution will allow for compulsory enlistment 'only in the case of necessity.' Ibid., p. 357.
67 Ibid., p. 384.
68 Ibid., p. 372.
69 Ibid., p. 384.
70 Ibid., p. 396.
71 Ibid., p. 384.
72 Ibid.
73 For example, if punishment of military personnel is required, such punishment is dictated by the nature of the offense as well as the political climate that is, in peacetime or in war. Ibid., p. 394.
74 Ibid., p. 393.
75 Ibid., p. 334.
76 This is contrary to what Bentham's idol, Catherine II of Russia, believed. She was uncompromising in her demands to have a warm water port, assuming not only that sea power was necessary, but that it was all the more so from particularly strategic and central locations.
77 Ibid., p. 335.
78 Ibid.
79 Ibid.
80 Ibid.
81 Ibid.
82 Ibid., p. 336.
83 Ibid.
84 Ibid.
85 Ibid.
86 *Discourses*, III, 41, p. 527.
87 UC XXV.22.

8   Bentham and the Colonies

> You will, I say, give up your colonies – because you have no right to govern them, because they had rather not be governed by you, because it is against their interest to be governed by you, because you get nothing by governing them, because you can't keep them, because the expense of trying to keep them would be ruinous, because your constitution would suffer by your keeping them, because your principles forbid your keeping them, and because you would do good to all the world by parting with them. In all this is there a syllable not true? – But though three-fourths of it were false, the conclusion would be still the same. – Rise, then, superior to prejudice and passion: the object is worth the labour. Suffer not even your virtues to prejudice you against each other: keep honour within its bounds; nor spurn the decrees of justice because confirmed by prudence.[1]

After his writings on international law and a type of international public opinion tribunal, Bentham's work on colonies is probably the best-known to international relations scholars. This is primarily because a substantial part of *Colonies and Navy*, one of Bentham's first pieces on the subject, is contained within *A Plan for An Universal and Perpetual Peace*, his most recognized work in international relations. This chapter evaluates Bentham's work on colonies to expand our understanding of his contribution to international relations literature. Bentham's writings on colonies are also one of the first and more important examples of a fundamental problem with his work on international relations: determining the extent to which his work contributes to, or can be situated within, the principles of any of the international relations theoretical traditions.

Others have explored Bentham's ideas on colonies. One of the most thorough investigations is by Donald Winch, whose general conclusion is that Bentham expresses a distinct ambivalence about the necessity for colonies. Lea Campos Boralevi responds with an argument that Winch's perspective does not take into account the philosophical perspective from which Bentham examined everything; Bentham's only measure of 'right and wrong' or 'necessity' is the principle of utility. This chapter will argue that both evaluations lack enough substance or explanatory power, and that although neither is wholly incorrect, both are inadequate if the goal is to understand Bentham's work, both on its own and in historical context.

After briefly looking at what some of Bentham's contemporaries had to say about colonies, and providing a more detailed presentation of the Winch and Boralevi analyses, I will examine the evidence, using in particular the two essays, *Emancipate Your Colonies!*, *Rid Yourselves of Ultramaria*, and the fragment *Colonies and Navy*. Other important excerpts from Bentham's works addressing related topics will be included, adding to the evidence Winch and Boralevi rely upon. Finally I will explain why both analyses, although useful to some degree, require more depth to provide adequate explanatory power.

Although Bentham did not believe he was breaking new ground by addressing the issue of colonies, he did not give some of his contemporaries, and especially his self-proclaimed mentor Adam Smith, much credit on this subject:

> On the encrease [sic] of wealth resulting from colonization I know no work which has spread so much light as a small publication of Dr. Anderson, published towards the end of the American war, entitled, *The Interest of Great Britain with regard to her American Colonies considered* (1782). The work of Adam Smith, which still is and deserves to be the textbook of political economy, contains almost nothing on the subject of colonies and on the greater part of the questions which are treated in the forementioned work.[2]

Like his own brief treatment of Smith's work on colonies, Bentham's contributions to the colonies debate has been similarly dismissed without much consideration by international relations scholarship.

Based on his 1960 doctoral dissertation, Donald Winch published his 1965 text *Classical Political Economy and Colonies* in 1965. In it he provides a very thorough account of Bentham's thinking on the colony issue and successfully brings to light the conflicting nature of Bentham's theorizing about the retention or emancipation of colonies:

> any examination of Bentham's contribution to the political economy of colonies and colonization entails an excursion from the mainstream of classical thought ... Bentham spent most of his life in the process of revising and occasionally contradicting positions he had reached earlier. His second-thoughts on colonial questions can be found in works dealing with other topics and also in his tangled manuscripts. Once these writings are taken into account, it becomes clear that Bentham had great difficulty in maintaining a consistent anti-colonial position; that, depending on the case under consideration, he alternated between emphasis on the drawbacks of colonial rule and awareness of the opportunities presented by the existence of Britain's overseas

possessions. This ambivalence is of interest not only as evidence of the private workings of Bentham's mind, but also because it epitomizes the ambivalence towards the empire felt by philosophical radicals as a group. It helps to explain Bentham's acceptance late in life of Wakefield's schemes for 'systematic colonization'; and, by implication, the involvement of philosophical radicalism with the Colonial Reform movement.[3]

As will be seen below, the conclusion that Bentham was ambivalent is more than self-evident. Winch successfully contested any notion that Bentham was strictly 'anti-imperial', but that is all. To conclude that Bentham was ambivalent is only to state the obvious. And this point is obvious only on a superficial level, as Boralevi argues.

Boralevi recognizes the contradictions in Bentham's thinking too, but she argues that it is not due to ambivalence but an examination of each case on the basis of its own merits. Bentham is in no way ambivalent and therefore inconsistent in his treatment of colonies; he is applying the principle of utility in every case. Boralevi:

> Bentham did not treat the problem of colonies and colonization as a single problem as we would today, but rather as two distinct problems: English, Spanish, and French colonies in America; Penal Colonies in Australia; and British India, all constituted different problems, towards which Bentham's attitudes changed in relation to his personal convictions and to particular circumstances ... This change of attitude has to be looked for instead, mainly in the transition from his original toryism to radicalism. In other words, Bentham later came to think that the greatest happiness of the greatest number was served better if the 'governing few' were prevented from pursuing their own sinister interests by submitting them to the strict control of the people ... The issue of oppression and the 'felicific calculus' which determined the quantities of happiness, are in fact the only perspective from which it is possible to reconstruct a line of continuity in Bentham's attitude towards colonies, which can be maintained even in these cases where, from the political or economic point of view, his position would appear to be contradictory.[4]

Boralevi examines Bentham's alleged lack of consistency, and does provide a plausible explanation for his apparent shift in position. Given the fact that on balance, Bentham's work favours emancipation, it does appear that his endorsement of colonies must be driven by particular circumstances rather than being a question of principle. An examination of the evidence, however, does not bear this conclusion out.

The bulk of Bentham's writings argue against the acquisition and retention of colonies. As stated above, two essays and one fragment are devoted to such arguments, and Bentham included this opinion frequently in many of his other writings. However, Bentham's initial opinion was not against colonies. When he began to put forward his position on this issue, he did not at first express the strong anti-colonial sentiments found in later writings.

The American War of Independence undoubtedly prompted Bentham and others to consider the importance of colonial emancipation.[5] Looking at Bentham's correspondence, one can see that his initial reaction was not a view on colonies per se. His strongest opinions on the American Revolution revolved around the nonsensical nature of the American Declaration of Independence. Bentham contributed to John Lind's pamphlet entitled *An Answer to the Declaration of the American Congress* (published in the autumn of 1776), where Bentham takes issue with the theory of government proposed, and later, the reason the Americans chose independence in the first place.

> 'hold to be inalienable'. This they 'hold to be' a (among truths) 'truth self-evident'. At the same time they are to secure these rights they are satisfied (content) that Governments should be instituted. They see not, or will not seem to see that nothing that was ever called government ever was or ever could be in any instance exercised save at the expence of one or other of those rights. That (consequently) in so far as many instances as Government is ever exercised, some one or other of these pretended inalienable rights is alienated. [*In margin:* It is thus they endeavour by a cloud of words to cover (veil) the atrocity enormity of their (crimes) (misdeeds) enterprizes.] If life is one the right of enjoying life be the unalienable right of all men, whence came their invasion of his Majesty's province of Canada, and the unprovoked destruction of so many lives of the Canadians inhabitants of that province? . . .
>
> 'Governments long established', they do vouchsafe to admitt, 'should not be changed for light and transient causes' – Can any cause be so light, as that which wherever Government has subsisted or can subsist has always and must continue to subsist. What was their original their only original grievance. That they were taxed more than they could bear? No, but that they were liable to be (so: more than they could bear. Is there any where, can there be imagined any where that Government whose subjects are not /so/ liable to be so taxed more than they can bear?[6]

Americans, therefore, were going to war solely because they feared greater taxes, and expressed these fears in the nonsensical notion of rights. Beyond that, Bentham's comments on the war were restricted to relating the latest military and political skirmishes to his friends, family, and colleagues.[7] He did not give much thought to the idea of colonies yet; at this point he was more concerned with the reliance the Americans placed on this elusive and nonsensical notion called rights (against which Bentham had a life-long battle), and less so with who should govern whom and why.[8]

If one wanted to argue that Bentham's position on colonies was contingent on either his age or his philosophical bent, then one would undoubtedly notice a discernible shift in position divided by some sort of development, for example his change from Toryism to radicalism, or the passing of the years. Bentham's colonial writings do not indicate either; as a young thinker he appears to be against colonies, in middle age he can see an argument in favour of them, in old age he is once again opposed to colonial possessions, and then a year prior to his death he once again seems to undergo a change of heart. If nothing else, one can at least discern a development of the ideas he first posed in the 1790s with *Colonies and Navy* and *Emancipate Your Colonies!*. His *Rid Yourselves of Ultramaria* includes more thought on economic arguments and much discussion of the political dimension when compared to the earlier pieces. The American Revolution had brought new attention to this issue for Bentham and his contemporaries. A chronological survey of Bentham's years of writing on this topic will illustrate the influences and issues affecting what he had to say on the matter.

Bentham's views on colonies first become formalized in his essay *Defence of Usury* (1787). Although he does not devote a great deal of time to the topic, this piece provides a glimpse into his future arguments not only on colonies, but on the related issue of, 'no more trade than capital'.[9] Although Bentham does not develop his ideas at this point, some very important features of his future arguments are already appearing: colonies are bad practice primarily on account of the economic disadvantages to the mother country. In general Bentham does not waver from this contention throughout his life, articulated as trade limited by capital. The inhabitants of the colony[10] are better able to govern themselves; and finally there is the impossibility of governing from a distance. It is especially this last point that will emerge most forcibly since the retention of colonies is to a great degree contingent on their distance from the mother country. Another interesting but lesser feature is Bentham's emphasis on the improvement of land in the mother country. The capital expended on colonies can only be considered as being taken away from agriculture at home; Bentham places more of an emphasis on land, therefore, than he does on other industries.

Bentham's comments on colonies in *Defence of Usury* hint at future arguments, especially his emphasis on the importance of agriculture and the cost of colonies:

PRACTICAL CONSEQUENCES OF THE PRINCIPLE 'NO MORE TRADE THAN CAPITAL' WITH RESPECT TO COLONIAL GOVERNMENT, ECONOMY AND PEACE.

What is it that would be the loss, suppose it to amount to anything, that a nation would sustain by the giving up of any colony? The difference between the profit to be made by the employing in that trade so much capital as would be employed in it were the colony kept, and the profit that would be made by the employment of the same capital in any other way, suppose in the improvement of land. The loss is nothing, if the same capital employed in the improvement would be more productive: and it would be more productive by the amount of so much as would go to form the annual rent: for deducting that rent, capital employed in the improvement of land produces as much as if employed in any other way. If the loss were any thing, would it then amount to the whole difference between the profit upon that trade, and the profit upon the next most profitable one? no: but only [to] the difference between so much of that difference as would be produced if the colony were retained in subjection, and so much as would be produced if the colony were declared free. The value of a colony to the mother country, according to the common mode of computation, is equal to the sum total of imports from that colony and exports to it put together.

From this statement, if the foregoing observation be just, the following deductions will come to be made:

The whole value of the exports to the colony.

So much of the imports as is balanced by the exports.

Such a portion of the above remainder as answers to so much of the trade as would be equally carried on, were the colony independent.

So much of that reduced profit as would be made, were the same capital employed in any other trade or branch of industry lost by the independence of the colony.

But the same capital, if employed in agriculture, would have produced a rent over and above the ordinary profits of capital: which rent, according to a general and undisputed computation, may be stated at a sum equal to the amount of those profits. Thence [arises a further deduction, viz. the] loss to the nation [caused] by employing the capital in the trade to the colony, in preference to the improvement of land, and thence upon the supposition that the continuance of the trade depended upon keeping the colony in subjection.

The other mischiefs resulting from the keeping of a colony in subjection, are:

1. The expence of its establishment, civil and military.
2. The contingent expence of wars and other coercive measures for keeping it in subjection.
3. The contingent expence of wars for the defence of it against foreign powers.
4. The force, military and naval, constantly kept on foot under the apprehension of such wars.

5. The occasional danger to political liberty from the force thus kept up.
6. The contingent expence of wars produced by alliances contracted for the purpose of supporting wars that may be brought on by the defence of it.
7. The corruptive effects of the influence resulting from the patronage of the establishment, civil and military.
8. The damage that must be done to the national stock of intelligence by the false views of the national interest, which must be kept up in order to prevent the nation from opening their eyes and insisting upon the enfranchisement [of the colony].
9. The sacrifice that must be made of the real interest of the colony to this imaginary interest of the mother-country. It is for the purpose of governing it badly, and for no other, that you wish to get or keep a colony. Govern it well, it is of no use to you.

   To govern its inhabitants as well as they would govern themselves, you must choose to govern them those only whom [they] would themselves choose, you must sacrifice none of their interests to your own, you must bestow as much time and attention to their interests as they would themselves, in a word, you must take those very measures and no others, which they themselves would take. But would this be governing? And what would it be worth to you, if it were? After all, it would be impossible for you to govern them so well as they would themselves, on account of the distance.
10. The bad government resulting to the mother-country from the complication, the indistinct views of things, and consumption of time occasioned by this load of distant dependencies.[11]

The importance of the notion 'no more trade than capital' becomes even more apparent in Bentham's intended postscripts to the second edition of *Defence*. He planned to add a number of postscripts to the second edition of *Defence of Usury*, for which the publisher soon began to press, and which he sums up as follows: '1. Short observations on the injustice and impolicy of forced reductions of the rate of interest. 2. Development of the principle *No more trade than capital*. 3. Practical consequences of the principle *No more trade than capital*, with respect to colonial government, economy and peace.'[12] His next work would explore this concept in much greater detail.

By 1790 Bentham had fleshed out his position on 'no more trade than capital' in the fragment *Colonies and Navy*. His argument on capital is the most thoughtful portion of the piece. As stated in Chapter 3, the introductory thirteen points of *Colonies and Navy* are contained within Bentham's better known but poorly edited work, *A Plan for an Universal and Perpetual Peace. Colonies and Navy* could constitute a small, coherent essay of itself were it not for the thirteen introductory points which Bentham failed to address in the subsequent text.

Colonies and Navy had both a general and particular audience at the same time: 'The ensuing sheets are dedicated to the common welfare of all civilised nations: but more particularly of Great Britain and France.'[13] Although Bentham did want to catch the attention of particular states, especially those whose interests most corresponded with his own, he also hoped for a broader audience. Bentham himself therefore debunks the notion that he only wrote to particular situations. He refutes it again when, after the thirteen points, he moves into his thoughtful account of 'no more trade than capital' by stating: 'The first of these principles, viz. That [the] trade of every nation is limited by the quantity of capital, is so plainly and obviously true as to challenge a place among self-evident propositions.'[14] Bentham mentions only once the French, and then the Irish, in the rest of the fragment, as illustrations for the ideas he is trying to convey. For the rest, he speaks to 'all civilised nations'.

Bentham's 'no more trade than capital' argument is also supplemented by comments on prohibitory trade measures and the lack of reason and economic sense that they imply. As Bentham briefly states in *Defence* and as he elaborates in *Colonies,* agriculture, and only that at home, is the most important productive industry. Bentham's point is that a nation's trade is restricted by the quantity of its capital and not the extent of its market.[15] For this reason, the mere acquisition of new territories as colonies will not increase a nation's wealth – only a capital investment in one of the five productive industries will do so: 'Productive industry may be divided into five main branches: 1. production of raw materials including agriculture, mining, and fisheries: 2. manufacture: 3. home trade: 4. foreign trade: 5. carrying trade.'[16] Investment in one industry means less investment in another. In turn, the encouragement of one industry through prohibitory measures means the discouragement of the rest. Such a project is carried out at the expense of the nation, whereas all the productive industries would thrive to the best of their ability if left alone.

Bentham also argues against the emphasis on manufacture as opposed to agriculture:

> Oh! but it is manufacture that creates the demand for the productions of agriculture. You can not therefore encrease the productions of agriculture but by encreasing manufacture. No such thing. I admitt the antecedent: I deny the consequence. Encrease of manufactures certainly does create an encrease in the demand for the productions of agriculture. Equally certain is it that the encrease of manufactures is not necessary to produce an encrease in that demand. Farmers can subsist without ribbons, gauzes, or fine cambrics [*sic*]. Weavers of ribbons, gauzes, or fine cambricks [*sic*] can not subsist without the production of agriculture. Necessary subsistence never can lose its value. Those

who produce it, are themselves a market for the produce. Is it possible
that provisions should be too cheap? Is there any present danger of it?
Suppose (in spite of the extreme absurdity of the supposition) that
provisions were growing gradually too cheap, from the encrease of the
quantity produced, and the want of manufacturers to consume them.
What would be the consequence? The encreasing cheapness would
encrease the facility and disposition to marry: it would thence encrease
the population of the country: and the children thus produced, eating
as they grew up, would keep down this terrible evil of a superabundance of provisions.[17]

Bentham argued that emancipation of the colonies would release capital
for reinvestment in agriculture, in itself a positive development: 'The loss
of the colonies, if the loss of the colony-trade were the consequence of
the loss of the colonies, would at the worst be so much gain to agriculture.'[18] Bentham did not think it likely that trade would terminate with the
emancipation of the colonies. Once a trade pattern had established itself
it would be very difficult to prevent its continuation. Nevertheless, as agriculture provides the basis to economy according to Bentham, then any
losses incurred in colonial emancipation would be easily made up when
capital is invested in agriculture.

Following quickly on the heels of *Colonies and Navy*, Bentham wrote
*Emancipate Your Colonies! Addressed to the National Convention of
France, Aô 1793, shewing the uselessness and mischievousness of Distant
Dependencies to an European State*, shortly after the French Revolution
and the granting of an honorary French citizenship to him.[19] Bentham
now expanded the arguments he first introduced in *Defence of Usury* and
Colonies and Navy. He included some arguments based on notions of justice
as opposed to a strictly economic approach, although ultimately the balance
of the essay is devoted to economic disadvantages. With the argument
from the point of view of justice he included a consideration of the 'other
people's' position of being ruled from afar: 'You choose your own government: why are not other people to choose theirs? Do you seriously mean
to govern the world; and do you call that *liberty*? What is become of the
rights of men? Are you the only men who have rights? Alas! my fellow
citizens, have you two measures?'[20] Whether Bentham is speaking only of
the colonists of French extraction or of the population at large is not
absolutely clear, but it seems, contrary to Boralevi's position, that it is the
latter. Boralevi requires that Bentham refer only to interests of French,
English, or Spanish colonists, depending on the work in question, and that
this, in part, explains the alleged inconsistency in Bentham's response to
the colony question. Thus far *Defence of Usury*, *Colonies and Navy*, and
now *Emancipate Your Colonies!* appear to have a broader audience in
mind – the colonizers as well as the colonized. *Emancipate Your Colonies!*
refers to 'the colonists' but questions whether they ought to be, or are,

considered Frenchmen, and further, who has the right to govern them. Bentham also wonders why the French would even 'govern a million or two people you don't care about'[21] and then decides that the 'French' are adequate to govern themselves but if it is determined that the others need masters, then so be it.[22]

Bentham begins *Emancipate Your Colonies!* with a discussion of the importance of justice, honour, and self-governance for those in the colonies, but he quickly changes tack: 'Think not that because I mentioned them first, it is for their sake in the first place that I wish to see them free. No: it is the mischief you do yourselves by maintaining this unnatural domination; it is the mischief to the six-and-twenty millions, that occupies a much higher place in my thoughts.'[23] The focus of the discussion once again becomes economic. Although he does emphasize his 'no more trade than capital' argument,[24] he expands this into a debate between colonial versus free trade. He argues that it is illusory for a country to think that it gains from a monopoly of trade with a colony, that the former derives an income from the latter, and that monopoly reduces prices of imported goods.[25] Finally, Bentham briefly addresses the view that colonies enhance power. He contests this on the basis that the mother country's power, militarily speaking, is vastly diminished. Military resources are spread thinly between France and the colony, and that makes France even more vulnerable to attacks from others, for example, from Britain.[26]

Bentham's next formal essay on this question did not appear until the 1820s and is based substantially on arguments he had already developed in *Emancipate Your Colonies!*[27] However the inconsistencies Winch noted and that Boralevi tried to explain have already begun to appear. Justice and economics reappear in the 1820's, but even in *Emancipate Your Colonies!* Bentham has hinted that an argument could be made for a pro-colony stance. To the extent that Bentham does advocate the possession of colonies, his strongest arguments appear in his 1801–1804 writings. He does not, however, devote full essays or fragments to this pro-colony position; his comments in this regard are still surrounded by arguments against colonies in general. It becomes evident that Bentham is divided. On principle, he argues against colonial possession: 'A man who could not bear the idea of inflicting the smallest injustice or the smallest personal injury on his neighbour, will send millions of men to be slaughtered, a smile on his lips and satisfaction in his heart, in order to conquer distant islands or to found a colony which will eat up revenue and yield nothing.'[28] Yet consistent with his preoccupation with security allows for the existence of colonies, albeit under more restricted circumstances. For the reasons that Bentham gives in the following paragraphs, any colony could find its justification for existence.

Between 1801 and 1804 Bentham continued to express a variety of opinions on the issue of colonies. In 1801 Bentham wrote *The True Alarm, Of the Balance of Trade*, and in 1804 he finished a substantive work on political economy entitled *Method and Leading Features of an Institute of Political Economy (Including Finance) Considered not only as a Science but as an Art.* These last years of writing on political economy are intriguing and significant;[29] the works that emanate from the period of 1801–1804 reveal an attitude of reserve and a level of 'Toryism'[30] that is generally not recognized in Bentham's economic works.

Stark considers *Institute of Political Economy* to be the 'last important work [Bentham] ever wrote on economic science',[31] in that

> 'we see quite clearly that Bentham was for once within an inch of final achievement: the pages written in 1804 were essentially a filling-in of the gaps left over from 1801, and one short month – in fact, a part of one short month – had sufficed to supply practically all that was still wanting. Even so, Bentham found it impossible to finish this book: ... Bentham was a brilliant man, but he was all his life a little like a child that plays with a favourite toy for a time but then throws it aside and forgets about it, whatever its attractiveness may have been in the past.'[32]

It is very interesting that Stark believed *Institute of Political Economy* to be such a potentially pivotal work for Bentham, and yet, at least for the international theorist, *Institute* expressed some themes of which 'ten years later [Bentham] would probably have been ashamed ... and disowned them'.[33]

It is only fair to consider the passages on colonies written in the period 1801–1804 to be a modification of Bentham's previous and subsequent position; he still readily argues that colonies are an expense to the mother country, and that it is useless to have to expend the money and energy on travelling great distances when it is possible to accomplish a similar, if not identical, result at home:

> Land is worth nothing, but in proportion as labour is applied to it. Land at a distance is worth less than land at home, by the amount of all the distance. Of the mass of labour which is employed in lessening the expence of carriage – in reducing the expence of carriage from a great distance to a level with the expence of carriage from a less distance. If it could be done without destruction to existing capital, and above all without vexation, and destruction of security of property, wealth might be encreased by taking the existing population, and transporting it from greater distances with reference to the metropolis, to lesser distances.
>
> Land newly acquired to a nation, especially in the way of colonization, is acquired at a greater distance. [The] foundation of a colony is an introductory expence; government of it a continual standing

expence; wars for the defence if it an occasional one. All this requires money: and money is not to be had for it but from taxes. To the mother country, the positive profit from it is equal [to] 0: the negative profit, the loss to, [or] the defalcation from, national wealth, consists in the amount of taxes.*

*When, at the expence of a war, and of a hundred millions, and a hundred thousand lives sacrificed in that war, England has got another nation or another colony to trade with, – the foreign nation main-taining itself at its own expence, the colony to be maintained at the mother country's expence – whatever portion of wealth in the shape of capital is *transferred* to the new spot, the Englishman considers as *created*. For a few *negative* hundred thousands a year, he looks upon the positive hundred millions as well bestowed. On the strength of this negative encrease in opulence, the Englishman encreases in insolence; the German envies him, the Frenchman would devour him, thus it is that wars are never to have an end.

But though, in the way intended, no good is done, good is done in another way, in which it is not intended. By the export of capital, a check is applied to the virtual income tax, imposed upon fixed incomists, by the reduction effected in the rate of interest by the contin-ually encreasing *ratio* of that part of the mass of money which is employed in the shape of capital, to the remainder which is employed in the shape of expenditure of income.

If, from the acquisition of a colony, any real advantage were derivable to the mother country, whence would it arise? From the diminution in the burthen of taxes: from the amount of taxes paid, by the inhabitants of the colony, to the government of the mother country, over and above what they would have paid, had they staid [sic] at home: the expence of governing and defending the colony being first defrayed by them. But it is a maxim, that by or for the mother country, colonists, as such, are not to be taxed at all: and thus it is that the inhabitants of the mother country are benefited by the acquisition of colonies.[34]

Thus far, Bentham's comments and conclusions do not differ radically from his previous position regarding colonies, except that now there is the possibility of a tax break. Other than this the only benefit in acquiring colonies is in the enjoyment of the exotic products they might produce, and the only way this increases wealth is as a source of enjoyment which increases value, if not quantity. Colonies are otherwise merely an inordinate expense.

For the most part Bentham's arguments against colonies are quite simple, and more often than not revolve around the expenses incurred by the mother country in the planning, acquisition, and retention of colonies. Essentially, one gets more from one's money when one works and shops at home.

Bentham considers this view to be logical, and if one remains within the realm of what is considered logical (at least when thinking in a Benthamic vein) then it is more than likely that no colonies would have been acquired. However, Bentham never addresses that for which colonies are, arguably, most desired: power. Not simply power measured in purely monetary or economic terms, but power in terms of influence, possession and control. It is not that Bentham did not recognize the existence of such power, but he refused to give it its due. Bentham provides a very simple, rational argument against the acquisition of colonies, but does not take into account the equally simple, albeit perhaps less 'rational' issues of power and dominance.

The arguments for generating greater accumulation of wealth at home reappear regularly, as will be seen below. He recognizes the problems he is up against, the common beliefs regarding wealth: 'The ideas of encrease of money and encrease of territory are so strongly associated in the minds of men with the idea of an encrease in real wealth, that it appears almost impossible to separate them. The distinction between these ideas becomes clear for everyone who takes the trouble to reflect, but many generations will perhaps pass by ere the opinion of thinking men becomes the opinion of the public.'[35] Also, if wealth is to be gained in the colonies, Bentham claims that the encrease is to the colonists – to the individual occupiers of the fresh land, not to the mother country. Taxes they at first can not pay, and afterwards will not pay'.[36]

However, a different approach develops in Bentham's writings with his concessions about the benefits to be gained from colonies. We again see some of the more redeeming qualities of colonial possession. Bentham exclaims that the true benefits of colonies are received not by the mother country, but by the colonized:

> It is desirable for mankind that offsets should be taken from the most flourishing and soundest root: that the races propagated every where in parts of the earth as yet vacant, should be races whose habits of thinking in matters of government should be taken from that constitution from which the greatest measure of security has been seen to flow, and whose habits of acting in the sphere of domestic economy and morals should be taken from that society which, in those respects, is in the most improved as well as improving state.[37]

Colonies, therefore, can consider themselves advantaged owing to the privilege of receiving the wise and advanced guidance, high moral values and exceptional standards of the colonizer.[38] As a matter of fact, the action of colonization now becomes more of an altruistic tendency on the part of the colonizer in that it not only bestows on the colonies its great wisdom, but the colonizer also incurs the cost of the activity.

The creation of wealth is a topic extensively explored by Bentham, but within his examination are certain contradictions regarding a nation's wealth. Although most of his writings specifically on colonies argue that their acquisition in no way increases a nation's wealth, he can also be found to admit the opposite, for example, in *The True Alarm*:

> It would be the object of a rather intriguing speculation to examine what the progress of wealth would have been if several modern causes which have contributed to its encrease had not existed: such as the augmentation of the precious metals by the discovery of the mines of the New World, ... As far as real wealth is concerned, its progress would not have been so rapid without the accession made, by these various means, to productive capital.[39]

However, Bentham does state that Britain's increase in wealth over the years would not have been considerably less than it is now, had the 'discovery' of the New World not taken place with its subsequent colonization. In his words, '[I]ts actual composition would have been a little different, but I do not see any decisive reason why it should have been less.'[40] He does not offer any suggestions as to how the increase in wealth, would have otherwise come into being, as produce from the New World has greatly contributed in the actual case. Finally, in *Institute of Political Economy* Bentham states, 'The operations by which an encrease of the matter of wealth is produced or promoted, may be thus enumerated under the following principal heads, viz ... Discovery of this or that portion of land, considered as the source from which portions of matter in an unimproved state, [i.e.] raw materials, are extracted.'[41] Bentham slowly but surely concedes that the acquisition of new land has financial benefits. This evidence is confusing because later on such notions are, once again, refuted. This is less a reflection of ambivalence than a complete reversal of what Bentham originally stated. The principle of utility also offers no help here. Wealth creation is wealth creation, and how one *generates* wealth is not linked to the ways in which that wealth should be used for the greatest good. However Bentham had already hinted in previous works at the features he considered to be important. Land, as always, is the key to wealth creation, and land acquisition through discovery to extract new materials or use for agriculture will generate wealth. It is distance that is key. Nevertheless, by 1804 it appears that 'taking futurity into the scale, the well-being of mankind appears to have been promoted upon the whole by the establishment of colonies'.[42]

There is yet one more circumstance under which colonies do impart a benefit to the mother country, according to Bentham, and that is through emigration. Over-population was a burden to many well-established European nations, and the acquisition of these newly acquired territories was seen to facilitate the management of these population crises. 'If we consider further the rapid encrease of population such as it has been even during the war, if we observe that it would soon, by its natural course, reach the point where it exceeds the means of subsistence which the two isles could produce, it will be recognized that the emigration of men and capital is a real good in the present state of Great Britain.'[43] In addition Bentham noted that 'We have seen in another place how the Sinking Fund distributes each year a mass of productive capital the effect of which could be to produce a superabundance of money, *if the emigration of men and capital did not offer a natural remedy for this evil* [italics mine].'[44] Here again we find an argument that seems to endorse colonization, and in this case the argument is made in a text which at other points would seem to suggest the reverse.[45]

Boralevi thinks that part of the explanation for Bentham's contradictory statements on colonies stems from his philosophical change from Toryism to radicalism.[46] At this time (1809) Bentham was more likely to articulate interests in terms of the sinister interests of the ruling few versus the universal interests of the subject many. In 1818 he wrote:

> In everybody of which men are the members, the most concentrated will, in the ordinary course of things, dissolve and swallow up the more dilute [?] interest. The interest of the few prevails over the interest of the many, the interest of the one over the interest of the few. Scarcely will you see that empire that has not in the heart of it one still more powerful by which, in a manner still more irresistible, the universal interest, the common interest of the governors and governed, is overborn[e] and sacrificed. In the vast East India monopoly, the millions of subjects are preyed upon by the thousands of proprietors, the thousands of proprietors by the confederacy of Directorys, and controuling Ministers.[47]

Although the notion of a sinister interest does come into play in Bentham's subsequent writings of the 1820s, his transformation to radicalism does not satisfactorily account for the differences of opinion at varying times. Most importantly, this would not account for the fact that Bentham's next work, *Rid Yourselves of Ultramaria*, is substantially based on arguments already developed in *Emancipate Your Colonies!*[48]

Following two preliminary drafts entitled *Emancipation Spanish* and *Summary of Emancipate Your Colonies* respectively, Bentham reorganized his research and material to eventually produce *Rid Yourselves of Ultramaria: Being the Advice of Jeremy Bentham as Given in a Series of Letters to the Spanish People* by the spring of 1822.[49] *Rid Yourselves of Ultramaria* is a far more detailed evaluation of colonies, although it still contains many similar arguments found in his previous works. Bentham's completion of *Rid Yourselves of Ultramaria* was, unfortunately, not timely:

Bentham came to recognize that his hopes of persuading the liberal government of both the undesirability and the impossibility of re-establishing Spanish dominion were unlikely to be realized. In Spain itself there was little dissent concerning the need to maintain Spanish hegemony over the Empire. The bulk of the political élite in Spain, whether the *serviles*, who had supported the absolute monarchy, or the newly restored liberals, wished to retain the Empire, refused to accept that its loss was inevitable, and only differed in their analyses of the causes of the discontent and thus their preferred policies for dealing with it . . . New Granada, Venezuela, Quito, Mexico, and Guatemala effectively secured their independence, Peru came near to doing so, while such influential foreign powers as Great Britain and the United States of America were increasingly sympathetic to the aspirations of the new states. Meanwhile divisions in Spain meant that she had neither effective politics nor the necessary means to crush the revolutionary movements.[50]

Additionally a Decree issued by the Cortes on 13 February 1822 ended all discussion on the matter of emancipating colonies. It relinquished any and all claims of independence contingent on the Treaty of Córdoba of 24 August 1821 and considered foreign recognition of such claims to be a violation of treaties.[51] Even so Bentham felt it an important enough topic to give it his full attention for the moment.

One of the more significant differences between this work and *Emancipate Your Colonies!* (1793) can be found in the detailed constitutional arguments Bentham now included in the latter. Additionally, where he stated that figures would be of no use to one's argument as they are so malleable,[52] he included various tables indicating the expenses incurred, over time, on the part of Spain in respect of her colonies. Beyond that, *Rid Yourselves of Ultramaria* is a broadly developed and complex essay arguing against the possession of distant colonies. Bentham's hope was that the Spanish people would petition their government to explore the benefits and deficiencies of holding colonies: 'behold now what I venture to propose: – a *motion* in the Cortes – nothing more. For the production of this effect, on the part of what number of wills is compliance necessary? A single one and no more. – Object of the motion, a set of *Estimates* – nothing more'.[53] Bentham also moves on from his earlier arguments over the questionable economic benefits of colonial possessions and explores how Spain's constitutional arrangements defeat any advantage Spain would otherwise gain in retaining her colonies.[54]

Bentham begins with a lengthy discussion of the 'Injury to Spain from the Claims in Her Name on Spanish Ultramaria', and makes plain that his points take the shape of pecuniary and constitutional arguments. The bulk of the essay is directed toward peninsular Spain's interests, with a few additional letters at the end outlining how possession of the colonies is also in conflict with the interests of the Ultramarians. Apparent in Bentham's writing is the notion of sinister interest; he explains here why colonies have thus far remained part of the political and social landscape. They serve the interests not of the common Spaniard, nor of the people of the colonies, but of the ruling few. Bentham very briefly gives a nod to the notion of honour and how it is bestowed upon the nation that relinquishes her colonies. The argument is almost identical to that in *Emancipate Your Colonies!*, except for his comment on the ruling few and their sinister enterprise.[55] He does attempt to reach out to those of the ruling few who may discover that they have a greater interest in the universal interest than in their narrow, sinister interest, and that they may take the lead for emancipation of the colonies.[56]

Bentham explores in greater detail the supposed profits to be made through colonies, identifying these sources of profit as taxation, mine-rents or mine-taxes, sale of lands, emolument from Ultramarian offices, and men for military service. He proceeds one by one with arguments to show how each profit-making source is illusory, or, if not illusory, how the profit does not maximize the greatest happiness for the greatest number, and how all profits fall into the hands of the ruling few. Any revenue generated from the first four sources is either unconstitutional or used by those in power. As for more men in the military, Bentham argues that Spain would be much better off financially to hire from neighbouring countries, if necessary, rather than incur the huge cost of shipping men from Ultramaria.[57] In the letters that follow, Bentham continues meticulously to detail and discuss the constitutional and financial pitfalls of Spain's dominions, arguments which are intricately woven together. For instance, although one might argue that Spain will derive a profit from the dominions in the shape of taxes, the constitutional code prohibits the government from doing so as it declares all Spaniards to be equal and therefore one group is required to shoulder the financial burden of another. Bentham's arguments in *Rid Yourselves of Ultramaria* are essentially all in this vein, and it is in this way that the essay, besides its larger scale, differs from *Emancipate Your Colonies!*. His arguments here are much more complex and deeply intertwined with an analysis of the Spanish constitution and the ways in which it limits Spain's profit-making opportunities.[58]

If Bentham considered colonies to be an evil, his opinion was primarily based on the costs and inefficacy of governing from afar; the issue of distance eliminated, the difficulty with colonial possession is considerably diminished. Bentham is clear about this distinction in *Rid Yourselves of Ultramaria*:

> But (says somebody) these arguments of yours, do not they prove too much? In case of other nations – not to say all other nations – profit is encreased as dominion is encreased, diminished as it is diminished. This you will not deny to be the case in those instances. Then why

should it be otherwise in our instance? What is it that makes the difference? If there be any such difference, what cause or causes can you find for it?

I answer in one word – *distance*. By distance – distance between the seat of government and a country subject to it, uselessness and burthensomeness to the governing country are produced – irremediably produced – in every way imaginable. On the one part, discontent is produced; on the other part, the means of suppressing it, whether by gentle measures or by forcible ones, are excluded. Exercised by imported strangers, subordinate power exercises itself by acts of oppression: or at any rate, what to this purpose comes to the same thing, is thought to do so: superior rulers at the seat of government, whether they be [willing] or unwilling to afford redress, the distance of itself, by excluding them from the knowledge of the grievance, suffices to render redress at their hands impossible. Before one grievance, with its discontent, has reached their ears, another grievance, with its discontent has succeeded: and thus matters go on, ill-will accumulating on both sides. Be the grievance what it may, if the newly acquired territory were in contiguity with the seat of government, no sea at all or no considerable sea intervening, the inhabitants will submitt to it, seeing no remedy but in patience and supplication: the sovereign's known approbation of every thing that is done in his name prevents so much as the birth of hope. But in the other case, the sovereign being supposed to be all goodness, on every occasion hope is continually raising itself up, and almost as continually beaten down by disappointment: till at last the very germ of hope being killed by experience, despair takes its place, and a settled despondency, or series of insurrections, is the ultimate result.

In another Letter I shall have occasion to shew you how it is that by distance, sooner or later, discontent ending in insurrection is sure to be produced. On the present occasion, an enquiry of that sort is not yet in its place: for what can not be denied is – that by no degree of discontent on the part of subjects, where effectual resistance is hopeless, can encrease of revenue and effective power to the rulers be prevented.[59]

It appears, therefore, that with regard to contiguous colonies or those more readily accessible, there is an argument to be made about their profitable nature.[60] Bentham repeatedly makes the point that distance makes the retention of colonies impossible for both parties; the mother country only ends up with the expense, and the colony suffers from poor governance. When Bentham tries to provide various arrangements to relinquish Spain's colonies, one suggestion he makes is the sale of such colonies to another 'host' country or foreign power. In the Spanish case Bentham suggests the United States because 'they have this great natural advantage – vicinity'.[61]

Yet another indication that distance is integral to the colonial question, Bentham states:

> So much for the profit side: now as to the loss side: namely the expence. The expence, being the first in the order of time, should on that account have been in the first instance brought to view. But in the profit, real or imaginary, you have the inducement – the sole inducement to the expence.
>
> Barbary is next door – Morocco is next door. Distance much less from Spain to many a part of Barbary, to many a part of Morocco, than from many a part of Spain to many another. Distance, meaning in place: and the distance in time abridged by that element which has no bad roads in it.
>
> Compared with a voyage to Peru or Chili, what is the length of voyage to any part of Barbary or Morocco? What therefore the expence of it?[62]

It would be incorrect to infer from these passages that Bentham endorsed the possession of colonies if the distance issue could be solved, but it is important to recognize his argument that without the expense, the arguments against are substantially reduced.

Otherwise, colonies will not do. *Rid Yourselves of Ultramaria* is specifically addressed to Spaniards (of Peninsular Spain, not Ultramaria) because it makes constant reference to the constitutional code. It is striking that Bentham does this not only because his argument readily refers to potential abuses of power in Ultramaria, as if the average Spaniard, so far away, would even give such abuse a moment's thought.[63] Additionally Bentham repeats often the 'fact' that Ultramarians would never pay taxes to support Peninsular Spaniards, either because constitutionally Ultramarians are Peninsular Spain's equal (so one cannot be expected to support the other)[64] or that Ultramarians would never submit to such taxes.[65]

Bentham relies upon the assumption that some or all Ultramarians are familiar with the Spanish constitutional code and would recognize their subjection as a blatant contravention. On this basis, if no other, Ultramarians would inevitably feel inclined to revolt.[66] Never mind the hypocrisy of Spain: 'Think of the task which, on this occasion, Spain has set herself – think of her undertaking to keep in subjection a population more than equal to her own, and in the teeth of those precepts of equality which, by Articles 4 and 13, she is professing all the while.'[67] Lastly, Bentham provides an interesting and paradoxical argument as to why relinquishment would be profitable for Spain. Spain and its dominions share language, religion, laws, and customs,[68] and for these reasons free trade should automatically result between parties who have so much in common.[69] Bentham could not say it more succinctly than he does here: 'in *language, institutions, customs, religion*, she is already yours'.[70]

Bentham's argument here is important not only as a reason to emancipate, but also as a clue as to whom he is actually speaking. The determination of whether Bentham is concerned about the welfare of the colonists per se (people descended from Spain), the natives, or both is very difficult to discern. Bentham writes so imprecisely at times that it is unclear whether he is discussing the Spanish colonists or the colonized indigenous peoples, or both. Nonetheless, his audience, or at least the people about whom he is concerned, is crucial to Boralevi's argument regarding Bentham's overall stance on the question of colonies. As noted in *Emancipate Your Colonies!*, although he occasionally spoke of 'colonists', at the same time he spoke of some colonies requiring a continued servility. Likewise in *Rid Yourselves of Ultramaria*, precisely who it is that Bentham intends to emancipate is often unclear and confusing. While Bentham argues that trade with one's former colonies is virtually guaranteed because of similar cultural background, he also refers to those in the colonies as strangers: 'True it is, that in the language of the Code, these strangers and you are designated by one and the same name: these strangers – for kinsmen as they are many of them, yet so distant are they in kindred as well as in place – so distant and so compleatly unknown, they are not the less strangers.'[71] In this case, only 'many' of these strangers are even kinsmen; an obvious acknowledgement that 'others' exist and are considered as well.

According to the Spanish constitutional code, these strangers would also have the power, by virtue of their numbers, to determine the constitution of the Cortes. 'Taken to the extent of the claim, supposing the design declared in the Constitutional Code effected, the effect would be to place in the Assembly of Cortes sitting in Spain, at present composed of Members the majority of whom are natives of the Peninsula, chosen by the inhabitants of the Peninsula, i.e. in the plain, original and true sense of the word *Spaniards*, a majority composed of, or at any rate chosen by, Ultramarians.'[72] Although Bentham is speaking to the colonists he includes the native population:

> But in these same three hundred years, the population of Spain has not, for any thing that appears, experienced any encrease.
> *Even if the Aborigines and the imported Negroes be deducted, still the encrease will be found very considerable.*[73] [My emphasis]

Bentham was not so ignorant as not to know that the colonies were populated prior to colonization. The issue of whom Bentham is speaking of in these passages is important because it does, as Boralevi claims, partly explain his alleged ambivalence. However, the principle of utility is also not adequate as an explanatory tool. Although he desires emancipation for almost everybody, Bentham was fearful of the consequences of granting freedom to peoples about whom he was less informed. He cannot help but propose a means by which some may seek emancipation and others may not. However, the difficulty lies in the fact that the people who 'deserve' emancipation and the people who would 'benefit' from further guidance live in the same area. He cannot resolve this.

Bentham's emphasis on the ancestral linkage and a common political culture is also significant. It is an integral part of his argument for the emancipation of the Spanish colonies. Implicit in this argument, however, is a need for colonization in the first place. The only way that these links originated was through the process of colonization. The benefit of emancipation requires this link to be established, otherwise continued mastery is required until such time that circumstances become more favourable. Again, this scenario reveals Bentham's need to ensure security; this is defined and maintained by the cultural values imposed upon the colonies at conquest. This security would also, he hoped, guarantee appropriate, culturally-instituted behaviours in international relations once the colonies are released.

Even though Bentham has acknowledged in previous works, some of the benefits of colonial possession, he now gives the occasional nod to the more sinister reasons why most mother countries do not emancipate colonies. Most detail is provided on the advantages colonies offer to the ruling few. This discussion still results in a rather short letter, which is suggestive.[74] It is obvious that Bentham is not oblivious to arguments of profits for the ruling few, and the subsequent augmentation of their power; he will not, however, give it much time or due. Bentham recognizes the influence of this power but will not address its significance. Perhaps he assumes that more time devoted to arguments against colonies will ultimately convince his readers of his position, but it is difficult to tell. With all of his efforts to claim the opposite, even Bentham cannot deny that thus far, colonial powers were not in the habit of relinquishing the dominions.

> If *after* the relinquishment of her dominion over that portion of English America, the quantity of money or money's worth drawn by England from that same region through the channel of trade – and this too even the very next year – was greater than *before*, – what should render the advantage less to Spain, in the event of her relinquishing *her* portion of dominion in that same distant continent? – *If so ample was the advantage where the emancipation was the result of sad necessity, extorted from adversary by adversary as the price of peace*, [my emphasis] – how much more ample may it not be expected to be, if, as here proposed, it be the result of spontaneous wisdom and benevolence, given freely and gratuitously, by kinsman to kinsman – by friend to friend – for hope of mutual encrease?[75]

And later:

> 'Yes' (men would be saying of you to one another) Yes: they gave up what they could not help giving up: but they keep every thing they are able to keep: the bad principle, the morbid appetite, with the folly of seeking to gratify it, still remain: still are they on the watch for every chance of gratifying it: of gratifying it, once more, at our expence. No: the peace they have been pretending to give us is, in their hearts, no better than a truce: for tormenting us again and again nothing is wanting to them but opportunity: and to eyes so eager, opportunity will be continually presenting itself.[76]

Bentham's only way out of this difficulty is to forward his plea to the 'common' Spaniard,[77] as it is only the people of Spain who could compel their rulers to relinquish the colonies:

> No: neither in this shape nor in any other, on this occasion or any other, without strong and general reluctance, will men in their situation, whoever they may be, make any the smallest sacrifice, of what in *their* eyes are their interests, to yours: to bring them to it must be *your* task: and to this end no peaceable exertion that you can make can be superfluous.[78]

One can only assume that Bentham believes the Spanish people, if at all compelled by the arguments of the ruling few that colonies enhance the power of Spain, will subsequently be compelled by his own counterarguments. But how he expects the Spanish people to rise above arguments of power is remarkable since,

> All this is *human*, and of course more particularly *regal*, nature: pride forbids the confession of miscarriage; love of power forbids the parting with any the least scrap of the fascinating appendage, how troublesome so ever, so long as any the faintest hope of keeping it can be kept.[79]

Given the fact that throughout his writing Bentham is not adverse to admitting the above perspective about humanity, this too can be seen as an excuse for falling back on that which appears to ensure security, both of property and lifestyle.

Bentham ends his essay with a brief look at 'Injury to Spanish Ultramaria from the Claims Made of Dominion Over Her in the Name of Spain'.[80] Much of it repeats previous arguments, but now slightly reflecting Ultramarian interests. He claims that where the previous government was able to keep Ultramarians relatively ignorant of their subjection, the new constitutional code inevitably reveals to them the injustices they have endured.

> While it kept all hands in shackles, the former government kept a gag
> in every mouth, a bandage over all eyes. By the present Constitution,
> these same instruments of tyranny – shackles, gag, and bandage – are
> all cast forth: cast forth not less compeatly [sic] in the one hemisphere
> than in the other.[81]

Bentham had already listed the various reasons for which Ultramarians
would revolt in a previous letter, and he explains these reasons more fully
in this section.[82] Again, the greatest difficulty arises from the vast distance
between government and governed. Distance denies the rights and proper
procedures allowed to all Spaniards: 'In this case – nay in almost all cases
– *distance* suffices of itself to render any thing better than despotism and
misrule impossible.'[83]

Bentham's arguments rarely have a moral perspective since economic
and constitutional considerations always take precedence. At one point,
however, he does resort to an appeal to the colonizers to put themselves
in the place of the colonized: 'think but on the indignation which the bare
anticipation of them would excite in your breasts if you yourselves were
placed in this same situation in which the Code undertakes to place your
kinsmen in Ultramaria'.[84] Finally, it appears that although the scourge of
colonialism was detrimental to those in the colonies (colonists and native
population alike), at least some benefit accrued to those in Spain, albeit a
minority.[85]

Rid Yourselves of Ultramaria was the last substantive essay Bentham
wrote about colonies, but it was not the last we hear from him on the issue.
In 1829 he added a postscript to *Emancipate Your Colonies!*, which
Bowring included in the *Works*. In it Bentham states:

> An argument, that had not as yet presented itself to the view of the
> author when penning the accompanying tract, is furnished by the con-
> sideration of the quantity of the matter of *good*, operating to the effect
> of *corruption*, in the shape of *patronage*.
>
> As a citizen of Great Britain and Ireland, he is thereby confirmed
> in the same opinions, and accordingly in the same wishes. But, as a
> citizen of the British Empire, including the sixty millions already under
> its government in British India, and the forty millions likely to be
> under its government in the vicinity of British India, not to speak of
> the one hundred and fifty millions, as the Russians say, of the con-
> tiguous Empire of China, – his opinions and consequent wishes are
> the *reverse*.[86]

That Bentham was not comfortable with emancipation for all peoples is
now more obvious than ever. Not only does this reflect his age and era,
it also conforms to his need for security and fear of the unknown. Therefore, emancipation of various parts of the British Empire, it became clear,

could only be had by those who have assumed the 'civility' of the mother country.

It is also in this postscript that Bentham mentions Australia and the likelihood that the colonies there would gain independence by the end of that century, adopting the government of a representative democracy.[87] Australia is also the topic for Bentham's last words on the subject of colonies. In 1831 (a year before his death), Bentham wrote a proposal entitled 'Colonization Society Proposal, being a Proposal for the formation of a Joint Stock Company by the name of the Colonization Company on an entirely new principle intituled [sic] the vicinity-maximizing or dispersion-preventing principle'. In it he 'examines all of the features of the proposal thoroughly, from its aims and financing down to the question of providing for the emigrants on the voyage "decent and comfortable bedding during the night and means of exercise and recreation in the daytime"'.[88] Bentham also notes that the colony would provide for an increase in the market of the mother country, a thought that contradicts earlier statements regarding trade limited by capital.[89] But where Winch sees this as a reflection of Bentham's ambivalence, and Boralevi confuses it with earlier comments on penal colonies in New South Wales, it is not difficult to understand from a security standpoint. Such a proposal would take care of any problems of over-population, and mirror the project of the East India Company, an enterprise with which Bentham had little difficulty.[90]

What Winch calls 'ambivalence' Boralevi refers to as a 'change in his opinion'.[91] Even if this change of opinion is the result of the application of the principle of utility, the rationale is still unsatisfactory. The application appears arbitrary. In order to explain this through the role of security or the disappointment-prevention principle, Bentham's arguments no longer need to be considered ambivalent or mere changes of opinion; his arguments are contingent on the extent and quality of security that he considers necessary. In the next chapter, this same trend is evidenced in Bentham's other, lesser known, works on economics.

It is security that distinguishes the civilized man from the "savage", this same savage who is allowed self-determination if the colonizing attitude sees fit, and when such self-determination would not be seen to threaten the existence of the colonizer. Bentham, the liberal, believes in progress and this progress is no less applicable to security than to anything else. As a matter of fact, the progress of civilization is contingent upon the progress of security:

> North America presents to us a most striking contrast. Savage nature may be seen there, side by side with civilized nature. The interior of that immense region offers only a frightful solitude, impenetrable forests or sterile plains, stagnant waters and impure vapours; such is the earth when left to itself. The fierce tribes which rove through those

deserts without fixed habitations, always occupied with the pursuit of
game, and animated against each other by implacable rivalries, meet
only for combat, and often succeed in destroying each other. The beasts
of the forest are not so dangerous to man as he is to himself. But on
the borders of these frightful solitudes, what different sights are seen!
We appear to comprehend in the same view the two empires of good
and evil. Forests give place to cultivated; morasses are dried up, and
the surface, grown firm, is covered with meadows, pastures, domestic
animals, habitations healthy and smiling. Rising cities are built upon
regular plans; roads are constructed to communicate between them;
everything announces that men, seeking the means of intercourse, have
ceased to fear and to murder each other. Harbours filled with vessels
receive all the productions of the earth, and assist in the exchange of
all kinds of riches. A numerous people, living upon their labour in
peace and abundance, has succeeded to a few tribes of hunters, always
placed between war and famine. What has wrought these prodigies?
Who has renewed the surface of the earth? Who has given to man this
domain over nature – over nature embellished, fertilized, and per-
fected? That beneficent genius is *Security*. It is security which has
wrought this great metamorphosis. And how rapid are its operations?
It is not yet two centuries since William Penn landed upon those
savage coasts, with a colony of true conquerors, men of peace, who
did not soil their establishments with blood, and who made themselves
respected by acts of beneficence and justice.[92]

It is a liberal premise that progress can happen at all; however, the basis
for that premise should be equally important. The basis for Bentham is
security, and constant security at that. Not unlike a realist, Bentham realizes
that security issues are ever-present, and even though prosperity may
increase and humanity may progress beyond the war of all against all that
he believes exists among 'savages', the slightest provocation can bring the
structure of security crumbling down again, and Bentham is very conscious
of this.

Notes

1 Jeremy Bentham, *Emancipate Your Colonies!* (London: Effingham Wilson, Royal
   Exchange, 1838), p. 18.
2 Bentham, *The True Alarm*, in *Jeremy Bentham's Economic Writings*, Vol. 3, ed.
   W. Stark (London: George Allen & Unwin, 1952), pp. 142–3.
3 Donald Winch, *Classical Political Economy and Colonies* (London: London
   School of Economics and Political Science, 1965), pp. 25–26.
4 Lea Campos Boralevi, *Bentham and the Oppressed* (Berlin: Walter de Gruyter,
   1984), pp. 121, 122, 130.
5 The American War of Independence marked the beginning of a long succession
   of secessions and independence movements and was therefore the first action
   against colonialism about which Bentham would have been able to offer opinions:

'But when independence for the American states was followed in turn by the emancipation of Latin America from Spain and Portugal and by mass decolonization in the twentieth century, the broader trends of historical explanation emerged and human culpability diminished: the American revolt then appeared as the first in a series of national colonial risings rather than the unique occurrence it had once seemed.' Roy Porter, *England in the Eighteenth Century* (London: The Folio Society, 1998), 459–60.

6 Bentham, *Correspondence*, Vol. I, 1752–1776, ed. Timothy L. S. Sprigge (London: Athalone Press, 1968), Letter to John Lind 2(?) September 1776, pp. 341–4. Bentham also helped Lind compose *Remarks on the Principal Acts of the Thirteenth Parliament of Great Britain* (1775) 'which included a defence of the Government's American policies' (*Correspondence*, Vol. I, p. 161, n2). Later on Bentham had hopes of accompanying George Johnstone, one of three peace commissioners to negotiate with the American Congress in 1778, as his assistant. Johnstone was a naval officer and a member of Parliament who strongly defended his Government's policies. He was very impressed by Bentham's *Fragment on Government* (1776) and on that basis Bentham hoped Johnstone would choose him. Through Bentham's friend John Lind, Johnstone intimated that he was interested in the idea if his first choice was unable to participate. Bentham never heard anything further on the subject. (*Correspondence*, Vol. I, pp. 94–95, n. 2)

7 *Correspondence,* Vol. I, p. 322; Vol. II, pp. 23, 26, 36, 49, 67, 153, 157.

8 Bentham tried to organize a 'colony' with his brother Samuel in Russia, under Prince Potemkin's authority. It was to employ Scottish farm workers from the estate of the economic and agricultural author James Anderson (1739–1808). (*Correspondence*, Vol. III, pp. 270, 285, 287, 291).

9 Werner Stark notes: 'this last section of the intended postscript [of *Defence of Usury*] is of interest because it concerns a topic to which Bentham attributed great importance: colonial policy, or rather colony-holding, of which he was a sworn enemy. The matter, as has been indicated, is more fully expounded in *Colonies and Navy*, a fragment which we shall have to consider in a moment; and it is the sole subject of two pamphlets which he drafted, one addressed to his friends in France – *Emancipate your Colonies* (*Works*, Vol. IV) – and the other to his friends in Spain – *Rid yourselves of Ultramaria*. Bentham's contention – which does not seem to be borne out by the history of the British Empire – is that both mother-country and colony are benefited if the link of dependency is dissolved. His arguments are here conveniently summed up. They are in good part political rather than economic; but there is one economic point which deserves a short glance and scrutiny.

  Bentham claims that if the trade with a colony were given up, the capital formerly invested in it and now freed could be used to greater advantage in Britain, "in the improvement of land".' (Stark, 'Introduction', *Jeremy Bentham's Economic Writings*, Vol. 1, pp. 37–38.) Stark claims that Bentham's arguments are strongly political; he is correct, but only to a degree. Bentham makes the choice to emphasize economic arguments, and this choice is a very political one as will be argued below. His decision adds to the confusion as to how Bentham's works are to be evaluated within the context of international relations theory.

10 Boralevi contends that Bentham only speaks of colonists, and not necessarily the native peoples of the land. It is hard to determine from where she gets this idea; although the native people are not colonists, are they not inhabitants of the colony? Bentham is not clear on this point but there is evidence in future writings that would suggest an acknowledgement of the native population. This will be further discussed below.

11 Bentham, *Defence of Usury*, *Jeremy Bentham's Economic Writings*, Vol. 1, pp. 202–4.
12 Stark, 'Introduction', *Jeremy Bentham's Economic Writings*, Vol. 1, p. 36.
13 *Colonies and Navy*, *Jeremy Bentham's Economic Writings*, Vol. 1, p. 211.
14 Ibid., p. 212.
15 The statement that extent of market is not central to trade actually appears in his next work, *Emancipate Your Colonies!*, but it is already implied here by his emphasis on the importance of the quantity of capital.
16 *Colonies and Navy*, p. 214.
17 Ibid., pp. 215–6.
18 Ibid., p. 218.
19 *Emancipate Your Colonies!* was printed in 1793 but not published until 1830 by Bowring (Vol. IV, pp. 407–418). It was also reprinted as *Canada. Emancipate Your Colonies! An Unpublished Argument, by Jeremy Bentham*, with a dedication to the Right Honourable Lord Viscount Melbourne by 'Philo-Bentham', (London: Effingham Wilson, Royal Exchange, 1838). The latter printing does not include the postscript of 24 June 1829 included in the Bowring edition. Bentham was granted an honorary French citizenship in 1792.
20 *Canada. Emancipate Your Colonies!* p. 1.
21 Ibid., p. 2.
22 Ibid., p. 16. Bentham also distinguishes between 'the people' and 'the good citizens', implying the latter are French and the former the greater population. Either way, at least at this point in the essay, both deserve emancipation. (ibid., p. 4) Later he speaks of the financial burden of maintaining forces to keep the colony under France's subjection: 'to pay the expense of a marine capable of blocking up all their ports, and defending so many vast and distant countries against the rival powers, *with the inhabitants on their side*' (Italics mine, ibid., p. 12); and 'Go then to those colonists, go with liberty on your lips, and with fetters in your hands, go and hear them make this answer. – *Frenchmen, we believe you intend liberty for us strangers, when we have seen you give it to your own brethren.*' (Italics mine, ibid., p. 15).
23 *Emancipate Your Colonies!*, p. 5.
24 It is in *Emancipate Your Colonies!* where Bentham states 'Yes – it is *quantity of capital*, not *extent of market*, that determines the quantity of trade.' (ibid., p. 7).
25 These concepts are further explored in *Rid Yourselves of Ultramaria*.
26 Although the reason why Britain is considered so powerful compared to France is hard to understand; Britain may have lost the United States but it still had numerous other colonies which would undoubtedly reduce Britain's strength as well, according to Bentham's argument.
27 '[*Rid Yourselves of Ultramaria*] is a work of sustained and coherent argument, which builds on those general principles against colonization which Bentham had first outlined at the time of the French Revolution.' Philip Schofield, 'Editorial Introduction', *Colonies, Commerce, and Constitutional Law*, (Oxford: Clarendon Press, 1995), p. xvii.
28 'Of the Balance of Trade' (1801) in *Jeremy Bentham's Economic Writings*, Vol. 3, p. 243.
29 In addition to being a legislative theorist, Bentham's 'career' as an economist approximately spanned the years 1796–1804, and it was only in 1820–1 that he once again took up the pen regarding colonies in order to persuade the Spanish to relinquish their colonies.
30 Stark, 'Introduction', *Jeremy Bentham's Economic Writings*, Vol. 3, p. 43.
31 Ibid., p. 7.
32 Ibid., pp. 45, 47.

33 Ibid., p. 44.
34 *Institute of Political Economy*, Vol. 3, pp. 352–3. 'The capital employed in the exportation and maintenance of the colonists and their stock would, if employed at home, at any rate have added something to the annually growing wealth* [*Bryan Edwards, *The History, Civil and Commercial, of the British Colonies in the West Indies* (1793), Vol. II, p. 260, even in magnifying the utility of colonies, makes the rate of profit upon capital so employed but 7 per Cent: the common calculation gives, for the profit on capital employed within the mother country, 15 per Cent. Whatever capital is bestowed upon this employment, is so much taken from other more lucrative ones.] as well as population, and thence the defencible security of the home territory, by the whole amount of it. Of the produce of the colonists when settled in the colony, it is only a part that would be exported to the mother country and be added to the mass if its wealth.
    In point of wealth and population, Europe has lost by colonies. The only gain, if any, is that which consists in mere enjoyment, and that so far, and no further, as it depends on novelty and variety in regard to the articles or instruments of enjoyment.' Ibid., p. 354.
35 *The True Alarm*, in *Jeremy Bentham's Economic Writings*, Vol. 3, p. 178.
36 *Institute of Political Economy*, in *Jeremy Bentham's Economic Writings*, Vol. 3, p. 353.
37 Ibid., p. 355.
38 Ibid., p. 43.
39 *The True Alarm*', *Jeremy Bentham's Economic Writings*, Vol. 3, p. 141.
40 Ibid., p. 142.
41 *Institute of Political Economy*, in *Jeremy Bentham's Economic Writings*, Vol. 3, p. 178.
42 Ibid., p. 355
43 *The True Alarm*', in *Jeremy Bentham's Economic Writings*, Vol. 3, p. 68.
44 Ibid., p. 193.
45 Earlier in *The True Alarm* Bentham states, but without providing any illuminating examples, that the acquisition of colonies did not increase a nation's wealth more than any other resource. This passage indicates that, even indirectly, colonization through the emigration of men and capital is necessary to the restriction of paper money and therefore to the increase of a nation's wealth.
46 See Boralevi above.
47 UC II.1–12 (c.1818). Provided by Stark, 'Introduction', Vol. 2, p. 69. Donald Jackson writes: 'There was a major change in Bentham's thinking after 1808 ... Traditionally, Bentham had accounted for irrationality in government on the basis of indolence and intellectual ineptitude of individual governors and office holders, but never in terms of general mendacity, improbity, or the influence of what he called *sinister interest* such as he had recently discovered to be the basis of maladministration in the judicial department.' D. Jackson, 'Halevy Reconsidered: The Importance of Bentham's Psychological Epistemology in His "Conversion" to Democracy', (New Orleans: Fifth Congress of the International Society for Utilitarian Studies 1997), p. 4.
48 Bentham states, 'I conclude this Introduction with a more particular reference to my own opinion, as above spoken of, applied as it was, in the only direct purpose of it, to the case of *France*.
    The work, in which the grounds of it are briefly developed, is a pamphlet of 48 8vo pages, headed *Jeremy Bentham* to the *National Convention of France*. Better would it have been characterized by the three words of exhortation that occurr in the first sentence – *Emancipate Your Colonies*. It was printed in the last month of 1792 or the first of 1793: it has incidentally found its way into various hands: but has scarcely ever been exposed to sale. A copy of it was,

along with others of my works, presented to the late Cortes, by which the same regard was paid to it as to your liberties and your welfare.

Among the representatives of your neighbours, those works, such as they are, have not been alike unfortunate.' *Rid Yourselves of Ultramaria*, in *Colonies, Commerce, and Constitutional Law*, ed. Schofield, p. 22.

And earlier: 'I will shew you the same positions maintained by the same arguments, not less than 27 or 28 years ago, by a writer who is not altogether unknown to you . . .' *Emancipation Spanish*, 204.

In her book *Jeremy Bentham: An Odyssey of Ideas, 1748–1832* Mary P. Mack argues 'that Bentham had become a full-fledged democrat and parliamentary reformer by 1790, made a Fabian retreat after 1792, and then resumed his previous position in 1809–10, a view successfully challenged by J. H. Burns in 1966.' Quoted in Jackson, p. 2. If one thought that Bentham had this many reversals of opinion then it might explain the *Emancipate Your Colonies!* and *Rid Yourselves of Ultramaria* connection. However, the argument that he had such reversals appears to be unsubstantiated.

49 *Emancipation Spanish* and *Summary of Emancipate Your Colonies* were earlier drafts of the major work, *Rid Yourselves of Ultramaria*: '[*Colonies, Commerce, and Constitutional Law*] also includes two earlier versions of the work, which represent significant stages in its drafting, and form discrete, coherent, and complete essays in their own right . . . "Emancipation Spanish", which Bentham had completed by the middle of July 1820; the second is "Summary of Emancipate Your Colonies", which began as a précis of 'Emancipation Spanish', but came to rival it in length, and which is reproduced in the state it had reached by the end of August 1820.' (Schofield, 'Editorial Introduction', *Colonies, Commerce* p. xvii.) Although these two previous drafts do constitute essays in their own right, their arguments of interest are contained within the major work. Evaluation of Bentham's ideas during this period are therefore confined to *Rid Yourselves of Ultramaria*.

50 Schofield, pp. xvi–vii.

51 *Rid Yourselves of Ultramaria*, p. 30, n2.

52 *Emancipate your colonies! Addressed to the National Convention of France, Aô 1793, Shewing the Uselessness and Mischievousness of Distant Dependencies to an European State.* In Rights, Representation, and Reform: Nonsense Upon Stilts and Other Writings on the French Revolution edited by Philip Schofield, Catherine Pease-Watkin and Cyprian Blamires. Oxford: Clarendon Press, 2002. p. 305.

53 *Rid Yourselves of Ultramaria*, p. 115.

54 *Rid Yourselves of Ultramaria*, p. 25.

55 However, the government that best exemplified the Greatest Happiness principle was 'the Anglo-American States' (ibid., p. 27). Bentham also provides a lengthy explanation of sinister versus universal interest in his second letter to the Spanish people (pp. 31–53).

56 Ibid., p. 52.

57 Ibid., pp. 55–61.

58 It is interesting to point out that Bentham's arguments are contingent on the fact that Spanish citizens, in general, are supposed to be even remotely aware of what their constitution says. He often argues that with reference to particular parts of the constitutional code, Penninsular and/or Ultramarian Spaniards would not stand for such behaviour. What is the likelihood that the average citizen had the reading and comprehension skills required to make such judgements?

59 Ibid., pp. 64–65.

60 It also appears that today it would be more profitable and beneficial to have a dominion since, 'Upon what theory – upon what hypothesis – can the expectation

of money to be drawn from Ultramaria into Spain have been grounded? That Ultramaria and Spain are contiguous; that Ultramaria is upon wheels, and may be drawn and pushed off at pleasure; *or that between them is stretched a rope along which letters may be passed in no time*' (italics mine, ibid., p. 104). Apart from Bentham anticipating the invention of email, it is again apparent that the possibility of retaining colonies becomes desirable if the colonies are close by.

61 Ibid., p. 151.
62 Ibid., p. 188.
63 Ibid., p. 69. Bentham reveals how difficult it is for Ultramarians to protest against abuses of power, given the distance.
64 Ibid., pp. 55, 104.
65 Ibid., p. 71.
66 This is, again, noting that much of Ultramaria had already gained independence and the rest were going to be flatly denied it if the Cortes had any kind of control.
67 Ibid., p. 110.
68 Ibid., p. 118.
69 For example: '*Customs*, which, in so far as they stand clear of laws and institutions, are free, have in the nature of the case, on that account, a better chance for permanence. The *fandango*, having neither been made obligatory nor been instituted by law, might still continue in use, when every law and every institution had long been changed.' (Ibid., p. 119). Bentham's emphasis on common ancestry as an incentive for future trade relations is also quite strong (ibid., pp. 120, 127).
70 Ibid., p. 126.
71 Ibid., p. 76.
72 Ibid., p. 77.
73 Ibid., p. 80. Where in one paragraph the Ultramarians are kinsmen, in the next they are strangers. To foment mistrust between the two parties Bentham even goes so far as to say, 'Of him who framed this Article together with Articles . . ., of those by whom it was adopted, what was the persuasion in matters of religion? Not to speak of Catholicism, was it really Christian? Was it not rather Mahometan? Their blood, is it altogether free from Moorish contamination? In their conception, have the female individuals of humankind each of them a soul belonging to it?' (Ibid., p. 173).
74 Ibid., pp. 74–75.
75 Ibid., p. 121. (last italics mine).
76 Ibid., p. 134.
77 Or, at least, the Spaniard who was literate and well versed in constitutional arguments, and in some way capable of influencing the government.
78 Ibid., p. 136.
79 Ibid., p. 137.
80 Ibid., p. 154.
81 Ibid., pp. 154–5.
82 Ibid., p. 73 (Letter 5).
83 Ibid., p. 160. The injustice to the Ultramarians is the inefficacy of appeals when required: 'Oppression follows oppression at the distance of a day: Relief follows oppression at the distance of 365 days: Oppression is a dromedary: Relief, a tortoise.' (Ibid., p. 161).
84 Ibid., p. 164.
85 Ibid., p. 180. 'Known – universally known – that the money, when collected, is – a great part of it – to be sent out of the province, sent to a Distant region, there to constitute, at the expence of the people of the province, the means of luxurious living to a set of utter strangers, whom the greatest part of the people

in the province will never see: in such a state of things, much more watching, and a considerably greater number of watchmen, and those with higher pay, would be necessary, than if there were no such dominion would be thought necessary.' (Ibid.) Again Bentham acknowledges that someone does benefit and profit from the colonies.

86 *Works*, Vol. IV, p. 418.
87 Ibid.
88 Winch, p. 128.
89 Ibid., p. 129.
90 *Emancipate Your Colonies!*, p. 16, and Boralevi, p. 121.
91 Boralevi, p. 124.
92 *The Theory of Legislation*, pp. 118–9.

9 Bentham the International Political Economist

> Maximizing universal security; – securing the existence of, and sufficiency of, the matter of subsistence for all the members of the community; – maximizing the quantity of the matter of abundance in all its shapes; – securing the nearest approximation to absolute equality in the distribution of the matter of abundance, and the other modifications of the matter of property; that is to say, the nearest approximation consistent with universal security, as above, for subsistence and maximization of the matter of abundance: – by these denominations, or for shortness, by the several words *security*, *subsistence*, *abundance*, and *equality*, may be characterized the several specific ends, which in the character of means stand next in subordination to the all embracing end – the greatest happiness of the greatest number of the individuals belonging to the community in question.[1]

Bentham's economic writings are rarely, if ever, highlighted by international relations scholars. When Bentham's work is referred to it is usually with reference to his writings in international law. Although some of his ideas in economics are familiar to us, this work has not been adequately explored from the international relations perspective to show its development and evolution. This chapter shows how Bentham believed economics to be fundamental to the peace and harmony of a state; economics dictate whether a state tends towards peace or war, and are contingent upon security of expectation, or the disappointment-prevention principle. If Bentham's writings on international political economy are not more significant than his thinking in international law, they are at least equally important and deserve to be considered as a major part of his contribution.

Bentham's work in economics is somewhat familiar to international relations scholars, but it is his writings in the area of colonial policy that are best known. This makes sense given the fact that *A Plan for an Universal and Perpetual Peace* is partially composed of the essay *Colonies and Navy*. After briefly discussing the economic theories current in Bentham's time, and examining the basis of Bentham's economic thinking, this chapter will continue with a survey of his views on topics such as free trade, the costs of war, and economics as it is linked to security.

The discourse of economics in the late eighteenth and early nineteenth centuries:

Many contemporary IPE scholars refer to at least three 'traditions', 'ideologies', or 'theories' of economics: Liberalism, Mercantilism, and Marxism.[2] These are often recognized as the springboards for current theoretical approaches, as like-minded descendents, such as rational choice theory emerging from liberalism[3], or critical evolutions.[4] Debates on the efficacy, accuracy, and salience of these categories are reflected in Bentham's work but to a significant extent they hinder the analysis of Bentham's work. Bentham was familiar with mercantilism which had a foothold in the political economy of states, and liberalism was still the fledgling tradition to which Bentham was to contribute. It is important to have an adequate understanding of these two political economy approaches as they affected, and were affected by, Jeremy Bentham's work.

Most of Bentham's economic writings were reactions to the practices of the government of his day, practices that, more often than not, reflected the mercantilist approach. This approach dictated the supremacy of the state over economic activities. Robert Gilpin, writing about it many years later, describes mercantilism:

> All [mercantilists] ascribe to the primacy of the state, of national security, and of military power in the organization and functioning of the international system. Within this general commitment two basic positions can be discerned. Some [mercantilists] consider the safeguarding of national economic interests as the minimum essential to the security and survival of the state. For lack of a better term, this generally defensive position may be called 'benign' mercantilism. On the other had, there are those [mercantilists] who regard the international economy as an arena for imperialist expansion and national aggrandizement. This aggressive form may be termed 'malevolent' mercantilism.[5]

Jacob Viner's oft-quoted passage notes that mercantilism reflects the historical and social context in which it was practised, but there are characteristics of this approach which have remained constant:

> I believe that practically all mercantilists, whatever the period, country, or status of the particular individual, would have subscribed to all of the following propositions: (1) wealth is an absolutely essential means to power, whether for security or for aggression; (2) power is essential or valuable as a means to the acquisition or retention of wealth; (3) wealth and power are each proper ultimate ends of national policy; (4) there is long-run harmony between these ends, although in particular circumstances it may be necessary for a time to make economic sacrifices in the interest of military security and therefore also of long-run prosperity.[6]

A central feature in the realization of mercantilist goals is the institution of industrialization, or rather the establishment of manufactures.[7] Doing so eliminates the necessity of the state having to rely on others for products essential to state-building and survival. The balance of trade and the accumulation of precious metals as stores of wealth are equally important. It becomes necessary for the state to impose various tariffs and trade barriers upon exported material in order to persuade domestic consumers to focus on domestically manufactured products. As noted above, the pursuit of industrialization (wealth and power) is intrinsically and positively linked to military security; 'it is the basis of military power and central to national security in the modern world.'[8] The mercantilist perspective, as an IPE perspective, is closely related to the international relations theory tradition of realism. Inter-state relations are inherently conflictual, and in this case, economic relations are not based on mutual state interest. It was to the mercantilist approach that Adam Smith, Jeremy Bentham and David Ricardo responded. The liberal perspective was in its infancy at this time, but was on its way to being one of the most influencial economic and moral discourses in the Western world.

Where the state once reigned supreme, the individual now takes hold as the primary unit of analysis. To allow free and unfettered competition to take place between individuals in markets is to create an environment where a 'natural' balance occurs, and 'utility' is maximized for all. The state is reduced to a mechanism for the maintenance of law and order, ensuring that competition between individuals remains free and unfettered: 'Liberalism is thus permeated with a concern for enhancing the freedom and welfare of individuals; it proposes that humankind can employ reason better to develop a sense of harmony of interest among individuals and groups within the wider community, domestic or international.'[9] Freedom is expressed through the acquisition of private property and the ability to build capital and profit without state intervention. Economically speaking this means that the market ought to be allowed to function and fluctuate as demand and supply see fit. In this way the 'natural' balance assents itself.

Given the fact that things do not always function ideally, liberals do not deny the state any opportunity to intervene at all; there can be occasions where intervention is warranted: 'Liberal economists do accept that there may be a case for some state intervention to correct market imperfections, but only if the state has sufficient knowledge to do this, and if administrative costs are not too high.'[10] This is still a much more qualified and restricted intervention than allowed by mercantilism, and it is a crucial differentiation point between the liberal and mercantilist approach.

At the international level, where the realist/mercantilist sees competition between states resulting in an insecure, fractured, anarchical and potentially war-torn environment, the liberal sees individual competition continuing internationally, and actually promoting peace by generating and encouraging mutual interests. Such 'free' trade and the attendant increase in communication would ultimately lead to each economic arena (state, firm or individual) providing its particular good or sct of goods at the cheapest possible cost, allowing all individuals to obtain a variety of goods, for the lowest prices, from among the various economic arenas participating in this trade regime.

> To give the monopoly of the home-market to the produce of domestic industry, in any particular art or manufacture, is in some measure to direct private people in what matter they ought to employ their capitals, and must, in almost all cases, be either a useless or hurtful regulation. If the produce of domestic can be brought there as cheap as that of foreign industry, the regulation is evidently useless. If it cannot, it must generally be hurtful. It is the maxim of every prudent master of a family, never to attempt to make at home what it will cost him more to make than buy.[11]

The belief that certain interests should be protected is not consistent with a liberal perspective. The less interference in the organization and function of the market, the better life is for everyone.

Establishing economic policy

> The underlying idea of it was, of course, to be the greatest-happiness principle, and the greatest happiness of the race was, in his opinion, to be achieved by establishing universal security, guaranteeing subsistence, maximizing abundance, and reducing, as far as possible, inequality . . . security and equalization of property are of paramount importance to the economist.[12]

Security, subsistence, abundance, and equality (or more accurately, the reduction of inequalities) are all subordinate ends of Bentham's universal principle of utility, or greatest-happiness principle. According to Bentham, these four components are essential to ensuring any one human being's happiness, and they ought to be considered constantly by those who engineer the economic policies of the state.

Bentham's approach to wealth and the accumulation thereof was quite simple; wealth was constrained by the amount of capital available and the particular use made of that capital.[13] That wealth is dependent on the amount of capital available is a crucial 'given' in Bentham's work; it justifies, if not demands, the relinquishing of colonies and is used in his arguments against prohibitory trade practices. The limitations of capital and the ways in which a community can increase wealth are therefore fundamental to Bentham's recommendations.

Bentham's view of the role of wealth is also integrally linked to security, both with regard to prosperity and also, and more importantly, to a state's defence.

> The enhancement of wealth is one of the most legitimate and one of the most reasonable ends which a government can have in view. In the polity of Sparta which excluded money, the legislator did not by any means exclude the augmentation of wealth: wealth is not only a means of enjoyment, but a means of security and [of adding to the] population: the more products there were, the more consumers: the more citizens, the more arms there were for the defence of the city.
>
> The encrease of wealth, its encrease as well as its preservation, is then an object which should, under all systems of government, attract the attention of the legislators. The encrease of money would be [an] equally proper [object] if money were wealth: but money is not wealth ... the augmentation of wealth will be equal to the [national] production minus the portion consumed for subsistence, for enjoyment, for security, and the part put in reserve for the purposes of future reproduction. The encrease of production is thus the primary aim ... And yet it is money, and not wealth, exchange and production, which has been the object of the solicitude of government.[14]

Wealth provides a state with security, not only for material comfort but also crucially for defence. Wealth, according to Bentham, is best understood in terms of how it is used: as subsistence, defence and enjoyment.[15]

> [The] uses of the matter of wealth [are]: 1. provision for subsistence – present subsistence, and security in respect of future; 2. provision for security in respect of defence, viz. against (*a*) external adversaries, (*b*) internal adversaries, and (*c*) calamities, to which, without human design, the community is exposed; 3. provision for enjoyment, viz. mere enjoyment, as far as distinguishable from that share, which is the natural, and more or less inseparable, accompaniment of subsistence and security.[16]

It is important to note the evident overlap of concepts between the uses of wealth and the subordinate ends of the greatest-happiness principle. Economics includes a distinct security feature; an economically viable state, and its defence, is expected by those residing within the state. The principle of utility seeks to ensure the ends of subsistence, abundance, equality, and security, which can only be met by integrating the interests of the community with an expectation of state security. Bentham expresses the importance of the interconnectedness of political and economic concerns in his discussion of political economy:

It may be said, there is a science distinct from every other, which is called *political* economy: the mind can abstractly consider everything which concerns the wealth of nations, and form a general theory concerning it: but I do not see that there can exist a code of laws concerning political economy, distinct and separate from all the other codes. The collection of laws upon this subject would only be a mass of imperfect shreds, drawn without distinction from the whole body of laws.

Political economy, for example, has reference to the penal laws, which create the species of offences which have been called *offences against population*, and *offences against the national wealth*.

Political economy would be found connected with the international code by treaties of commerce, and with the financial code by the taxes, and their effects upon the public wealth.[17]

Security is linked to economics; not just the security of wealth, but also the security of the state, as political economy impinges upon penal and international codes, among others.

Because security is such an integral part of the legislator's role, and is a pivotal concept in our understanding of theories of international political economy, it plays a great part in trying to determine Bentham's contributions to the field. Although subsistence, security, abundance and equality are subordinate ends of the greatest-happiness principle, they also affect, and are affected by, one another. It is this causal chain, as Bentham presents it, that becomes problematic and adds to the difficulty in recreating the perspective through which Bentham views international politics.

The responsibility of the legislator lies in the establishment and maintenance of security[18] and in 'the enhancement of wealth.'[19] As a matter of fact, '[T]he encrease of wealth, its encrease as well as its preservation, is then an object which should, under all systems of government attract the attention of the legislators.'[20] If this is the case, just how broad are the legislator's parameters in handling the economy, for the purpose of 'encrease' and 'preservation'?

Bentham's causal chain functions in this manner: continually improving security breeds opulence which, in turn, breeds populousness. Therefore security is directly responsible for the success of another subordinate end, abundance, which is composed of both opulence and populousness.[21] Populousness is advantageous to security from a defence point of view; a state benefits from the increased troop potential. Security, abundance and equality are all dependent upon subsistence as the population must be able to survive to thrive. At the same time, subsistence is dependent upon security since a population cannot take advantage of subsistence without some level of security.

Assuming 'adequate' security is established and opulence increases, a problem arises. Although populousness is a result of opulence, Bentham also argues that increased populousness results in decreased opulence.[22]

In essence, the two factors which make up abundance actually work against each other; as populousness increases, opulence decreases, and as populousness decreases, opulence increases. However, security benefits from increases in both, since opulence leads to a greater proportion of income allowed for luxury goods (which are easily exchangeable for defence measures,[23]) and increased populousness provides for more troops. Finally, equality is affected by, and affects, the other ends such that, according to Bentham, equality is reduced as opulence increases, but, as inequality increases, security is reduced.[24]

Through these assumptions, associations, and causal links, Bentham has established a precarious and often contradictory arrangement that requires an intricate balancing act of the subordinate ends for the principle of utility to have any ability to function. Inherent in these subordinate ends, and in the greatest-happiness principle itself, is a notion of progress. In this sense this elaborate arrangement is liberal in its intentions. However, it is also difficult to avoid the importance of security and how it must pervade a substantive portion of a community's life; it is necessary to establish and increase opulence, but then also to reduce inequality and maintain subsistence. The question is: when does the notion of security traverse the boundary between that required for the liberal thinker, and that required by the mercantilist? Mercantilism focuses on national security; the benefactor of security is the state. The liberal provides security for the individual to carry out, safely and freely, her or his activities.[25] It is difficult to ignore the pervasiveness of security in Bentham's system. Does it really differ from mercantilist requirements? Security and the increase of wealth are the purview of the legislator (who is part of the state mechanism), and security is fundamental to the attainment and maintenance of the subordinate ends, and therefore to the greatest-happiness principle. It can be argued that the principle of utility must necessarily be under the strict guidance of the state (or legislator). This argument speaks to the development of the disappointment-prevention principle, which articulates Bentham's need to intervene in the political system to ensure security of expectation.[26] The subordinate ends strive to meet the community's expectations for subsistence, abundance, and to a certain degree, equality. Ensuring the expectation of these ends produces the greatest happiness for the greatest number. Bentham's emphasis on security is clear, and begs the question: to what extent does this emphasis on security for the state impinge on the state's economic position with regard to other states?

Government interference

A substantive distinction between the mercantilist and liberal perspectives is the role, or lack thereof, of the government in economic activity. The extent to which Bentham advocates government interference, and under what circumstances, provides us with further insight into Bentham's thinking and his position on this 'theoretical continuum.

Security is fundamental to the mercantilist perspective, but is also well entrenched within Bentham's thinking, as it is the primary, subordinate end of the greatest happiness principle. Security is the primary goal of the legislator, as it is intrinsic not only to the safety and freedom of the individuals composing the community, but also to the increase of wealth.[27]

> [B]y what means and how far the comparatively inferior ends of extra-security for subsistence, opulence, and equality might be attained in the utmost degree of perfection without prejudice to the superior interests of security, in comparison of which every other blessing is but a feather in the political scale.[28]

Bentham's tone is realist, but one might argue that security is equally necessary for the purposes of liberty, and for liberalism. Although security is paramount, it exists for the individual and not the state. This point is apparent in Bentham's work, but not continuously. Additionally, the example of another subordinate end of utility, equality, which cannot be achieved under conditions of extensive liberty, illustrates Bentham's struggle. In this case Bentham attempts a balancing act between notions of liberty and equality, especially as they relate to security, which provides much ambiguity and confusion in the interpretation of his work.

Nevertheless, Bentham appears to be the consummate liberal, given his well-known position on government intervention as an evil. It is still a necessary evil, and most of Bentham's work is directed towards the legislator and how he ought to legislate. Ideally, the areas, according to Bentham, where the legislator, and hence government, has no authority, are the following:

> If the end could be accomplished without any interference on his part, so much the better: and so much as will be done without his interference, so much he will [if he is wise] suffer to be done. The whole course of legislation, though a necessary evil, is still an evil: the legislator can not stir, but what he does is felt in the shape of hardship and coercion somewhere.[29]

With regard to economics, 'Government ought not to give bounties, much [less enforce] prohibitions &c, for [the] encrease of wealth, as they can't encrease wealth because they can't encrease capital.'[30] These thoughts are consistent with liberal ideals, but to what extent does Bentham play these ideals through?

In *Institute of Political Economy*, certain ambiguities come into play as Bentham, although adamant about the troublesome nature of government interference, qualifies this position in a small, but obviously significant paragraph:

> That the uncoerced and unenlightened propensities and powers of individuals are not adequate to the end without the controul and guidance of the legislator is a matter of fact of which the evidence of history, the nature of man, and the very existence of political society are so many proofs.[31]

It is not necessary to immediately conclude that Bentham advocates total government control of individual action, but it is understandable that many Bentham scholars are ambivalent about the extent of Bentham's liberal ideals. Another question is raised when Bentham, throughout his economic work, discusses the four subordinate ends to the greatest-happiness principle; subsistence, abundance, security, and equality (or the minimization of inequality).[32] These ends are very similar to the ends or uses of wealth: subsistence, enjoyment, security, and 'encrease'.[33] A circular argument appears in Bentham's use of the four subordinate ends. Security plays a primary role, the other ends are dependent upon it, especially opulence, which is directly related to the generation of wealth; security is also the central focus of government intervention, as the purpose is to alleviate as much mischief and crime as possible which would interfere in the creation and accumulation of wealth. Under proper legislation, a community would find itself in a condition of continually improving security,[34] which leads, in turn to increasing opulence.[35] Opulence is central to the *relative* wealth of the nation, as the population of the community increases, opulence decreases, or when the population decreases, opulence increases: 'opulence is *relative* wealth, relation being had to population: it is the ratio of wealth to population'.[36] In Bentham's scheme wealth and happiness are close to being the same thing. It is possible to extrapolate broad parameters for the legislator, meaning government interference in the economy, as the 'guarantor' of wealth enhancement, and therefore happiness. This is no longer a reflection of a liberal position.

International trade

Bentham did not devote much time to the idea of foreign trade.[37] However, in the places where he does address this question, the emphasis is on the unnecessary and destructive quality of prohibitive measures, or any measures at all for that matter, which are effected by government to influence foreign trade. Bentham's ideas on foreign trade were remarkably consistent. On this topic he differs very little from his predecessor, Adam Smith, and his ideas are often repeated *Manual of Political Economy* (1795), to *Institute of Political Economy* (1804), and finally in *Observations on the Restrictive and Prohibitory Commercial System* (1821):

It may be laid down as a universal maxim, that the system of commercial restriction is always either useless or mischievous; or rather mischievous in every case, in a less degree, or in a greater degree. In the judgement of the purchaser, or the consumer, the goods discouraged must be either better than those which are protected, or not: if not better, (of course better for a fixed equivalent,) they will not be bought even though no prohibition exist: here then is uselessness, or mischief in the lesser degree. But the case, and the only probable case, in which the fictitious encouragement will be applied, is that where the goods excluded are better, or in other words cheaper, than those sought to be protected: here is unqualified mischief, mischief in the greater degree.

[...]

The persons for whom this favour is intended, what title have they, what title can they ever have, to such a preference; to a benefit to which a correspondent injury, not to say injustice, to others, – an injury, an injustice to such an extent, – is unavoidably linked?

And in point of numbers, what are the favoured when compared with the disfavoured? – Answer, The few; the few always served, or meant to be served, at the expense of the many.[38]

As a result, the nation imposing the prohibitory measures falls prey to higher costs, inferior quality, reduced demand for home-produced products, loss of tax on those products, increased smuggling, increased animosity from foreigners, and increased animosity toward the nation's ruling few from 'the subject many'.[39]

In the works that touch on foreign trade (*Manual of Political Economy, Of the Balance of Trade, Defence of a Maximum, Institute of Political Economy*, and *Observations on the Restrictive and Prohibitory Commercial System*) Bentham provides a number of interesting (although not extensive) arguments against mercantilist practices. He frequently demands that trade be allowed to proceed on its own, such that as little government intervention as possible may take place. He argues against bounties on production and exportation. In the case of the former, Bentham discussed the inefficacy of supporting a trade with bounties; the only way a trade would be truly successful and not burden the community in which it is being carried out is to let it function on its own. This can particularly be seen with bounties on exportation since, as Bentham states, this means a loss to the community exporting the goods and

'is a continuance for getting foreigners slily to receive tribute of [the exporting state] without their knowing of the matter' . . . In the instance of the bounty given on exportation, no advantage can be reaped by anybody in the nation in any case: in any case, whatever is given is either so much sunk and wasted as if it had been thrown into the sea, or else given to foreigners.[40]

Bentham is very concerned with the state as a whole, and not just the individuals who compose it. Government policies affect the state negatively where prohibitory measures are concerned.

Anticipating twentieth-century opinions, Bentham refutes the notion that one state's gain in trade is always at the expense of another's loss: he argued that since no one gives away their produce for nothing, any trade must result in some gain for all. It does not matter that one nation's earnings are greater than those of another: that both have increased wealth is what is important.[41] This relates to Bentham's discussion of the balance of trade:

> By *balance of trade* is meant the excess, in terms of value, of the goods exported out of the country over the value of the goods imported . . . But is not long and positive experience against this theory? Taking a country as a whole and over a certain length of time, there cannot exist what is called a *losing* trade.[42]

The mercantilists insist on using notions such as favourable or unfavourable balances of trade. Bentham claims it is a deception used for political rather than economic reasons:

> Another distinction which is no less necessary and no less difficult to bear in mind, is that between what is called the balance of trade and the balance or difference of profit or loss in the books of this or that person engaged in trade. The term *favourable balance* does not mean the same thing in its political and in its commercial sense: it has not the same significance. A merchant and indeed all merchants may have carried on a trade more lucrative than ever before in the same period in which what is called the balance of trade has been unfavourable. They may in the same way have carried on a trade less lucrative than ever before in the same period in which the balance of trade has been favourable.[43]

The stockpiling of gold and silver is crucial to the mercantilist, and Bentham finds difficulty with this practice as well. As he puts it, 'If an individual has need of money, it is to exchange it for all the things which he likes. Would he regard it as a favour if, to the possession of the money, you were to add the stipulation that he must never spend it?'[44] To Bentham, wealth is not solely composed of precious metals, but of all goods that are produced and exchanged.[45] If the legislator has a role to play here, since wealth enhancement is part of the legislator's jurisdiction, it does not include imposing taxes, barriers, or incentives allegedly to assist the home market.[46]

Bentham devotes one of his chapters, in *On the Balance of Trade* among other essays, to arguments against the mercantile system. In this chapter Bentham argues against the accumulation of money as an end unto itself. He considers this the same as granting an individual a sum of money with 'the stipulation that he must never spend it'.[47] In this chapter Bentham states that money has only one purpose – exchange. Hoarding money is an 'absurdity' and serves no other purpose than to disrupt the peace between states, causing commerce to be interrupted and real wealth to dry up at source while this 'phantom' is pursued.[48]

It is true that the above represents the bulk of ideas Bentham had to offer on the topic of foreign trade, but as in so many of the issues he addressed, there are always exceptional instances. Bentham would curtail export in the event of a shortage, and more so to prevent any insurrection and 'various mischiefs' that would probably occur due to a lack of supply. Under these circumstances it would be logical and necessary for the government to forbid export since that supply would be needed in the home market.[49] Additionally, Bentham advocates magazining, not only by individuals[50] but by government as well, so that 'you are sure you have'.[51] If a country has the forethought to have full magazines, then any restriction upon trade would again be unnecessary. Such trade measures are in any case less desirable since these regulations cost money and do not provide the same level of security as stockpiled supplies in magazines. To what extent does this differ from the mercantilist practice of stocking up on precious metals? It is true that Bentham is not hoarding gold and silver for the security of the nation, but rather he hoards corn for the same purpose. Is the difference really so great?

Werner Stark alerts his readers to some notes made by Bentham while writing *Manual of Political Economy*. In gathering ideas for his treatise Bentham compiled some thoughts about 'eligible modes of encouragement' on the part of government. Stark points out:

> The one deals with technological problems in the narrower sense of the work, the other rather with questions of export technique and financial steering. Here is the former list of ideas: '[1.] Inventing methods of applying the natural *primum mobiles* with encreased advantage: *1*. Men's force. *2*. Animal. *3*. Water. *4*. Air. *5*. Artifical vision. 2. Diminishing the unhealthiness or disgustfulness of certain trades' (64). Bentham probably thought that the government should foster research along these lines. He did not expect the individual always to play the part of the forlorn hope of technical advancement. The second set of suggestions is still less in line with the free-trade point of view. It reads as follows: '1. Securing of existing markets for manufactory – with or without competition – foreign or colonial. 2. Acquisition of new markets – with or without competition – foreign or colonial.' How far could Bentham have gone in this respect without abandoning the definite position he had taken up in *Colonies and Navy*?[52]

It should be remembered that these are just notes, and did not carry across into the body of Bentham's *Manual*. However, they do provide a useful insight into Bentham's thoughts and the directions that he was apparently willing at some point to take in his designs for ideal economic interaction between states.

A few thoughts on war

Bentham often tries to make plain the horrible and useless nature of war, 'mischief upon the largest scale'.[53] But again, there are frequent occasions where Bentham provides ammunition against his own case. His economic writings frequently point out the necessity and utility of financial planning in the event of war; arguments stating the economic and moral rationale for avoiding war do not eliminate plans to financially manage affairs of state when a war takes place. Among his ideas to safeguard the state's finances is the development of a new Sinking Fund. This fund would compensate for the lack of surplus occurring during war years, and would differ from the old Sinking Fund in that it would be fed by interest and not by principal, the latter 'being a mere fiction, which neither is, nor ever can be, realized'.[54] Additionally Bentham saw a context for his annuity note proposal in discussions regarding war and peace. His rather bizarre and very complicated plan consisted of circulating annuities instead of fixed-value bank notes, such that the value of the annuities, which were to be used daily, consisted of a different value each day they were used. A table would be provided on the annuity note which would indicate the value of the note that day for the convenience of the persons conducting financial transactions, from buying simple foodstuffs to complex stock transactions. These new notes could be simultaneously currency and capital, depending on the need of the moment. Bentham's intention, by issuing these notes, was to increase national wealth and eradicate the national debt. To support his plan against arguments of increased inflation, Bentham used the example of peace and war to illustrate how his annuity notes were to be used; in times of war the notes would act as currency since the government of the day would be required to hoard as much of the scarce cash as possible to finance the high expenditure of war, whereas in times of peace the notes would be withdrawn from circulation as they would be primarily used for purposes of investment.[55] Bentham supposed his system would work so smoothly that excess capital or currency would never become a problem.

Whether a state is at war or peace is secondary to the circulating annuities proposal, however it provides an interesting insight into the scope of Bentham's thinking. As much as he had written against the efficacy of war, he was enough of a realist to be prepared for it, at least financially. If all else failed at least the state would not become bankrupt in the process. Bentham deals with modern warfare as a financial problem, taking all of a state's resources into account in times of conflict, anticipating the development of 'total war'.

Bentham's contrasting views are remarkable. While often echoing the liberal notions of his mentor Adam Smith, and fervently arguing against state intervention so that free trade may result, Bentham continually demonstrates that he cannot accept these liberal principles under all circumstances. First and foremost security, and security of expectation or disappointment prevention, must be adequately maintained. This may, or may not, involve state intervention. The point is that the liberal notion of non-interference in economic questions is not the driving force behind Bentham's initiatives, it is only a result under conditions where security needs are adequately met, and expectation can be enhanced by free-trade practices. When expectation is reduced by the same practices, or if preparations for war warrant it, mercantilist practices come into play through magazining, or directing resources towards defence needs. In either case the disappointment-prevention principle is the key to understanding Bentham's ambivalence and inconsistency in his work.

Notes

1 Bentham, The Philosophy of Economic Science, in Economic Writings, ed. W. Stark, Vol. 1, p. 92.
2 The latter, Marxism, is not applicable in Bentham's case, as Marx developed most of his ideas after Bentham's death.
3 George T. Crane and Abla Amawi, The Theoretical Evolution of International Political Economy: A Reader (New York: Oxford University Press, 1991), p. 22.
4 Ibid., p. 19. Authors who recognize these three traditions as distinctive include Robert Gilpin, The Political Economy of International Relations (Princeton: Princeton University Press, 1987); Crane and Amawi, eds., The Theoretical Evolution of International Political Economy, p. 4; and for a critique of this practice of holding to three fundamental traditions, see Susan Strange: 'But for the rest, all we have, so far, are competing doctrines – sets of normative ideas about the goals to which state policy should be directed and how politics and economics (or, more accurately, states and markets) ought to be related to one another. This is enough to satisfy ideologues who have already made up their minds. They may be realists who want to think narrowly about the means and ends of national policy at home and abroad; or they may be liberal economists who want to think about how the world economy could be most efficiently organized, or they may be radicals or Marxists who want to think about how greater equity and justice could be achieved for the underdogs.' Susan Strange, States and Markets, 2nd edn (London: Pinter Publishers, 1994), p. 16.
5 Robert Gilpin, pp. 31–32.
6 Jacob Viner, The Long View and the Short: Studies in Economic Theory and Policy (New York: Free Press, 1958), p. 286. In Gilpin, p. 32.
7 Alexander Hamilton, 'Report on Manufactures', in G. T. Crane and A. Amawi, eds pp. 37–47.
8 Gilpin, p. 33.
9 Geoffrey Underhill, 'Conceptualizing the Changing Global Order,' in Political Economy and the Changing Global Order, Richard Stubbs and Geoffrey Underhill, eds. (Toronto: McClelland & Stewart, 1994), p. 27.

10 Stephen Gill and David Law, The Global Political Economy: Perspectives, Problems and Policies (Baltimore: Johns Hopkins University Press, 1988), p. 43.
11 Adam Smith, 'Of Restraints Upon the Importation from Foreign Countries of Such Goods as Can Be Produced at Home' in An Inquiry into the Nature and Causes of the Wealth of Nations (London: Ward, Lock & Tyler, 1812), pp. 354–55.
12 Stark, 'Introduction,' Jeremy Bentham's Economic Writings, Vol. 1, pp. 17–18.
13 Manual of Political Economy, in Jeremy Bentham's Economic Writings, Vol. 1, p. 228. All references to Bentham's economic writings are taken from the above compilation, unless otherwise noted.
14 Of the Balance of Trade, Vol. 3,pp. 239–41.
15 The True Alarm, Vol. 3, p. 72.
16 Institute of Political Economy, Vol. 3, pp. 318–9.
17 The Philosophy of Economic Science, Vol. 1, p. 94.
18 Institute of Political Economy, Vol. 3, p. 311.
19 Of the Balance of Trade, Vol. 3, p. 239.
20 Ibid.
21 Institute of Political Economy, Vol. 3, p. 307.
22 Ibid., pp. 318, 361.
23 Ibid., pp. 321, 327.
24 Ibid., p. 327.
25 The individual cannot pursue his/her interests if the state is not secure, but once security is established, the primacy of the individual can come to the fore.
26 These interventions can include those that maintain the political status quo, or slowly introduce reforms.
27 Of the Balance of Trade, Vol. 3, p. 239; Institute of Political Economy, Vol. 3, p. 311.
28 UC XX.180–1. Provided by Stark, 'Introduction', Vol. 1, p. 63.
29 Institute of Political Economy, Vol. 3, p. 311.
30 Manual of Political Economy, Vol. 1, p. 269.
31 Institute of Political Economy, Vol. 3, p. 311.
32 Stark, 'Introduction', Vol. 1, p. 18.
33 Manual of Political Economy, Vol. 1, p. 226.
34 Defence of Usury, Vol. 1, p. 180; Institute of Political Economy, Vol. 3, p. 310.
35 Institute of Political Economy, Vol. 3, p. 318.
36 Ibid., p. 318.
37 Ibid., p. 27.
38 Observations on the Restrictive and Prohibitory Commercial System, Vol. 3, pp. 386, 388.
39 Ibid., pp. 391–403.
40 Manual of Political Economy, Vol. 1, p. 249.
41 Of the Balance of Trade, Vol. 3, p. 222.
42 Ibid., p. 221.
43 Ibid., pp. 226, 227.
44 Ibid., pp. 243–4.
45 Institute of Political Economy, Vol. 3, p. 319.
46 Observations on the Restrictive and Prohibitory Commercial System, Vol. 3, pp. 385, 386, 389, 391.
47 Of the Balance of Trade, Vol. 3, p. 244.
48 Ibid.
49 Manual of Political Economy, Vol. 1, p. 267.
50 Bentham still believed that magazining by individuals would be a more productive approach than leaving provision in the hands of government. Nevertheless, the government is also expected to provide full magazines for the nation, and

Bentham is not clear on what sort of balance should be achieved between government and individuals in this regard. See Stark, 'Introduction', Vol. 1, p. 54.
51 Ibid.
52 Ibid.
53 UC XXV.22.
54 On the Form of the Supply to the Sinking Fund, BM Add. MSS 31235, p. 27. 23 July, 1800. Supplied by Stark, 'Introduction', Vol. 2, p. 44.
55 Stark, 'Introduction', Vol. 2, p. 60; Bentham, Circulating Annuities, Vol. 2, pp. 261–7, 310, 421; Paper Mischief [Exposed], Vol. 2, p. 456.

10 Bentham's Contributions to the Human Security Debate

Though incomplete, the following list reveals some of the critical items that make life worth living and working to sustain: 1. Continuing improvement in human welfare. 2. Sufficient food, clothing, shelter, and belongingness. 3. Liberty, equity, equality, and justice. 4. The existence and maintenance of the rule of law and democracy. 5. A clean and safe environment. 6. Personal peace, safety, and security. 7. The maintenance, protection, and promotion of human rights and responsibilities. 8. Achieving and sustaining human longevity. 9. The ongoing pursuit of human factor development. 10. Personal development (i.e., spiritual, intellectual, moral, physical, etc.). The pursuit of these ideals has now become the strongest motivating factor in people's endeavors. As people go about their social, economic, political, and educational activities and programs, they do their best to make sure that human effort is directed toward the attainment of these ideals. Since the desire is to live longer and enjoy the good life, public policy is often aimed at the achievement of these ideals.[1]

Attaining and maintaining a 'good life' is a goal taken for granted by many, denied to many more, but aspired to by almost all. This goal, articulated by the above quotation, reflects years of liberal thinking, in particular, and has become global in nature due to the dominance of liberal ideals in hegemonic orders and international institutions. Although the definition of what it is to have 'a good life' has shifted over time according to the philosophical and ideological influences of the day, this goal nevertheless continues to have much in common with the designs of early liberal thinkers, including those of Jeremy Bentham.

The opening quotation was intended by its authors to reflect the current expectations of individuals around the world. Its accuracy may be questioned, but it nevertheless illustrates a common belief about the nature of the good life and how it ought to be attained. The dominance of these and similar beliefs are expressed through myriad public policy measures, one of which will be the focus of this chapter: human security. From its rather vague beginnings as a policy framework designed by the United Nations Development Programme in 1994, human security has rapidly grown both as a concept and as a policy measure.

The concept of human security has become increasingly popular, as well as controversial, among international relations practitioners and theorists alike. In a twenty-first-century world where notions such as human rights, the free market economy, international law, and international organizations regularly compete for the spotlight in the predominantly liberal discourse of international politics, a new conception of what constitutes security has taken root, and now informs many foreign policy agendas as well as theoretical debates on the meaning and efficacy of a concept rooted in the security of the individual.[2] The result has not been the 'death' of traditional conceptions of security that place the state at the centre of security concerns. Rather, it appears that the idea of security is at a crossroads; the dominance of traditional security interests is now, conceptually at least, at loggerheads with a new security referent, the individual.

Relatively new though this concept is, human security finds much of its foundation in liberal ideas. Two features of Bentham's writing make his work relevant to this examination of human security. Although Bentham's work in international relations remains an important, although often misunderstood, contribution to international relations theory, including coining the word 'international' itself,[3] one of his most useful contributions to IR theory is that which is least often recognized – his demonstration of the important relationship between the individual and the state. Bentham makes it clear that the individual and her interests are paramount in determining the good life, or the greatest happiness for the greatest number. However, he pays close attention to the role of the state and how the state, through the legislator, works to promote the interests of the individuals who constitute the subjects of the state. In addition, Bentham's writings are of particular interest in this context because he explicitly articulated the importance of security as understood from the level of the individual, not unlike the modern expression of human security. Bentham's 'security of expectation' is firmly rooted at the level of the individual albeit operationalized at the state level, with the express purpose that expectations are provided for and remain stable.

Although Bentham does not explicitly address the relationship between the state and individual as it affects security, at least in his international writings, his work demonstrates, primarily through security of expectations, the importance of this link, a demonstration and recognition of the individual–state relationship that is currently lacking in human security literature. The human security agenda, a growing theme among foreign policy mandates throughout the world, presents a concrete policy and conceptual example of the conflict between the security of the individual versus that of the state, and Bentham's contribution to security and international relations theory can be used to assist the development of human security, identifying areas of weakness, with the intention of developing a more effective overall conception.

I will reiterate a number of points I have made throughout the book to both review and highlight these points and to apply them to the theme of human security. begin with examining the nature of security itself, especially with reference to traditional conceptions. This is followed by the evolution and definition of human security, along with some of the attendant debates surrounding the notion, which will set the stage and context for discussion of the relevance and applicability of Bentham's writings in international relations, and the lessons that might be learned from Bentham's work, insights, and struggles.

What is security?

Defining security is a challenging problem. In the international arena, security has largely referred to the security of the state, and therefore the security of those residing within the state is taken as a given. This assumption continues to dominate, as individual and state or national security, continue to be conflated: 'What is required to promote justice or *human welfare, or our national security, welfare*?' [italics added].[4] In the study of international security, the pre-eminent position of the realist has had little competition, thereby reifying the definition of international security as the sole purview of the state, and largely military in character.[5] Stephen Walt has been credited with providing a strong and succinct definition of security in this traditional framework: 'He argues that security studies is about the phenomenon or war and that it can be defined as "the study of the threat, use, and control of military force."'[6] The process of securitization, or bringing an issue or agenda into the security framework, requires a level of state mobilization that would otherwise not be called upon to address this issue.[7] Such mobilization is relegated to the level of high politics or the paramount priority of the state. This mobilization needs to be differentiated from state action which is taken at the political level (such as social security or economic policy), that is at the level of politicization or 'low politics', and not perceived in terms of an immediate or extraordinary threat to the existence of the state itself, and by association, its inhabitants. 'Traditionally, statesmen concerned themselves with grand strategy, diplomacy, alliances, and balance-of-power politics: 'high politics'. Left to their underlings were the more routine day-to-day dealings in the realm of trade relations: 'low politics''.[8] As such, the state has a central role, and addresses the threats to its existence by eliminating any fear that such threats would successfully overthrow the state and its apparatus.

Human security

Debates over the definition of human security were stimulated by the 1994 United Nations Human Development Report,[9] and since then researchers have attempted to refine and streamline the definition to render it more workable. Little agreement has been reached on what constitutes an ideal definition, and the concept has sometimes suffered as a result. Human security entails freedom from fear and freedom from want, and consists of four essential characteristics; it is taken to be universal, interdependent, easier to ensure through early prevention, and people-centred.[10] The UNDP report stated that although the list of threats to human security was long, the most universal threats could be encapsulated within seven primary categories of security: economic, food, health, environmental, personal, community, and political.[11] From the outset the report clearly stated that the intent was to broaden the notion of security; for too long the focus of security had been too narrowly concentrated on the interests of states, to the detriment of the people residing within them.

Since 1994 the debate has been whether or not the UNDP report, and subsequent definitions were too broad or still too narrowly focused. When the security referent is placed upon the individual, security, it is argued, becomes personal and only definable in terms of each separate individual. As such, human security definitions have recently attempted to reduce their scope to address only threats of a political or criminal nature. Research and policy measures restricted to these conventional security threats are undoubtedly important as they address the threats that are most obviously causing harm. The question still remains as to whether it is possible to broaden these parameters without losing their scholarly application.

Moving the focal point from the state to the individual is significant, and does, in fact, change the parameters of what security means and how it should be effected. Security for the individual is considerably more complex. We know this because in over two hundred years of liberal thinking we have been told that each individual is capable of determining her or his own interests, and should be free to pursue these interests bound only by the restriction that they cause no harm to others. As such, a restrictive definition for a concept that is intended to reflect the varying and diverse needs of individuals works against to the very purpose that it is trying to promote.

Problematizing security – the individual versus the state

What makes an issue into an international security issue? As has been shown, the referent object of security has been, and continues predominantly to be the state. Human security, by definition, would not be considered an aspect of the international dimension from the traditional security point of view because the referent is not the state but the individual. Nevertheless, advocates of human security envision this new referent as one with international importance. But from where does a referent acquire its legitimacy?

In traditional and even in wider international security circles it is collectivities, whether they be in the form of a state, a firm, national economy, a religion or individual species (the whole of humankind, or whales, for example), that assume legitimacy as referent objects: 'We are not dealing here with a universal standard based in some sense on what threatens individual human life.'[12] The assumption is that individual security is addressed on the basis of 'low politics' through internal structures and policies. Threats to individuals can and do take place, but are handled by internal law enforcement or similar structures which are designed to safeguard individuals from one another in the event of conflict.

But what if these structures are insufficient? What if they do not safeguard individuals, either due to inadequacies on the part of these internal agencies, or because these agencies themselves pose a threat to the individual? Eventualities such as these cannot be addressed by traditional security parameters. The state may not be the object of the threat, but the individual can nevertheless be threatened by the state. Additionally, the state apparatus may be so weak that it is incapable of providing the required protection to individuals to ensure their safety and security. Just as individuals cannot be considered as acting in isolation of the state, the state cannot function, and promote security and development in isolation from individuals:

> Therefore, the popular belief and political rhetoric that state creation brings development closer to the people is absolutely false, if development is defined as improvements in living standards – better education, food security, improved health care, more employment opportunities, access to good water, and reliable means of communication. These basic needs can hardly exist without the active participation of citizens in productive activity, which finds expression in improvements in agriculture and industry.[13]

The relationship between the individual and the state was actively explored by Bentham, and it is the understanding of this relationship that could possibly move human security past the crossroads at which it currently stands. The subsequent discussion will focus on Bentham's treatment of the individual, state, and security, as in his work many of the central problems of human security have already been explored, if not resolved.

Bentham and security

For Bentham, the referent of security is the individual.[14] The state has a role in representing and providing security for the community, but neither the state nor community would exist without the amassing of individuals. To each individual Bentham endowed 'security of expectation', later articulated as the disappointment-prevention principle, which is rooted, for the most part, in maintaining the status quo, or in gradually altering expectation so that no insecurity results from reforms, and in particular with regard to property. The notion of 'security of expectation' is the offspring of a fundamental underlying concern throughout Bentham's work, but has been completely overlooked by international relations theorists who have drawn on Bentham's contributions in international relations.

This principle is a reflection of Bentham's concern over the place of security in legislation. The disappointment-prevention principle 'might be said to form, for Bentham, under the overall authority of the greatest happiness principle, a principle of justice'.[15] Security and justice become intertwined. 'If, for Bentham, happiness in its basic sense means the establishment of security (as opposed to the simple satisfaction of wants), the disappointment-prevention principle, in providing security of property, would seem to operate as a necessary condition for happiness.'[16] The state, through proper legislation, offers such security to the individuals that compose it, recognizing the diverse forms in which a threat can arise:

> Security admits as many distinctions as there are kinds of actions which may be hostile to it. It relates to the person, the honour, to property, to condition. Acts injurious to security, branded by prohibition of law, receive the quality of offences.[17]

Although not every threat defined by each and every individual can be reflected in legislation, it is the role of the legislator to secure 'a pattern of expectations which enables each individual to secure his own conception of well-being'.[18] The relationship between security, the state, and the individual is the departure point for Bentham's principle of utility, and his subsequent work in international relations. Bentham wishes to secure expectations, not just for present conditions but also for the future. When and if security is threatened, and security is directly linked to self-preservation, then law acts on behalf of individuals and hence security is maintained. Law protects individuals and property through a sacrifice of liberty.[19] At the same time, however, law can also ensure that other liberties can be obtained; these liberties are often known as civil liberties.[20] As Fred Rosen states, 'Bentham recognizes that liberty has this second sense, but he distrusts the way that other writers and supporters of liberty fail to see that the creation of civil liberty requires the sacrifice of "natural" liberty.'[21] Bentham therefore replaces this second notion of liberty with his idea of 'security':

> As to the word *liberty*, it is a word, the import of which is of so loose a texture, that, in studied discourses on political subjects, I am not (I must confess) very fond of employing it, or of seeing it employed: *security* is a word, in which, in most cases, I find an advantageous substitute for it: *security* against misdeeds by individuals at large: *security* against misdeeds by public functionaries: *security* against misdeeds by foreign adversaries – as the case may be.[22]

Bentham used a very broad conception of security, which included security at the individual, state, and international levels.

The impact of security in liberal ideas – the struggle between the individual and the state

When Bentham closely re-evaluated the principle of utility, or the greatest happiness principle, in order to address any deficiencies,[23] it is arguable that his evaluation was, in part, prompted by the struggle that is evident throughout his work. Bentham's writing, at least with regard to international relations issues, is beset with a continuous debate over the nature of security. How much security is necessary to produce the greatest happiness for the greatest number? That he later associated the importance of security with establishing the greatest happiness through the disappointment-prevention principle illustrates the importance of security, and is directly linked to Bentham's concerns in international affairs; state territory, sovereignty, international relations and law. Athough he demonstrated a recognition of this important relationship, and more importantly linked it to the concept of security, he did not find an easy reconciliation between them. This should not be understood as an inherent problem with Bentham's work, rather than an inherent struggle faced by liberal ideas themselves:

> Liberalism has operated primarily within countries. This is an important point to remember when liberalism is applied to the realm of world politics, because liberal theory treats the domestic circumstances of states as crucial variables in explaining their international behaviors.[24]

Bentham, and liberalism in general, take the individual for their referent while still utilizing and assuming the importance of the state:

> The fictional technique is invoked in every field with which the legislator or psychologist is called upon to deal. Thus Security may be considered with reference to the objects which are secured, and with reference to the objects against which they are secured: – 'Taking human beings individually considered, these are the only real entities considered as being secured. But when a particular and practical application comes to be made of the word security, certain names of fictitious entities in common use must be employed to designate so many objects, to and for which the security is afforded. Person, reputation, property, condition in life – by these four names of fictitious entities, all the objects to which, in the case of an individual, the security afforded by government can apply itself, may be designated.'[25]

Bentham aptly recognizes the various constructs, or fictions, we endow with security for the purpose of securing the individual. But these constructs support as well as complicate the security dynamic. This undeniably causes a struggle, though not necessarily in domestic politics, as various safeguards for the individual can be created to ensure that the state acts on the individual's behalf (at least in constitutional democracies): 'The first sub-ordinate end of good government is internal and external security.'[26] However, turning towards the international stage, the state inevitably becomes a greater problem. It may act against individual security when acting in favour of state security. This struggle is emphasized here to illus-trate some of the issues that must be faced when adhering to a concept or policy rooted in the individual and applied in the international arena.

This struggle can be illustrated, for example, in Bentham's approach to the relationship between security and liberty, and the extent to which the state acts to ensure security. Again, this relationship impacts on domestic as well as international levels of security. On the one hand, one might understand that Bentham's preoccupation with security is merely his way of ensuring that particular liberties are available that otherwise would not be if the legislation did not exist. Liberty becomes central to Bentham's whole system. On the other hand, '[M]aterial security, like health and knowledge, may be a condition for liberty, suggests Berlin, but to provide for increasing security is not the same thing as expanding liberty.'[27] The liberty, and therefore security, that Bentham sought through adequate legis-lation requires obligation, not freedom, to obtain it. The question is, how extensive do these obligations need to be in order to provide the security that Bentham expects, such as security against foreign invasion, hunger, or crimes against one's property?

Sovereignty – central to the liberal relationship between the state, individual, and international arena

Clearly, the state must have the authority to act on behalf of its security interests, and ideally of those individuals that compose it. The relationship between individuals and the state is very much dependent upon the nature of sovereignty, or the supreme authority. Although the diversity of inter-national actors may have changed considerably since Bentham's time, the state still remains one of the predominant, if not the paramount, agency in international relations. The relationship between the individual, state, and security is illustrated in Bentham's development of the concept of sovereignty. His point of departure is the individual where sovereignty resides.[28] Bentham's emphasis on the individual in this sense developed later in his career, and it had an important although poorly elucidated impact on a central feature of his writing, his *Constitutional Code*. His object was to protect individuals from abuse of power by the state appara-tus, creating a situation of 'shared'or divided sovereignty, allowing for a division in sovereign power in relation to the people through a constitu-tional democracy.[29] Fred Rosen notes, however, that Bentham did not explicitly delineate how individuals were precisely to exercise their sover-eignty as they were endowed with neither legislative nor executive power, and were 'limited to electing and dismissing various authorities' and were therefore very functionally prescribed.[30] The relationship between the individual and the state becomes rather complex, but nevertheless reflects the ideal that the individual is paramount. What results is a continuous, if not uneven, devolution of responsibilities; the individual is sovereign, endows upon other authorities the power to distribute and enforce law and order within the state (and presumably represent the individual internationally) through a legislature, judiciary and administration, who are all subject to election or dismissal by the sovereign people. As Rosen states, 'the sovereign people obey as well as direct the government'.[31] This relationship is more or less assumed from Bentham's writing rather than explicitly stated, as it is unclear whether Bentham actually meant for individuals to have unlimited sovereign power, and how he would have otherwise defined the individual's role in the running of the state apparatus as a whole.[32]

Assuming the above adequately describes Bentham's view of the relationship between the individual and the state, it helps to examine how this might be manifested in an international setting. In Bentham's earlier, international writings of *Persons Subject*, he explored such a relationship. He distinguished between jurisdiction – that which applies to the relationship between the individual and the state – and dominion – the supreme authority or sovereignty which applies to the state in relation to other states.[33] Jurisdiction is related to diverse, autonomous responsibilities, such as those held by the legislature and judiciary for example, but all these jurisdictions would nevertheless be contained within the dominion of one sovereign.

Bentham engages a number of factors in determining the relationship between the state and the individual. He already distinguished between a 'habit of obedience' and a 'habit of conversancy' to first determine the relationships between the individual and state, and state to state in his work *A Fragment on Government*.[34] In the first instance, individuals act in a subservient manner to a higher authority, such as a sovereign, and therefore are obedient to, and coerced by, that supreme authority. In the second instance, Bentham applies the 'habit of conversancy' to the relationship between states. They are not obliged to obey one another, or a supreme authority, but the 'habit of conversancy' reflects a voluntary dialogue that may or may not lead to non-binding agreements such as treaties. When speaking of dominion, Bentham illustrates how each dominion relates to individuals according to which dominion each individual is obliged to pay obedience.

In *Persons Subject* Bentham expanded on the relationship between states. Part of the exercise of sovereignty is determining which persons ought to be considered under the dominion of each sovereign, again establishing the relationship of the individual to the international realm through the state. It is dependent in particular upon territorial dominion over which the sovereign has absolute power due to its physical capacity in 'occupying and traversing a given tract of land, insomuch that he can effectually and safely traverse it in any direction at pleasure at the same time that against his will another sovereign can not traverse the same land with equal facility . . .'.[35] Bentham further distinguishes between *standing* or *ordinary* subjects of the sovereign and *occasional* or *extraordinary* subjects. Here expectation comes into play, such that the sovereign *expects* to have dominion over certain persons and not others, and certain persons *expect* to pay obedience to a particular sovereign.[36] Extraordinary or occasional subjects/citizens are those who are temporarily within the territory of a sovereign other than their own, nevertheless subject to the laws of the land, but not expected to be in a continual and permanent habit of obedience.

Bentham took pains to ensure that the individual played an integral part in the determination of sovereignty, albeit ideally in a constitutional democracy. Bentham's basic perceptions of sovereignty are still applicable in today's international setting. States are weak, strong, failed, or burgeoning, they may not be the only actors on the international stage, many are non-democratic and abusive to their citizens, but they nevertheless dominate as the only institutions that are explicitly connected to individuals while at the same time assuming a unitary role at the international level. Focussing on the individual as the security referent, as Bentham does, places the individual at the forefront of security concerns, but Bentham's insistence on developing a relationship explicitly between the individual and the state acknowledges the important role the state still has as an active participant in the human security paradigm.

The only way in which the individual bypasses the state to have effect in the international arena, and therefore speak on behalf of his or her security, is through public opinion. This is a concept with which Bentham has often been credited but which was never very well developed in Bentham's international writings. Nevertheless, to the extent that the individual can have immediate 'contact' with the international realm, it is largely through public opinion that this would be manifested. Likewise, Bentham recommends that all treaties and negotiations in which the state is engaged be made available to the public.[37] Eliminating secrecy at the state level ensured individual security of expectation by constantly revealing to the community in what ways its security was being sought, and ideally for the community to respond through public opinion. This is yet another instance in which Bentham's writings illustrate the importance of the role of the state. Even when Bentham arranges for an ideal method through which the individual may participate beyond just electing and dismissing state representatives (assuming such an individual lives in a constitutional democracy), there are still some circumstances in which the state would be acting appropriately by withholding information from the community. In this respect Bentham articulates classic security concerns when he allows for secrecy on behalf of, among others, the Defensive Force (Army and Navy Bis-subdepartments) and the Foreign Relation Subdepartment.[38] These departments which are directly linked to the state's interactions internationally must act in such a manner as to ensure both state and individual security, and therefore are permitted to act in secrecy, at least for a limited period of time.[39] In this respect Bentham exhibits a typical struggle between what could be considered as the conflicting security concerns of the state and the individual. It is assumed that the state, by withholding information, is likewise acting on behalf of the security of the individual. The challenge is the extent to which the individual can be certain that her security concerns are indeed being safeguarded by the state. Bentham tries to ensure this, again, through the securities designed within his framework for a constitutional democracy. Nevertheless, the state is provided significant leeway if it declares some information classified on the basis of security.

Bentham and human security

Bentham's definition of security does not discriminate between various units such that security means one thing at the individual level, another at the state level, and yet another at the international level. As the state is merely composed of individuals, it is the individual that is pre-eminent in the legislator's concern – both domestically as well as internationally. The individual is on the one hand merely one separate unit among many others, and on the other hand a citizen of the world, or the greatest possible community. Security is also, however, the purview of the state. It is the legislator who is endowed with the responsibility of ensuring security: 'Security is more especially and essentially his work: in regard to subsistence, opulence, and equality, his interference is comparatively unnecessary.'[40]

Bentham's work can contribute on a number of levels to the literature on human security. He attempted to focus as much as possible on the individual and the security of the individual through security of expectation. Within his framework however, he illustrates, if not explicitly acknowledging it himself, the important role the state plays in establishing security of expectation for the individual by establishing the pattern of expectations upon which individuals could construct their own secure surroundings. The use of 'security of expectation' recognizes that individuals look to various institutions, most importantly the state apparatus, to establish their security needs. This point could not be better illustrated than in today's politics, where individuals and groups of individuals such as 'minorities' and women, as well as individuals from all walks of life who participate more and more in public opinion, look to the state apparatus to ensure that their diverse, particular, and necessary security needs are met.

Bentham's work, especially when establishing the relationship between the individual and the state, can be easily construed as idealistic, but it is no less an ideal than the concept of human security itself. Although the individual–state relationship that Bentham designs requires the sort of constitutional democracy that many states, one hundred and seventy five years ago as well as today, have not instituted, it remains one of the few acclaimed political systems that has the best chance of ensuring human security.[41] Bentham describes the various ways in which the individual can express security of expectation within and through the state, as well as through public opinion. However, because many states do not allow for such expression does not mean that the state apparatus is therefore irrelevant, or that individuals do not still look to their state to secure expectations. To simply proclaim human security as a goal is meaningless unless a mechanism is in place to ensure it. By and large this mechanism remains the state.

The problem is that the role of the state must be considered integral to the pursuit of human security. Whether this is achieved in non-democratic states through various international pressures (which can and do include 'humanitarian intervention', adding yet another controversy to the human security debate), securing expectations one at a time, or through political reform within states, these institutions are pivotal to any hope of seeking security at the individual level. Most importantly, understanding human security in reference to 'security of expectation' makes the concept more inclusive. Whereas the concept of human security at present subject to a narrowing of definition for the sake of scholarly precision (hence a focus on the military and political security aspects as opposed to broader economic, environmental, and other concerns), Bentham's 'security of expectation' necessarily broadens the definition including all individuals in all states. Clearly, those individuals subject to immediate violence and terror require equally immediate attention within the discourse of human security. But security of expectation goes one step further, beyond encouraging action only at those times when violence erupts. It acts to prevent such violence by recognizing the very foundations of security itself:

> There is, first, the primeval indispensable principle of economic security, subsistence and abundance. A starving man will fill his stomach before he thinks about civil rights. Political security therefore rests on economic. This was so obvious a truism, Bentham thought, that it needed no discussion. It was true in fact and true by definition. If civilization is measured by radius of social reference, a starving man is a savage, for he is blind to everything but his urgent need for food.[42]

Human security sought on the basis of security of expectation is truly ideal, but also truly secure.

Notes

1 Senyo B-S. K. Adjibolosoo, ed., *International Perspectives on the Human Factor in Economic Development* (Westport, CT: Praeger Publishers, 1998) p. 3.
2 The Canadian and Norwegian governments spearheaded the initiative to use 'human security' as the foundation of their foreign policy agendas, and were soon joined by a number of other countries (the Netherlands, Austria, Greece, Mali, and others) who have expressed a commitment to this agenda. It has, however, not been adopted without controversy, often attracting criticism from traditional security circles both in policy as well as academic arenas.
3 Bentham's credit for coining the word 'international' has been questioned, most recently by Peter van den Dungen, 'The Abbé de Saint-Pierre and the English 'Irenists' of the 18th Century (Penn, Bellers, and Bentham)' in *International Journal on World Peace*, Vol. 17, No.2, (June 2000), pp. 5–31). Dungen claims that Saint-Pierre actually preceded Bentham in coining the word 'international', but subsequently notes that no proof of this usage has yet been found in Saint-Pierre's writings (it has only been asserted by other authors who do not indicate any sources).
4 Michael W. Doyle and G. John Ikenberry, eds., *New Thinking in International Relations Theory*, (Boulder, CO: Westview Press, 1997) p. 7.
5 Miles Kahler, 'Inventing International Relations: International Relations: Theory After 1945' in *New Thinking in International Relations Theory*, Michael W. Doyle, and G. John Ikenberry eds. (Boulder, CO: Westview Press, 1997) p. 35; Barry Buzan, Ole Waever, and Jaap de Wilde eds. *Security: A New Framework for Analysis*, (Boulder,CO: Lynne Reinner Publishers, 1998), pp. 2–3.
6 Buzan, *et al.*, p. 3.
7 Ibid., p. 4.
8 Charles L. Robertson, *International Politics since World War II: A Short History* (Armonk, NY: M.E. Sharpe, 1997), p. 183.
9 Lloyd Axworthy, 'Introduction' in *Human Security and the New Diplomacy: Protecting People, Promoting Peace*, Rob McRae and Don Hubert, eds. (Montreal and Kingston: McGill-Queen's University Press, 2001), p. 3.
10 UNDP Human Development Report, 1994, pp. 22–23.
11 Ibid., pp. 24–25.
12 Buzan, pp. 21–23.
13 Adjibolosoo, ed., *International Perspectives on the Human Factor in Economic Development*, p. 103.
14 Bentham, *An Introduction to the Principles of Morals and Legislation*, J. H. Burns, and H. L. A. Hart, eds. (New York: Clarendon Press, 1996), p. 12.
15 Ibid.
16 Ibid., p. 105.
17 Bentham, *The Theory of Legislation*, pp. 96–97.
18 Paul J. Kelly, *Utilitarianism and Distributive Justice: Jeremy Bentham and the Civil Law* (Oxford: Clarendon Press, 1990), p. 8.
19 Ibid., p. 69.
20 Ibid.
21 Ibid.
22 Ibid. From Bentham's *Letters to Count Toreno on the Proposed Penal Code* in Bowring, Vol. VIII. pp. 509–10.
23 Ibid., p. 104.
24 James N. Rosenau and Mary Durfee, *Thinking Theory Thoroughly: Coherent Approaches to an Incoherent World* (Boulder, CO: Westview Press, 2000), p. 34.

25 C. K. Ogden, *Bentham's Theory of Fictions* (London: Paul, Trench, Trubner, 1932), p. cxiii. Quoted from *Works*, Vol. IX, p. 11.
26 Stephen Toulmin, 'A New "Art and Science". Science and Scientific Method,' in *Jeremy Bentham: An Odyssey of Ideas* (New York: Columbia University Press, 1963), p. 286.
27 Ibid., p. 71.
28 Bentham, *Constitutional Code*, Fred Rosen ed. (Oxford: Clarendon Press, 1994), p. 25. Bentham's placing of sovereignty in the people occurred fairly late in Bentham's writing career. A historical account of the development of Bentham's ideas on sovereignty can be found in H. L. A. Hart, 'Bentham on Sovereignty' *The Irish Jurist*, 1967, and J. H. Burns, 'Bentham on Sovereignty: An Exploration', *Northern Ireland Legal Quarterly*, Vol. 24, No3, (Autumn 1973), for an examination of sovereignty as it applies largely at the domestic level. See also F. Rosen, *Jeremy Bentham and Representative Democracy: A Study of the Constitutional Code* (Oxford: Clarendon Press, 1983).
29 See above articles.
30 Rosen, *Jeremy Bentham and Representative Democracy*, pp. 47–48.
31 Ibid.
32 Ibid.
33 *Persons Subject,* UC XXV.10; Bowring, Vol. II, p. 540.
34 Bentham, *A Fragment on Government* (Cambridge: Cambridge University Press, 1988), p. 40.
35 UC XXV.13; Bowring, Vol. II, pp. 541–2.
36 UC XXV.14: Bowring, Vol. II, p. 542.
37 UC XXV.50; Bowring, Vol. II, p. 554. This essay in its original form is entitled *Cabinet No Secrecy*, but was made a component of the well-known *A Plan for an Universal and Perpetual Peace* which is actually a compilation of four separate essays originally written by Bentham. See Gunhild Hoogensen, 'Bentham's International Manuscripts Versus the Published *Works*' in *Journal of Bentham Studies*, Number 4 (2001), available at http://www.ucl.ac.uk/Bentham-Project/journal/jnl_2001.htm.
38 *Constitutional Code*, pp. 163–4.
39 Ibid., p. 57.
40 Stark, *Jeremy Bentham's Economic Writings*, Vol. 3, (London: Allen & Unwin, 1954), p. 311.
41 Rob McRae, 'Human Security in a Globalized World' in *Human Security and the New Diplomacy*, p. 15.
42 Stephen Toulmin, 'A New "Art and Science" Science and Scientific Method,' in *Jeremy Bentham: An Odyssey of Ideas* (New York: Columbia University Press, 1963) p. 314.

11 Conclusion

> Like so much that Bentham wrote, the work was smug, parochial and simplistic, making sweeping generalizations on the basis of minimal knowledge.[1]

Bentham's work has suffered as a result of his personal failings; he was his own worst publicist. In his younger years he shunned any direct communication with the very figures whose attention he sought, and in his later years his vanity overwhelmed any sensible assessment of the man or his work. Often reduced to caricatures or, as above, bluntly dismissed, careful scrutiny of his work was neglected. The 'Auto-Icon' sits to this day in a corner at University College London, its original head now placed in a safe rather than between its legs.[2] Bentham's post-mortem wishes are often better known than the work he compiled over his eighty four years, although he hoped that his utilitarianism would be the world's philosophy by 2032. Such a goal is undoubtedly another failed aspiration, but even so Bentham's writings on political and juridical reform have been influential and a source of debate.[3] There has been an attempt in recent years to overcome the awkward and peculiar reputation of the philosopher, and give due attention to the massive store of manuscripts that was also Bentham's legacy. The revised and carefully edited *Collected Works* are slowly replacing the dismal edition of John Bowring, enabling many scholars to accurately examine Bentham's work for the first time. Bentham's writing on international relations has not yet benefited from this careful treatment, until now receiving only superficial attention.[4]

It is plain that Bentham's contribution to international relations theory is important to scholars, as his work continues to be included in some of the most recent compilations on the subject. Although some scholars have moved well past the humble origins of international relations theory and do not bother to pay acknowledgement to philosophers long gone, there are others who recognize the importance of revisiting the works of classical theorists to glean insights on today's international politics. Michael Doyle's latest text falls in the latter category, encouraging scholars to recall the important foundations laid by Thucydides, Machiavelli, Rousseau, Smith and Marx. Doyle includes Bentham as a contributor to the liberal tradition, and confidently labels him as 'homogeneously pacific'.[5] Doyle continues what appears to be a time-honoured tradition where Bentham is concerned; his brief discussion is only devoted to *Plan*, and he relies on a minimal number of secondary sources for his own analysis. The result is a familiar and unoriginal presentation, typically emphasizing oft-repeated comments on disarmament, international courts, secrecy in the foreign office, and public opinion. Torbjørn Knutsen employs similar tactics in *A History of International Relations Theory*, and even Stephen Conway, who is most familiar with Bentham's work in international relations as he has had access to the original manuscripts, does not effectively inform his readers either of the poor shape of *Plan*, or that Bentham's writing contains contradictions in theme and content.

Although these authors contribute to an important facet of international relations scholarship, often the treatment of Bentham's work is poor, and relies on weak research.[6] What they present is not necessarily incorrect, but what they neglect makes these presentations inaccurate. Further, this treatment is unnecessary as the work of F. H. Hinsley and Michael Howard illustrates; even on the basis of *Plan*, these authors were aware of at least some of Bentham's contradictory positions, and his awkward place within the liberal tradition. Howard aptly notes that Bentham was never a pacifist and had little difficulty with acquiring colonies that were contiguous rather than distant, and Hinsley recognized that disarmament was, at best, a subsidiary concern.[7] But all of these works lack the insight that can only be obtained through a thorough examination of Bentham's original manuscripts and the more recently edited *Collected Works*, exploring not only his many international relations essays but his *Constitutional Code* and his wealth of writing on economics. If Bentham's work is significant enough to warrant presentation, and it is according to the most recent explorations of international relations theory that this remains the case, then the repetition of past analyses will no longer suffice.

What is Bentham's contribution to international relations theory? Bentham's detailed examination of international law made an important contribution to international relations thinking, although *Plan* is probably the weakest source of this contribution, paling in comparison with *Persons Subject* and his draft of international law of 1830. His view of international law is meaningless, however, without a clear understanding of his position on sovereignty, the latter rarely receiving any attention by international relations scholars. Bentham walked a fine line between engendering cooperation and 'proper' behaviour between states, and maintaining absolute sovereignty within each state. This balancing act is problematic today, and although Bentham's work did not have the necessary depth to suggest solutions, his resulting reliance on the security of absolute sovereignty over international law cannot be ignored. Known for encouraging an international court to adjudicate in conflicts between states, Bentham was never ready to relinquish the sovereignty of the state to such a noble ideal.

Bentham's views on sovereignty, a neglected facet of his work by international relations scholars, has had an equal impact on debates over international political economy, another of his interests which has largely escaped the attention of many experts in international relations theory. Hinsley and Howard briefly speak to his work on colonies, a subject that occupied a substantial part of Bentham's time, especially from 1796 to 1804. Doyle misses this point altogether, but then Bentham's contribution to international political economy has been grossly underrated by most scholars. Bentham tangles with the contentious problem of free trade versus the sovereign state, and through colonial emancipation, the question of self-determination. His work of the 1780s, such as *Colonies and Navy*, is cited as illustration of his demands to emancipate all colonies and his claim that colonies have no trade value above free trade between sovereign states. Bentham was however always equivocal on this point.

Free trade and self-determination are not issues of the past: quite the opposite. It is significant that Bentham recognized the importance of these issues two hundred years ago. His views on these subjects were not exhaustive, as he did approach many topics in a simplistic fashion, and would often repeat, rather than elaborate on, the same arguments. However he did raise important points. Bentham looked at the difficult decision of granting independence; self-determination requires the initiative to gain independence, as well as having such independence granted and/or recognized. Bentham was far more hesitant in granting independence to a colony contiguous to the mother country, taking a contemporary example, a region such as Chechnya, but was more willing to grant independence to a distant colony such as Hong Kong. This is no less a problem today than in Bentham's time.

Not unrelated to Bentham's contribution to international relations theory is his place within the various theoretical traditions. The difficulty in situating Bentham has been a recurrent theme in this book, and although not explicitly stated, this difficulty reflects on the efficacy of the theoretical traditions as such. The previous ten chapters challenge superficial treatments of Bentham's work by carefully analyzing the key source for international relations scholars, *A Plan for an Universal and Perpetual Peace*, and providing a full and comprehensive presentation of Bentham's ideas on international relations. Although *Plan* is a flawed, but not entirely incorrect account of some of Bentham's ideas, it only provides one view of his work. This discussion has sought out Bentham's original sources, going beyond the material contained only within *Plan*, to gain an overall sense of Bentham's thinking on the subject.

From issues of sovereignty, through peace, war, colonization, and other important economic questions, Bentham's ideas appear to be wide and varied. It is clear that he debated continuously with himself throughout his lifetime, and this was not contingent on the period in which he was writing, or the philosophical position he was thought to hold. Bentham was ambivalent, and this is apparent throughout the many themes reviewed here. For example, at times sovereignty must be divided to prevent a sovereign from having absolute power, and at other times the power of the sovereign is unquestionably absolute. Yet the power and importance of the state is manifest in Bentham's work, and plays a fundamental role in his thinking on international relations. When he considers peace, war, colonies, or foreign trade, the ambivalence that appears in each circumstance is rooted in the security of the state, and the expectation that the state retain its power. Security of expectation, known by the late 1820s as the disappointment-prevention principle, is the measure by which state security is determined. Bentham's use of this principle is a leading cause for the confusion and ambivalence surrounding his work, and greatly affects perception of his place within the theoretical traditions in international relations as a result.

The categories into which we place thinkers and their ideas can oversimplify the complexities of their work. To say that a thinker is an idealist or a Kantian speaks volumes; through the traditions we understand the ideas a thinker proposes before having explored the ideas themselves. Traditions are necessary in that they provide us with intellectual impetus to understanding ideas, as well as to conceive our own. They show us how and through whom ideas are connected. But they also reify those ideas and the thinkers who explored them, and if we are not careful, we become trapped into an understanding that is no longer meaningful or even accurate.

The legacy of Bentham demonstrates that the work done in international relations by any thinker transcends the categories we have contrived to better understand certain concepts. He shows us that the battles between traditions need not take place between thinkers, between epochs, or between continents, but can take place, in an even more nuanced fashion, within the thinkers themselves. Through his work we can see that these ideas consist of a contest between various ideas. Influential in Bentham's writings are the works of Adam Smith, Niccolò Machiavelli, Hugo Grotius, Thomas Hobbes, and the Abbé St. Pierre, an ecclectic mix of liberal and realist traditions.

Bentham is steeped in idealism, and has much in common with the optimism of the Abbé St. Pierre when he speaks of the power of public opinion, and the extent to which public opinion can influence international affairs. Bentham's reliance on commerce as a purveyor of peace is completely consistent with the work of Kant, another thinker associated with idealism. Such views have nothing in common with the work of Machiavelli, or other realists. On the other hand, Bentham shares Machiavelli's fear of innovation and the stresses induced by unexpected change and reform in a political system. Fear of innovation is the motivation for Bentham's disappointment-prevention principle, or security of expectation, a fundamental feature of his thought. Other influences appear in his work on sovereignty; he strove to eliminate the absolute authority of the sovereign, especially in *A Fragment on Government*, yet in other works his concern for maintaining the absolute nature of the sovereign appears paramount, in some respects emulating his predecessor Hobbes. That Bentham is not Hobbes is clear enough, but as Bentham's work progresses, his need to wield authority through the legislator for the benefit of the community is equally clear. This tendency has been noted in various places, and has been addressed by Bentham scholars who debate the existence of the 'authoritarian' versus the 'liberal' Bentham. Bentham's work on international law brings him easily back into the liberal tradition, alongside Grotius, but their foundations for international law differ significantly; Grotius looks to natural law as the guide, a concept for which Bentham has no time. Bentham looks instead to self-interest, an approach which modern commentators such as Friedrich Meineke and Stanley Hoffmann have great difficulty in associating with anything but realism. One of the few thinkers to whom Bentham paid tribute, and acknowledged as an important influence, is Adam Smith. In Bentham's economic works in general, and in his international economic works in particular, Bentham often recognized the important contribution of Smith. But this self-confessed disciple of Smith still had a profoundly different outlook, particularly in questions of defence. Where Smith looked to a professional army to secure the needs of the modern state, Bentham could only allow for a small stipendiary force, and one which would be easily outnumbered by a citizen's, 'radical' force. His reliance on the citizenry to check the paid professionals owes more to Machiavelli than Smith.

It is difficult to look to one tradition over another to capture adequately Bentham's work in international relations. His writing on peace, war, colonies and foreign trade shows us that he contributed many ideas to the liberal tradition, but he is not a liberal. His realist side has not been recognized and bears examination. Even so, it would not be correct to call him a realist. Bentham's work is important to us because he cannot be categorized so easily. His ideas are dependent upon, and rooted in, the security of expectation, which results in a position that does not adhere to the strict dictates of international theory traditions. Bentham's conclusions often bypass these traditions, and as a result, present scholars with another perspective through which to understand and explain international relations.

Bentham did not have a broad-based theory of international relations, and in all likelihood cannot be considered one of the subject's greatest thinkers, but what he does have to offer is neither irrelevant nor insignificant. Today's world, and especially the liberal democracies, face precisely the same problems that Bentham attempted to grapple with two hundred years ago. As one of the original advocates of liberal attitudes – even though not limited to liberal ideals – Bentham helped create the world in which we live. Faced with the challenges of globalization, today's democracies must make choices as to the importance of sovereignty in relation to fair and open trade practices. In the face of public opinion, they must decide to support, ignore or reject independence movements. The demands of liberal ideals will always clash with harsh realism when national security remains the underlying concern.

Notes

1 Michael Howard, *War and the Liberal Conscience* (London: Temple Smith, 1978) p. 33.
2 The term 'Auto-Icon' was Bentham's own, an appropriate title, according to him, as he sat and inspired future disciples. Bentham has often mistakenly been thought of as a founder of University College London, but his corpse and manuscripts were willed to the school a few years after his death and shortly after University College first opened. C. F. A. Marmoy, 'The "Auto-Icon" of Jeremy Bentham at University College, London', *Medical History*, Vol. 2, 1958, pp. 77–86.
3 Bentham's work on the Panopticon has spurred many a discussion, for example.
4 Bentham's poor and scattered writing, combined with incompetent editing, has largely contributed to this weak treatment of his work.
5 Michael Doyle, *Ways of War and Peace: Realism, Liberalism, and Socialism* (New York: W. W. Norton, 1997), p. 209.
6 Conway's work is not included in this assessment as his project is primarily historical. Nonetheless, Conway does tend to emphasize Bentham's more pacifist side, as well his contributions to international law.
7 Howard, pp. 32–35; Hinsley, p. 85.

Bibliography

Manuscripts

Bentham Manuscripts in the University College London Library.
Milne, Taylor, A., ed., *Catalogue of the Manuscripts of Jeremy Bentham in the Library of University College, London*, London: Athlone Press, 1962.
Bentham Manuscripts in the British Library, Add. MSS 30151.

Bentham's Works

The Collected Works of Jeremy Bentham, general editors J. H. Burns and J. R. Dinwiddy, London, 1968 – (in progress).
Colonies, Commerce, and Constitutional Law: Rid Yourselves of Ultramaria and Other Writings on Spain and Spanish America, ed. Philip Schofield, Oxford: Clarendon Press, 1995.
Constitutional Code, Vol. 1, ed. Fred Rosen, Oxford: Clarendon Press, 1994.
The Correspondence of Jeremy Bentham, 1752–1776, ed. by T. L. S. Sprigge, London: Athlone Press, 1968.
The Correspondence of Jeremy Bentham, 1781–1788, ed. I. Christie, London: Athlone Press, 1968.
Of Laws in General, ed. H. L. A. Hart, London: Athlone Press, 1970.
An Introduction to the Principles of Morals and Legislation, New York: Hafner Publishing, 1965.
A Fragment on Government, eds J. H. Burns and H. L. A. Hart, with an Introduction by Ross Harrison, Cambridge: Cambridge University Press, 1988.
Canada. *Emancipate Your Colonies!* London: Effingham Wilson, Royal Exchange, 1838.
Jeremy Bentham's Economic Writings, 3 vols, ed. W. Stark, London: George Allen & Unwin, 1952–4.
The Theory of Legislation, New York, Havcourt Brace, 1931.
Works of Jeremy Bentham, ed. J. Bowring, Edinburgh, 1843; reprint, New York: Russell & Russell, 1962.

Other Books and Articles

Arblaster, A., *The Rise and Decline of Western Liberalism*, Oxford, Basil Blackwell 1987.
Austin, John. *The Province of Jurisprudence Determined.* (1832), New York, B. Franklin, 1970.

Bahmueller, C. F., *The National Charity Company*: Jeremy Bentham's Silent Revolution, Berkeley, CA, University of California Press, 1981.

Baumgardt, D., *Bentham and the Ethics of Today*, Princeton, NJ: Princeton University Press, 1952.

Beitz, C., *Political Theory and International Relations*, Princeton, NJ: Princeton University Press, 1979.

Boralevi, Lea Campos, *Bentham and the Oppressed*, Berlin: Walter de Gruyter, 1984.

Bowie, Norman E. and Robert L. Simon, *The Individual and the Political Order: An Introduction to Social and Political Philosophy*, New Jersey: Prentice Hall, 1977.

Bull, Hedley, 'Hobbes and the International Anarchy,' *Social Research*, 48, 1981.

—— Benedict Kingsbury, and Adam Roberts (eds), *Hugo Grotius and International Relations*. Oxford, Clarendon Press 1990.

Burns, J. H., 'Bentham on Sovereignty: An Exploration', *Northern Ireland Legal Quarterly*, Vol. 24, No. 3, Autumn 1973.

—— 'Bentham and the French Revolution', *Transactions of the Royal Historical Society*, 5th series, xvi, 1966.

Carr, E. H. *The Twenty Years' Crisis 1919–1939: An Introduction to the Study of International Relations*, New York: MacMillan, 1966.

Chambers Biographical Dictionary, Gen. Ed. Magnus Magnusson, asst. ed. Rosemary Goring, 5th ed., Edinburgh: Chambers, 1990.

Conway, S., 'Bentham on Peace and War' *Utilitas,* Vol. 1, No.1, (1989).

—— 'Bentham versus Pitt: Jeremy Bentham and British Foreign Policy 1789', *The Historical Journal*, Vol. 30, No.4, (1987).

—— 'Bentham, the Benthamites and the Nineteenth-Century British Peace Movement', *Utilitas*, Vol. 2, No.2, (1990).

Crane, George T. and Abla Amawi, eds., *The Theoretical Evolution of International Political Economy: A Reader*, New York: Oxford University Press, 1991.

Cranston, Maurice, 'Foreword' to Lea Campos Boralevi *Bentham and the Oppressed*, Berlin: Walter de Gruyter, 1984.

Crimmins, J. E., 'Contending Interpretations of Bentham's Utilitarianism,' *Canadian Journal of Political Science*. Vol. XXIX, No.4, 1996.

Dinwiddy, John, *Bentham*, Oxford: Oxford University Press, 1989.

Doyle, Michael, *Ways of War and Peace: Realism, Liberalism, and Socialism*, New York: W. W. Norton, 1997.

Edwards, Bryan, *The History, Civil and Commercial, of the British Colonies in the West Indies*, London: John Stockdale, 1794.

Gill, Stephen and David Law, *The Global Economy: Perspectives, Problems and Policies*, Baltimore: Johns Hopkins University Press, 1988.

Gilpin, Robert, *The Political Economy of International Relations*, Princeton: Princeton University Press, 1987.

Grotius, Hugo, *De Jure Belli ac Pacis Libre Tres*, (1625) in *International Relations and Political Theory*, Edited by Howard Williams *et al.* Vancouver: 1993.

Gunn, J. A. W., 'Jeremy Bentham and the Public Interest', *Canadian Journal of Political Science*, I (1968).

Hart, H. L. A., 'Bentham on Sovereignty', *The Irish Jurist* (1967).

—— 'Bentham and the United States of America', *The Journal of Law and Economics*, XXI, 1967.

Hinsley, F. H., *Power and the Pursuit of Peace*, Cambridge: Cambridge University Press, 1963.

Hinsley, F. H., *Sovereignty*, London: C. A. Watts, 1966.

Hobbes, Thomas, *Leviathan*, in *International Relations and Political Theory*. Edited by Howard Williams *et al.* Vancouver: UBC Press, 1993.

Hoffmann, S., *Contemporary Theory in International Relations*, New Jersey: Prentice Hall, 1960.

—— *Duties Beyond Borders: On the Limits and Possibilities of Ethical International Politics*, Syracuse: Syracuse University Press, 1981.

Howard, Michael, *War and the Liberal Conscience*, London: Temple Smith, 1978.

Hurrell, A., 'Kant and the Kantian Paradigm in International Relations', *Review of International Studies*, Vol. 16, 1990.

Jackson, D., 'Halevy Reconsidered: The Importance of Bentham's Psychological Epistemology in his "Conversion" to Democracy'. New Orleans: Fifth Congress of the International Society for Utilitarian Studies, 1997.

Kant, Immanuel, *Kant: Political Writings*, Edited by Hans Reiss, Cambridge: Cambridge University Press, 1970.

Knutsen, Torbjørn, *A History of International Relations Theory*, Manchester: Manchester University Press, 1997.

Long, D., *Bentham on Liberty*, Toronto: University of Toronto Press, 1977.

Mack, Mary P., *Jeremy Bentham: An Odyssey of Ideas, 1748–1792*, London: Heinemann, 1962.

Machiavelli, N., *The Prince and the Discourses*, New York: The Modern Library, 1950.

—— *The Art of War*, New York: Da Capo Press, 1990.

Meinecke, F., *Machiavellism: The Doctrine of Raison d'État and Its Place in Modern History*, New Haven, CT: Yale University Press, 1957.

Merriam, C. E., *History of the Theory of Sovereignty Since Rousseau*, New York: Columbia University Press, 1900.

Pocock, J. G. A., *The Machiavellian Moment: Florentine Political Thought and the Atlantic Republican Tradition*, Princeton: Princeton University Press, 1975.

Porter, Roy, *England in the Eighteenth Century*, London: The Folio Society, 1998.

Rosen, F., *Jeremy Bentham and Representative Democracy: A Study of the Constitutional Code*, Oxford: Clarendon Press, 1983.

Philip Schofield, 'The Constitutional Code of Jeremy Bentham', *The King's College Law Journal*, Vol. 2, 1991–92.

Schwarzenberger, Georg, 'Bentham's Contribution to International Law and Organization', *Jeremy Bentham and the Law,* G. W. Keeton and G. Schwarzenberger (eds), London: Stevens and Sons, 152–84, 1948.

Smith, Adam, *An Inquiry into the Nature and Causes of the Wealth of Nations*, London: Ward, Lock & Tyler, 1812.

—— *Lectures on Justice, Police, Revenue and Arms*, edited by E. Cannan, Oxford: Oxford University Press, 1978.

Stark, W., *History and Historians of Political Economy*, edited by Charles M. A. Clark, New Brunswick: Transaction Publishers, 1994.

Strange, Susan, *States and Markets,* 2nd ed. London: Pinter Publishers, 1994.

Taylor, A. J. P., *Rumours of Wars*, London: Hamish Hamilton, 1952.

Underhill, Geoffrey, 'Conceptualizing the Changing Global Order' in *Political Economy and the Changing Global Order*, edited by Richard Stubbs and Geoffrey Underhill. Toronto: McClelland & Stewart, 1994.

Viner, Jacob, *The Long View and the Short: Studies in Economic Theory and Policy*, New York: Free Press, 1958.

Waldron, Jeremy, ed., *Nonsense Upon Stilts: Bentham, Burke, and Marx on the Rights of Man*, London: Meuthen, 1987.

Wight, Martin, *International Theory: The Three Traditions*, ed. Gabriele Wight and Brian Porter, Leicester: Leicester University Press, 1991.

Winch, Donald, *Classical Political Economy and Colonies*, London: London School of Economics and Political Science, 1965.

Wolfers, A. and L. W. Martin, *The Anglo-American Tradition in Foreign Affairs*, New York: Yale University Press, 1956.

Index

References to end-of-chapter notes are indicated by 'n' followed by the note number.